# Interpersonal
# Violent Behaviors

**R. Barry Ruback, JD, PhD**, is Professor of Psychology and Professor of Criminal Justice at Georgia State University. He is Editor of the *Criminal Justice Review*, Research Director of the Georgia Statistical Analysis Bureau, and a member of the State Bar Associations of Georgia and Texas. He has authored or coauthored 50 articles and book chapters. He has been a Mellon Fellow, a Fulbright Fellow, a Visiting Fellow at the National Institute of Justice (U.S. Department of Justice), an Indo-American Fellow (Indo-U.S. Subcommission on Education and Culture), and a Fulbright-Hays Fellow (U.S. Department of Education).

**Neil Alan Weiner, PhD**, is a Senior Research Associate at the Sellin Center for Studies in Criminology and Criminal Law at the University of Pennsylvania and a Visiting Fellow at the National Institute of Justice at the U.S. Department of Justice. At the Sellin Center, he is Director of the Center for the Interdisciplinary Study of Criminal Violence. He was the Senior Research Associate on the Panel on the Understanding and Control of Violent Behavior of the National Research Council of the National Academy of Sciences and a Postdoctoral Fellow at the School of Public and Urban Affairs at Carnegie-Mellon University. He has edited several books and special journal issues on violent crime and has written about and conducted research on historical trends in urban violent crime, national patterns and trends in violent crime, situational dynamics of violence escalation, the prediction of violent crime, criminal-justice and public-health approaches to preventing violence, explanations of violent behavior, and using research on violent crime in applied settings.

# *Interpersonal Violent Behaviors*

## Social and Cultural Aspects

R. Barry Ruback, JD, PhD

Neil Alan Weiner, PhD

Editors

*Springer Publishing Company*

Copyright © 1995 by Springer Publishing Company, Inc.

No part of this publication may be reproduced, stored in a retrieval system, or transmitted in any form or by any means, electronic, mechanical, photo-copying, recording, or otherwise, without the prior permission of Springer Publishing Company, Inc.

Springer Publishing Company, Inc.
536 Broadway
New York, NY 10012

95 96 97 98 99/5 4 3 2 1

**Library of Congress Cataloging-in-Publication Data**
Interpersonal violent behaviors : social and cultural aspects /
   R. Barry Ruback, Neil Alan Weiner, editors.
      p.   cm.
   Includes bibliographical references and index.
   ISBN 0-8261-8510-X
   1. Violence.  2. Violent–Cross cultural studies.  3. Violence–
Research.  4. Violent crimes.  I. Ruback, R. Barry, 1950–   .
II. Weiner, Neil Alan.
HM281.I6  1994
303.6–dc20                       94-23169
                                  CIP

Printed in the United States of America

# Contents

# Contributors

**Dane Archer, PhD**
Department of Sociology
University of California
Santa Cruz, California 95064

**Martin Daly, PhD**
Department of Psychology
McMaster University
Hamilton, Ontario L8S 4K1
Canada

**Carol R. Ember, PhD**
Department of Anthropology
Hunter College, CUNY
New York, New York and
Human Relations Area File
Yale University
New Haven, Connecticut 06511

**Melvin Ember, PhD**
Human Relations Area File
Yale University
New Haven, Connecticut 06511

**Richard B. Felson, PhD**
Department of Sociology
University at Albany
Albany, New York 12222

**Rosemary Gartner, PhD**
Department of Sociology
University of Toronto
Toronto, Ontario M5T 1P9
Canada

**Candace Kruttschnitt, PhD**
Department of Sociology
University of Minnesota
Minneapolis, Minnesota 55455-0412

**Sylvia Lang, PhD**
Transportation Research Institute
University of Michigan
Ann Arbor, Michigan 48105

**John H. Laub, PhD**
Henry A. Murray Research Center,
Radcliffe College and
College of Criminal Justice
Northeastern University
Boston, Massachusetts 02115

**Janet Lauritsen, PhD**
Department of Criminology and
Criminal Justice
University of Missouri
St. Louis, Missouri 63121

**Patricia McDaniel**
Department of Sociology
Rutgers University
New Brunswick, NJ 08903

**Richard E. Nisbett, PhD**
Institute for Social Research
University of Michigan
Ann Arbor, Michigan 48105

**Gregory Polly, PhD**
Department of English
Harvard University
Cambridge, Massachusetts 02138

**James T. Tedeschi, PhD**
Department of Psychology
University at Albany
State University of New York
Albany, New York 12222

# 1

# Introduction

**R. Barry Ruback**
**Neil Alan Weiner**

Interpersonal violent behaviors, actions that intentionally threaten, attempt, or inflict physical harm on others, are caused by multiple factors at multiple levels, from the biological and psychological to the social and cultural. Although studies have been conducted at each of these levels, there are relatively few systematic investigations of how society and culture, especially traditional social and cultural ideas and their associated values and effects (Kroeber & Kluckhorn, 1952), condition violent behaviors. There is little sound empirical evidence about either the mechanisms of social and cultural influences or the degree to which these influences eclipse, or are eclipsed by, influences operating at other levels.

Further research on social and cultural factors may be especially important for the study of violent behaviors because of the insights that can be provided about some central and sometimes controversial hypotheses about these behaviors. For example, one common broad hypothesis is that, to some extent, violent behaviors have biological components. An important way to examine this hypothesis is to study the degree to which, for a particular biological trait or state, the frequency and severity of a specific violent behavior varies across social and cultural contexts and across situations within these contexts. Although conducting such a study poses some daunting problems, it is nevertheless essential for a valid test of the hypothesis.

Violent behaviors, in particular those that are not lethal in outcome, are defined, legitimated, and sanctioned in such dissimilar ways in different societies and cultures that their comparative study is considered by some scholars to be virtually impossible. These researchers have tended to focus only on the methodological flaws and the resulting interpretative ambiguities. The whole point of comparative analysis is to identify, through innovative if not perfect study designs, the extent to which social and cultural similarities and differences exist. Doing so is necessary for disentangling the various social and cultural pathways to violent behaviors.

The aim of studies of violent behaviors that span multiple societies and cultures is no different from the aim of any other scientific enterprise—the differentiation of general causes from those that are specific. Achieving this aim *requires* that comparisons be made.

Understanding how social and cultural influences operate entails as an essential aspect a comparative slant, distinguishing diverse social and cultural factors, processes, groups, structures, and institutions. Societies and cultures differ in their social (e.g., racial and ethnic heterogeneity, demographic composition, exposure to a broad range of beliefs and attitudes, levels of education and literacy, methods of child raising), political (e.g., geographical size, number and types of political parties, complexity of power structures, social inequality, democratic traditions, participation in the political process), and economic (e.g., modernization, industrial and economic development, economic inequality) dimensions (Jahoda, 1979; Murdock & Provost, 1973). To ignore these differences is to be a cultural chauvinist. Although we may think that the contemporary research on interpersonal violent behaviors is sophisticated because it generally involves one or another social or cultural comparison, in fact, much of what we know, or think we know, about the social and cultural origins of violent behaviors is provincial. What routinely passes as comparative knowledge is based mainly on data collected and on ideas circulating in modern Western nations, and, more limiting still, these ideas are nascent, commonly no more than 20 to 30 years in the making.

This volume, which grew out of a Special Issue of *Violence and Victims* [8(3), 1993 (Fall)], explores how the social and cultural sciences can more rigorously, systematically, and collaboratively pursue their investigations into the causes of violent behaviors. Scientific analyses of social and cultural influences have moved well beyond the evidence and insights of personal knowledge, but these explanations are still segmented, fragmentary, and weak, both for theoretical reasons and because of such practical limitations as research cost and logistics (e.g., availability of pertinent data, staff with the necessary skills). The goal of this volume is to begin to organize what we know from social and cultural standpoints about violent behaviors and to point out ways that might increase our knowledge base.

## THE PURPOSE OF THIS VOLUME

Adopting a comparative approach, this volume brings together several influential, provocative, and sometimes controversial lines of inquiry about how society and culture influence violent behaviors and how social and cultural scientists might organize themselves better to accelerate the pace of their work on this topic.

We knew from the outset that this project would be difficult, but we did not realize just how much so. As the book progressed, it became apparent, through the labors of the contributors, that a little analytical thought and research had embraced a truly comparative perspective with respect to the social and cultural origins of violent behaviors, especially nonfatal violence. We discovered that this impoverishment was as true for large surveys, whether cross-cultural or cross-national, as it was for ethnographies. The sparseness of the comparative research has meant that explanations of violent behaviors are still overwhelmingly tentative because they are conditional on the specific societies and cultures analyzed. The paucity of systematic work has spurred those involved in this volume to think long and hard about two broad critical issues: (a) the impediments to and pitfalls of comparative social and cultural inquiry and (b) the potentials of and opportunities for such inquiry.

Much of the work presented in this volume is seminal; therefore, the volume is introductory rather than conclusive, a departure point for future work rather than an exhaustive encyclopedic rendition. Notice that some important topics have not been covered, such as how violent behaviors are influenced by the interaction of environment, society, and culture. More basically, however, even with respect to those topics that have been selected, many of the questions raised about them cannot yet be adequately answered because of severely impoverished or flawed data. We are fortunate to be able to introduce papers by internationally recognized scholars whose writing spans many key issues: critical summaries of existing research; informed speculation about causal relationships; and discussions of the reasons for research deficiencies and ways to remedy them.

We asked the authors to address the following four points, to the extent that it was possible within their topic area: (a) the potential, unique contributions of the social and cultural sciences to understanding violent behaviors in the United States and elsewhere; (b) the most informative social and cultural theories and findings; (c) the strengths and weaknesses of these theories and findings; and (d) conclusions about what major gaps in knowledge exist, why they exist, and how they can be filled. In other words, we asked the authors to be, in equal measure, both critical and innovative and to stimulate discussion about violent behaviors from a comparative standpoint. Each chapter has met that challenge.

## AN OVERVIEW OF THE CHAPTERS

The chapters in this volume move from methodological issues to general theoretical perspectives to more specific types of research questions. Chapters 2 and 3 tackle daunting methodological issues. In chapter 2, "Methodological Issues in Cross-Cultural Large-Survey Research on Violence," Rosemary Gartner discusses the strengths and weaknesses of cross-national large-survey studies on violent behaviors; the kinds of data that are currently available for doing this type of research; what is presently known, descriptively and analytically, based on large-survey studies; new directions that this kind of inquiry might productively take; and the research strategies, methodologies, resources, and organizational skills and capabilities that will be needed to pursue aggressively these new directions. As Gartner notes, the enormous sweep and magnitude of the comparative theoretical and research issues requires basic, innovative changes in the way such studies are managed and conducted. Social and cultural scientists will need to experiment with the design and implementation of their research if they are to make breakthroughs in knowledge.

Chapter 3, "Issues in Cross-Cultural Studies of Interpersonal Violence," by Carol R. Ember and Melvin Ember, discusses the strengths and weaknesses of ethnographic data in general and of the Human Relations Area File in particular, the research implications of the differences between cross-national and cross-cultural analyses, the achievements and promises of cross-cultural ethnography, and the definitional and measurement hurdles that have had to be negotiated in the ethnographic study of violent behaviors. The chapter summarizes research findings on several topics, such as how child socialization, war, and social structure can influence involvement in violent behaviors. The chapter concludes with suggestions for improving, theoretically and methodologically, cross-cultural research on violence.

Chapter 4, "Violent Criminal Behavior over the Life Course: A Review of the Longitudinal and Comparative Research," by John H. Laub and Janet L. Lauritsen, examines the existing longitudinal, developmental research on violent criminal behaviors, identifying the precursors of aggression and violent behaviors. It also assesses the evidence pointing to the continuity of violent behaviors over the life course and traces patterns of change in individuals' propensity for aggression and violent behaviors. Only a handful of relevant studies could be located. Not surprisingly, then, the authors were unable to answer definitively the extent to which variations in violent behaviors across societies and cultures reflected differences in opportunity structures or differences in developmental pathways (trajectories) and role and status changes (transitions). The chapter concludes with specific recommendations for improving future comparative research (e.g., adopting a life course approach; examining a wide range of antisocial behaviors, including violent ones; looking at intra- and intersocietal variations in violent and related behaviors and their social and cultural correlates) in order to sort out the degree to which stability and change in violent behaviors over the life course is dependent upon a person's social and cultural placement.

Chapter 5, "Violence and Gender: Differences and Similarities Across Societies," by Dane Archer and Patricia McDaniel, examines the extent to which gender differences in the types and rates of aggression and violence can be explained by four different theoretical models: biology, society, environment, and culture. After reviewing research on each of these theoretical models, the authors frame specific, and sometimes rival, hypotheses about the differences between male and female aggression and violence within and across societies. Although the authors focus on gender, the discussion of the four theoretical models actually applies to other factors that might affect violent behaviors and that fall within the scope of more than one of the models (e.g., age, race, ethnicity). In order to begin their assessment of the relative validity of the theoretical models, the authors examine data from their own cross-national study of personal attitudes toward, values and expectations about, and justifications for aggression and violence. In their study, subjects were asked to write endings for 12 standardized open-ended stories. Although within societies males consistently ended their stories with greater aggression and violence, across societies there was substantial variation in the levels of males' and females' aggression and violence. The authors conclude that all four theoretical models have merit: (a) biology influences relative gender differences in aggression and violence within a society and (b) society, environment, and culture influence absolute quantities of attitudes, values, and expectations affecting the levels of aggression and violence within a society.

In chapter 6, "Violence by and Against Women: A Comparative and Cross-National Analysis," Candace Kruttschnitt synthesizes current cross-national research on women's violent offending and victimization. Although comparative knowledge about these issues is limited regardless of the person's gender, it is especially so with respect to women. Very few studies focus on how social and cultural contexts moderate violent involvements and how personal characteristics such as gender might affect the mediation of this violence. Kruttschnitt is especially helpful in explaining how different types of data can be used in investigating these issues: (a) individual-level data help spotlight characteristics (e.g., age, race/ethnicity) and situations (e.g., victim/offender relationship) that place women at risk of violence within particular nations, whereas (b) aggregate-level data concentrate on women's risk of violent involvements across nations and on how societal- and cultural-level factors might account for these risks. Despite the lower involvement of women in violent encounters, relative to that of men, both as offenders and as victims, the magnitude of this disparity can vary substantially by context, historical period, and type of violent behavior. Kruttschnitt suggests that the gaps in our understanding of violence by and against women can be filled by multilevel and multicontextual (social and cultural) research embracing long time periods, a wide range of violent behaviors, and nonofficial data sources.

In chapter 7, "An Evolutionary Psychological Perspective on Male Sexual Proprietariness and Violence against Wives," Margo Wilson and Martin Daly apply evolutionary biology to account for the origins and consistency across time and place of male violence against wives. The central hypothesis is that male proprietariness ("ownership"or "entitlement") over female sexuality and reproductive capacity, although diversely manifested in different cultures, reflects an evolved panhuman masculine psychology—a naturally selected trait representing reproductive "fitness." The evolved masculine psychology embodies a specific adaptation to the problem confronted by generation after generation, regardless of society and culture: enhancing fitness (i.e., outreproducing other members of one's species under conditions of limited reproductive resources). For human males, adaptation often involves the use of physical coercion. Cultural investigations can help identify those cues that trigger in a particular culture the sexually proprietary psychological mechanisms that result in violent behaviors. The salience and prevalence of these cues, both activating and inhibiting, influence the rates of violent sexual proprietariness. Using these ideas, the authors develop a series of hypotheses accounting for variations across societies and cultures in levels of violent sexual proprietariness.

In chapter 8, "Homicide and U.S. Regional Culture," Richard E. Nisbett, Gregory Polly, and Sylvia Lang argue that the high rates of homicide in the southern United States stem from "the culture of honor" embraced by the English cavaliers who settled Virginia but, more importantly, from the Scotch-Irish pig herders whose descendants dominate the region today. In response to insults, Southerners exhibit more violence than do Northerners, particularly when honor is involved. Also, homicides resulting from arguments (e.g., barroom brawls, lovers' quarrels) are much more likely to occur in the South than in the North. Importantly, the research program of which this work is a part combines both aggregate-level data (e.g., FBI Supplemental Homicide Reports by region) and individual-level data (e.g., attitudes and behaviors of individuals raised in the South and in the North). The individual- and aggregate-level data provide convergent support for the culture of honor hypothesis.

In chapter 9, "A Social Interactionist Approach to Violence: Cross-Cultural Applications," Richard B. Felson and James T. Tedeschi argue that, despite differences across societies and cultures in the specific forms that violent behaviors might take and in the technical means of pursuing these behaviors, violence is used by the members of all societies and cultures as a coercive technique to achieve three specific goals: (a) to produce obedience and compliance, (b) to restore justice through retribution, and (c) to assert and protect social identities. For each of these goals, the use of violence follows incentive-driven decision making. The social interactionist approach formulated by these authors underscores the importance of social factors in causing and moderating interpersonal violence. Specifically, they focus on how prior grievances and social control can prompt violent exchanges and on how the social dynamics of face-to-face interactions and the actions of third parties (e.g., mediators, inciters, bystanders) can trigger and fuel violent escalations.

As we note in chapter 10, these diverse and rich companion chapters stimulated our thinking about the social and cultural aspects of violent behaviors, the ways in which these aspects can be better investigated, and possible methods of controlling violent behaviors based on these improved investigations. We hope and expect others to be similarly stimulated.

## REFERENCES

Jahoda, G. (1979). A cross-cultural perspective on experimental social psychology. *Personality and Social Psychology Bulletin, 5,* 142–148.

Kroeber, A. L., & Kluckhorn, C. (1952). Culture: A critical review of concepts and definitions. *Papers of the Peabody Museum of American Archeology and Ethnology, 47,* 379–392.

Murdock, G. P., & Provost, C. (1973). Measurement of cultural complexity. *Ethnology, 12,* 379–392.

# 2

# Methodological Issues in Cross-Cultural Large-Survey Research on Violence

## Rosemary Gartner

Although many scholars acknowledge the importance of a cross-cultural perspective on violence, few agree on precisely how to advance such a perspective. Recognizing the risks this dilemma poses, this chapter briefly outlines potential contributions, as well as very real and well-documented limitations, of one type of cross-cultural research on violence: research based on large-survey data sets. There is also a review of the major sources of cross-cultural survey data on violence and a summary of research based on them. With this review as a framework, a conclusion is provided with suggestions for new directions in cross-cultural research using large-survey data on violence.

## CONTRIBUTIONS AND LIMITATIONS OF CROSS-CULTURAL LARGE-SURVEY RESEARCH ON VIOLENCE

Large-survey cross-cultural research offers some distinctive possibilities for the study of violence beyond those provided by cross-cultural ethnographic research or case studies. Serious forms of violent behavior are relatively rare in most societies; large-survey data capture enough of these acts for statistical analysis of trends over time and systematic comparisons of levels of violence across cultures. The range of societies that can be included for relatively low cost is greater when using large-survey data. Perhaps most important, some substantive issues are uniquely suited to large-survey research. Many who use large-survey data view rates of violent behavior as social facts—emergent properties of a group or society that cannot be explained simply by reference to the individuals comprising the group. Large-survey data allow consideration of properties of a culture or society that affect violent behavior but that can neither be reduced to individual or small-group characteristics nor uniquely identified in single-society studies. While rates of violent behavior are made up of the purposive actions of individuals, these actions occur in particular cultural, institutional, and structural settings and are shaped by group and systemic responses to them. Large-survey data are necessary for examining the processes that link violent behaviors at the micro-level with these macro-social influences.

Whether the limitations of existing survey data on violence preclude fulfilling this potential is controversial (Beirne, 1983; Christie, 1970; Newman, 1977). Several aspects of these data have discouraged some from conducting cross-cultural survey research and others from granting it credence. These include assumptions about the equivalence of acts classified by legal officials, medical officials, and researchers in different societies; the abstraction of violent acts from their interpersonal and cultural contexts; difficulties in documenting random and systematic measurement errors due to underreporting, misrecording, and overreporting; and the absence of information on forms of violence neglected by official control systems. Each of these raises questions about the validity and reliability of survey data on violence.

Reliance on data compiled by government bureaucracies also raises questions about appropriate sampling units and units of analysis. At present, most large-survey data on violence are collected by national agencies that delineate reporting areas by political boundaries. Even surveys on violence by independent researchers are defined by these political boundaries, because researchers often use data from government agencies to design sampling strategies or measure contextual variables. However, the cultural boundaries that identify populations of particular interest for violence research subdivide and overlap these political boundaries. Consequently, existing survey data on violence and the research based on them are not truly cross-cultural, but cross-national.[1] (See Ember & Ember in this volume for a discussion of the distinction between cross-national and cross-cultural.)

As valid as these concerns are, they are not unique to research on violence. Much cross-cultural survey research faces similar problems. Some are inherent in the measurement and data collection processes; others result from the limited resources and multiple, often conflicting purposes of organizations that collect data on violence. Our goal should be to increase sensitivity to the effects of these problems and to avoid uses of the data that exacerbate them—not to abandon cross-cultural survey research on violence. This may require, as I describe below, a shift away from conventional analyses of large-survey data and toward more innovative approaches to and methods of cross-cultural research.

## SOURCES OF LARGE-SURVEY DATA ON VIOLENCE

There are three sources of large-survey data on violence: official statistics, victimization surveys, and self-report surveys. They share many of the limitations described above; each also possesses particular advantages for the cross-cultural study of violence.

### Official Statistics on Violence

The major sources of cross-cultural official statistics on violence have received considerable scrutiny (Bennett & Lynch, 1990; Huang & Wellford, 1989; Redo, 1986; Vigderhous, 1978; Wolfgang, 1967). My review of these data is therefore brief and draws heavily from others' work. The most commonly used large-survey data on violence are compiled by the United Nations, INTERPOL, and the World Health Organization (WHO). The U.N. and INTERPOL collect data on various types of violent criminal acts and actors; WHO collects data on violent causes of death (regardless of legal designation). All three sources are oriented to interpersonal acts of violence rather than to collective, official, or societal forms of violence.

***United Nations***. Since 1946, the U.N. has compiled data on violent crime from its member nations, initially to inform policies on crime prevention and more recently to inform debates over human rights. In 1977, a series of systematic U.N. Crime Trends and Criminal Justice Surveys was begun. These are designed to collect data on broadly defined crime categories for descriptive analyses of crime trends. Member nations are invited to report officially recorded rates of intentional homicide (defined as death purposely inflicted by another, including infanticide and attempts), assault, sex crimes, robbery, and kidnapping, along with other crimes. Each of the three presently completed surveys covers a five-year period and includes over 50 nations from all regions of the world (Redo, 1986).

***International Criminal Police Organization***. INTERPOL has collected and published crime data from national criminal justice agencies since the early 1950s. Its violent crime categories have changed somewhat over time; recent annual reports include data for murder ("any act performed with the purpose of taking human life," including attempts, but excluding manslaughter and abortion), rape, and serious assault. Crime rates, clearance rates, and offender (arrest) data are included for each crime (e.g., INTERPOL, 1986). The number of nations reporting data and the amount of data they provide to INTERPOL varies substantially from year to year; during 1980-84, 145 countries were listed as members of INTERPOL, but no more than 85 reported crime data in a single year.

***World Health Organization***. Since 1948, WHO has collected mortality statistics, classified by cause of death, from national health organizations. Classification of homicides has varied somewhat over time; its basic definition ("deaths due to injuries purposely inflicted by others") has at times included deaths by legal intervention and deaths due to war. Raw and rate data on victims of homicide, broken down by age and gender, are reported for between 40 and 55 nations each year (e.g., WHO, 1989).

***Other Sources of Official Data on Violence***. Some researchers have compiled their own cross-cultural data sets on violent crime, drawing from the above sources, from data in national statistical abstracts, and from direct contact with criminal justice agencies in different nations. Two data sets are particularly extensive: the 110-nation Comparative Crime Data File (Archer & Gartner, 1984) and the Gurrs' data set on crime in 14 western societies (Gurr & Gurr, n.d.). Both contain data on murder, assault, robbery, and rape, although for varying time periods. Other researchers have collected more in-depth data from police forces and other official sources for a small number of countries (or cities within various countries) for specific research projects (e.g., Adler, 1983; Clinard & Abbott, 1973; Gurr, Grabosky, & Hula, 1977; Wikstrom, 1991); often these include detailed information on offenders, victims, and circumstances of the acts.

***Evaluating Data on Violence from Official Sources***. The advantages of data sets from official sources are obvious to researchers who use them extensively. They provide easily accessible data, often for a large number of countries, sometimes for extended time periods. Where nations are the units of observation, data on a wide variety of social correlates of violence can be assembled from published sources. Data reported annually allow replication of analyses for different years and time-series analyses of trends in violence. Finally, by using data from different sources, and based on different measures, analyses can use data quality controls to examine the robustness of findings.

Limitations of these data sets revolve around issues of the reliability and validity of their measures of violent behaviors or events. Violence that is non-criminal (e.g., official violence) or not direct and interpersonal (e.g., delayed deaths from workplace hazards) is largely excluded from consideration. Moreover, the criminal and interpersonal acts of violence that are measured are subject to under-reporting, misclassification, and variations in classification. Because the extent of these errors is difficult to establish and no doubt varies across societies, correcting for them has not been possible. Consequently, most researchers view as untenable analyses that directly compare societies on their rates of such violent crimes as rape, assault, or robbery.

Homicide is another matter, however. Because cross-national homicide data from official sources generally are considered to be reasonably reliable for many analytic or explanatory purposes[2] (Bennett & Lynch, 1990; Huang & Wellford, 1989; Vidgerhous, 1978), they have sustained a large body of research. Nevertheless, homicide data do have their limits, and their validity is design-specific (Archer & Gartner, 1984). Probably the most widely accepted use of official statistics on homicide is as indicators of trends in lethal interpersonal violence in time-series analyses. Time-series homicide data can also provide a standard of comparison for time-series data on nonlethal forms of violence. If, for example, rates of robbery, rape, and/or assault show similar trends to homicide rates, conclusions about changes in overall levels of violence can be made with greater confidence. Dissimilar trends raise more serious inferential questions, but can provide opportunities for examining variations in the relationships between different types of violent behaviors and the official and unofficial reactions to them (Gurr, 1989; Weiner & Zahn, 1989).

Unfortunately, researchers have not fully exploited official statistics as sources of data on reactions to violence—a use that would obviate many concerns over their reliability and validity as measures of violent behavior and encourage investigation of significant theoretical and practical problems. For example, although official data on rape are invalid for cross-cultural comparisons of violent behavior, they could be used to compare changes in the reporting and recording of rape over time. While such analyses face their own problems with data quality, at least they do not require the assumption that their data are adequate measures of violent behavior. Furthermore, analyses of reactions to violence would provide an important balance to the preponderance of cross-cultural survey research on homicidal behaviors.

## Victimization Survey Data

Victimization surveys, which were developed to correct for the limitations of official data on violence, are now fielded in several countries. A few countries have conducted surveys for over a decade; many others have recently experimented with victimization surveys. Most are modeled after the U.S. National Crime Victimization Survey but have been modified to reduce costs. These modifications include using more limited geographical areas (sometimes a single city), eliminating re-interviews, reducing sample sizes, using different sampling techniques, including few (or no) filtering questions, and asking about different types of victimizations (Block, 1984b). As a consequence, data from various surveys suffer from a lack of comparability.

To redress these problems, a coordinated International Crime Survey (ICS) was fielded in 1989 in 14 countries.[3] The ICS standardized the sampling procedure, interview method, series of questions, and data analysis across all 14 countries. The survey included questions about three general categories of violent acts: robbery, sexual assault, and other assault (including threats). Those reporting a victimization were asked about its location, harm, and police involvement, along with sociodemographic and life-style information. The survey was intended to provide descriptive data for comparisons of crime levels across countries and for comparisons with official data within countries.

In a report on preliminary findings from the survey, coordinators of the ICS also discuss its limitations (van Dijk, Mayhew, & Killias, 1991). The ICS shares several problems with other victimization surveys, including dependence on the discretion of respondents to report violent acts and a lack of information on offenders. But there are additional problems specific to the ICS. The goal of 2000 interviews in each country was not consistently achieved so that sample sizes range from 1000 – 5300. The use of telephone interviews produced non-response rates of 40 – 60% in some countries. Sampling error is large and varies across countries. Consequently, the survey undercounts violent victimization and is marred by systematic error. Further, intra-country variations (e.g., rural/urban, regional) in victimization are not adequately documented, limiting the value of the data for cross-cultural analysis.

Notwithstanding these problems, the ICS highlights the potential value of victimization surveys for cross-cultural research on violence. It provides opportunities to analyze information on violent acts not typically reported to officials, to assess the reliability of and specify the domain tapped by official data on nonlethal acts of violence, and to examine victims' perceptions of and reactions to violence. Nevertheless, growing awareness of the limitations of victimization surveys for studying violence (e.g., Reiss & Roth, 1993) argues against viewing the ICS or other victimization surveys as clearly superior to official statistics for measuring the "true" extent of violence in a society. At the same time, comparisons of data on violence from official and unofficial sources can remind us that an objectively identifiable and measurable set of violent behaviors does not exist. It is this socially constructed nature of violence that is both a challenge and justification for cross-cultural research.

**Other Survey Data on Violence**

Some researchers have fielded their own cross-cultural surveys on violence to address questions that cannot be examined using existing large-survey data. There are two types of these data sets: (1) self-reported survey data on specific types of violent victimization and offending, and (2) self-reported survey data on perceptions or definitions of violence.

An example of the first is Straus's Conflict Tactics Scales (CTS), which queries respondents about their involvement in violence in marital and other intimate relationships (Straus, 1979). Questions about verbal and physical aggression and violence cover acts ranging in severity from throwing things to assault with a deadly weapon. The CTS has been fielded in a number of countries, including the United States, Canada, Finland, India, Japan, Belize, Puerto Rico, and Israel (Steinmetz, 1981; Kumagai & Straus, 1983). Analyses of CTS data have been largely descriptive; more systematic analyses are precluded by nonrandom sampling designs, lack of conceptual equivalence in different translations, and variations in response categories.

Examples of the second type of survey include Newman's (1976) survey of perceptions of deviance in six nations, and Archer's (Archer & McDaniel, 1989) 11-nation survey of high school students' attitudes and justifications about conflict resolution. These two efforts are notable for both their substance and their methodology. Both are interested in how a wide range of (potentially) violent events—including national conflicts, collective protests, official violence, and interpersonal aggression—are perceived and evaluated. Both used a variety of techniques (including back translation, multiple pretests, and collaboration with foreign scholars) to ensure cultural equivalence while preserving variations in meaning across cultures.

These data collection efforts have expanded the range of questions that can be addressed in cross-cultural research on violence much beyond those addressing behavioral incidence or prevalence. Unfortunately, these largely individual efforts are few in number and necessarily restricted in scope; consequently, they have not yet supported extensive research literatures.

## RESEARCH BASED ON LARGE-SURVEY DATA ON VIOLENCE

Data from official sources, victimization surveys, and other surveys together have sustained a diverse body of research on violence in different societies. My discussion highlights only some of the consistent findings and general conclusions from this work. I differentiate studies by the size of their samples (i.e., large-*n* or small-*n* studies), and by their analytic purpose (i.e., descriptive or explanatory).[4]

### Large-*N* Survey Studies of Violence

By necessity, large-*n* research is based primarily on data from the U.N., INTERPOL, or WHO, because these are the major sources of data on a large number of nations. In these studies, data on violence are treated as measures of behavior; most focus on homicide because of concerns over data reliability and cross-cultural variation in definitions of nonlethal violence.

*Descriptive Studies.* Most of the descriptive work is done by official organizations, such as the U.N. and the U.S. Bureau of Justice Statistics (e.g., Kalish, 1988; U.N., 1985). Its authors typically caution against (but sometimes draw) direct comparisons of levels of violent crime across countries, instead concentrating on describing trends over time. General substantive conclusions from these analyses are that variation in violent crime across societies is probably greater than variation in violence within most societies; the United States has higher rates of violent crime than all other developed nations and many less-developed nations; violent crime rates appear to be higher in less-developed than in more-developed nations; and different types of violent crime track different trends over time and in different regions of the world. Important methodological conclusions are that single-year observations of a society's violent crime rate should not be relied upon, especially for less-developed nations; and that data from multiple sources should be compared and used for data quality control purposes whenever possible.

***Analytic Studies.*** Cross-sectional analyses of homicide predominate among analytic studies. Most attempt to identify macro-social correlates of homicide and/or test theories of national variation in homicide rates. Typically, countries are treated as the unit of analysis and the question asked is: "What explains differences in violence across nations?" Sometimes countries are treated as the context of analysis and the question asked is: "Is homicide associated with [some structural correlate] in the same way within different nations?"[5]

Variation among cross-sectional studies in their samples, time frames, data sources, and models have resulted in diverse, at times inconsistent, and often complex findings. Nevertheless, some conclusions are possible; since this work has been summarized elsewhere (LaFree & Kick, 1986; Neuman & Berger, 1988), I note only two. First, of the wide variety of political, economic, cultural, and social indicators included in these analyses, only one—income inequality—has shown a consistent (and positive) association with homicide rates (Avison & Loring, 1986; Braithwaite & Braithwaite, 1980; Krahn, Hartnagel, & Gartrell, 1986; Messner, 1980; 1989). Second, none of the theoretical perspectives tested in these studies has received strong support. For example, studies testing predictions derived from modernization theory do not find consistent relationships between homicide and urbanization, industrialization, or other measures of modernization (Groves, McCleary, & Newman, 1985; Kick & LaFree, 1985; McDonald, 1976; Messner, 1982).

Less common than cross-sectional studies are large-*n* time-series analyses of homicide rates. Adding the dimension of time allows tests of a wider range of theories and can increase the statistical power of an analysis, but requires attention to changes in data reliability over time. Some studies analyze time-series data for each nation separately and then combine and compare the results across nations; others use data that are pooled across countries and over time and analyzed simultaneously. A major advantage of a time-series approach is the ability to test causal hypotheses about social change and social process, which cannot be done in cross-sectional studies. Because time-series analyses are less numerous, few general conclusions from this work have emerged. Some findings, because they are consistent with the results from cross-sectional studies[6], are worth noting. Economic inequality, disrupted family structures, and cultural support for violence appear to be positively related to homicide rates, at least in developed nations. Nevertheless, age structure of the population and urbanization do not consistently predict levels of or trends in homicide across countries (Archer & Gartner, 1984; Gartner, 1990).

Partly as a response to the diverse findings from these studies, some scholars now analyze rates of violent crime disaggregated by age or gender of the victim or offender (Fiala & LaFree, 1988; Gartner 1990; 1991; Gartner, Baker, & Pampel, 1990; Hartnagel, 1982; Marshall, 1982; Messner, 1985). By working with more homogeneous categories of violent behavior, the hope is to develop explanations with narrower scope but greater empirical support. While promising, too little of this work exists to draw meaningful conclusions.

Large-*n* cross-cultural research has been criticized both for its mission and its methods.[7] Because it seeks to generalize about violence, large-*n* research tends to ignore the particular context in which violence occurs, abstracting it and assuming its equivalence across diverse contexts. As a consequence, nations are treated as collections of variables, without unique meaning, history, or existence, and sample sizes often are maximized at the cost of more theoretically-meaningful sampling. The emphasis on generality also justifies aggregating diverse acts into a few general categories that obscure the heterogeneity of violence.

While these features of large-*n* research can be defended in pursuit of generalization, others that result from constraints of data and method cannot. Because of the lack of appropriate data and difficulties in estimating multilevel models, large-n research has yet to specify and test for intervening causal mechanisms linking violent behaviors to their macro-social correlates. Furthermore, the conventional preference for linear multivariate statistical techniques means that causes tend to be treated as solely additive, as the same in all contexts, rather than as conditioned by sociocultural context. Finally, the analytic techniques used in large-*n* research assume that observations from different nations are statistically independent; but cultural contact and cultural diffusion among nations clearly challenge this assumption.[8] Together, these criticisms of mission and method provide implicit (and often explicit) support for studies based on smaller samples.

## SMALL-*N* SURVEY STUDIES OF VIOLENCE

These studies use both official and unofficial data to measure violent acts and reactions to and perceptions of violence. Consequently, the range of substantive issues addressed is much wider than in large-*n* studies, where violent acts are the primary interest. With fewer cultural contexts to consider, small-*n* studies can devote more attention to cultural differences in the meaning and definition of violence. Smaller samples also permit analyses of nonlethal violence, because detecting and correcting for cultural differences in definitions and reporting practices is feasible. In most cases, this work treats countries (or cities within them) as the context of study; here, primary interest is in examining and comparing the distribution and correlates of violence within a small number of strategically selected societies.

***Descriptive Studies.*** Because descriptive small-*n* studies vary greatly in data and method, their findings are not easily summarized. Many compare the social patterns, characteristics, and circumstances of violent crime in two or a handful societies. Wikstrom's (1991) analysis of official data on violent crime in Stockholm and Philadelphia is an example. Victimization data have been used for similar purposes (e.g., van Dijk et al., 1991; Block 1984a). This work suggests there are many similarities among societies in the social patterns and correlates of violent crime, despite large differences between societies in levels of violence (Gurr, 1989). For example, young people, urban residents, and males are consistently at higher risk of violent offending and victimization, regardless of the total amount of violence in a society.

Studies based on survey data on attitudes toward violence suggest the patterning of attitudes parallels that of violent behavior. For example, Archer's work (Archer & McDaniel, 1989; Archer, In Press) shows that the large differences across societies and between genders in expectations about the use of violence mirror societal and gender differences in violent behavior. Methodological insights into the relationship between violence and reactions to it have also emerged from these descriptive studies on attitudes and behavior. For example, victimization data reveal that although the reasons for not reporting victimizations to officials are the same in diverse contexts, the proportion of crimes that are not reported varies considerably across nations (Block, 1984b).

*Analytic Studies*. Researchers who do small-*n* analytic studies tend to choose their samples more strategically than do large-*n* researchers. For example, societies may be chosen to maximize similarities or differences either in violence or in the cultural and structural factors thought to be associated with it. Choosing societies based on their similarities (e.g., level of development) achieves a rough statistical control over variables that is not possible in small-n studies through more systematic procedures. Choosing societies based on their differences ensures greater variation in variables of interest and increases generalizability. Some small-*n* studies analyze relationships between violence and its correlates within societies and then compare findings across societies (e.g., LaFree & Birkbeck, 1991). Others treat societies as the objects of study and try to determine the factors that differentiate them on their patterns of violent acts and reactions (e.g., Adler, 1983).

Small-*n* studies that use cross-sectional designs combine attention to the complexity and uniqueness of each case with efforts to generalize from commonalities across cases (e.g., Adler, 1983; Clinard, 1978; Clinard & Abbott, 1973; Newman, 1976). The same features are present in time-series analyses of small-*n* samples, but these have the added potential to examine reciprocal relationships between violence and reactions to it. For example, Gurr and his colleagues (Gurr et al., 1977) have done exemplary work that traces trends in public order, crime, and crime control policies from the early nineteenth century in Stockholm, London, Calcutta, and New South Wales. What distinguishes this study are its examination of collective and official violence, as well as its close attention to issues of data reliability and validity—important advantages of its case-study design.

Other work uses time-series data to explore the historical, cultural, and structural basis for differences across nations in violent crime (Hagan, 1989; Lenton, 1989) or to analyze the relationships between trends in violent crime and its economic, demographic, or other social correlates within selected nations (Brenner, 1976; Gartner & Parker, 1990; Shelley, 1981; Zehr, 1981). Taken together, these diverse studies indicate that the factors associated with differences in levels of violence across nations, and those associated with changes in violence within nations, are not consistently the same.

Small-*n* studies of violence are subject to several criticisms. Concerns exist over the representativeness of the cases studied, the generality of findings, and their ability to test theories. What is gained through in-depth examination of a few societies may be counterbalanced by a loss of more general understanding of the causes and consequences of violence across diverse societies.

## GENERAL CONCLUSIONS FROM CROSS-CULTURAL SURVEY RESEARCH ON VIOLENCE

The research reviewed here is characterized by a wide variety of research designs, questions, and purposes. Nevertheless, some general conclusions are possible. Perhaps most basic is that there are immense and enduring differences among societies in their levels and types of violence. But we have only begun to identify the bases for these differences. We know that historical, demographic, political, economic, and other institutional factors are implicated, but the mechanisms linking these macro-social factors to the group and individual processes that produce violence have not been identified. Furthermore, no set of systematically and consistently measured macro-social factors has been found that distinguishes between societies with high and low levels of violence, or that explains changes over time in violence within diverse societies.

What this research makes apparent are the impediments to identifying macro-level causal relationships in the production of violence. For example, while few question that violence and its correlates are linked in complex feedback processes, researchers using cross-cultural data have yet to adequately model such reciprocal relationships. Similarly, the possibility of spurious relationships between violence and its macro-social correlates has been largely neglected. Yet some of the consistently observed relationships—such as that between homicide and income inequality—may be due to the mutual influence of a third variable, such as a sociocultural factor (see below) that may be exceedingly difficult to measure.

With these qualifications in mind, let me identify some general themes from the literature on cross-cultural differences in violence that are consistent with specific findings from the research reviewed above. These themes offer promising leads for future research because they draw from in-depth case studies of particular societies and from U.S.-based research on criminal violence, as well as from large-survey cross-cultural research.

Sociocultural contexts that appear to be least conducive to interpersonal and collective violence are those (1) with strong systems of informal social control backed by highly consensual normative systems; (2) where individuals are linked in networks of communal obligation and mutual interdependence; and (3) where social institutions encourage political integration and other ties that crosscut ascribed social groupings (see, e.g., Adler, 1983; Bayley, 1976; Braithwaite, 1989; Currie, 1985; Gartner, 1990; Horwitz, 1990; Messner, 1989). Societies with these characteristics tend to have a collectivist or communitarian orientation that is reflected in their social, political, and economic ideologies and practices. This orientation may represent the sociocultural factor crucial to explaining well-known societal differences in violence. Operationalizing this element for purposes of quantitative analysis is a critical challenge for cross-cultural research on violence.

The validity of these observations is limited, then, by the current absence of measures of a sociocultural context for violence. It is also limited by the types of violence that researchers using large-survey data sets have been able to study. Large-survey data sets have neglected most noncriminal forms of violence and criminal forms of violence that are less likely to come to the attention of officials or survey researchers. For example, nonlethal violence among family members and other intimates is systematically under-represented in these data sets. Furthermore, existing legal designations and classifications restrict possibilities for studying some conceptually and experientially meaningful categories of violence. Hate crimes against ethnic or religious minorities, for example, become indistinguishable from assaults or other violent crime in existing data sets. Whether the tentative observations offered above would hold for these diverse forms of violence is presently unknown.

## THE FUTURE OF CROSS-CULTURAL LARGE-SURVEY RESEARCH ON VIOLENCE

Cross-cultural research based on large-survey data clearly has yielded useful insights into the phenomenon of violence—and can continue to do so because of its particular strengths. Large-survey data provide unique opportunities to

- analyze violence and the reactions to it as characteristics of social groups and societies, not simply as individual behaviors;
- examine serious, but relatively rare, as well as non-serious violence;
- search for general trends and patterns in violence common across many cultures; and
- test theories of violence as a macro-social phenomenon affected by large-scale social processes and change.

Large-survey data therefore are ideally suited for cross-cultural research oriented to the goals of generalization and abstraction.

Unfortunately, research based on large-survey data has failed to achieve its full potential because of the limits of existing data sets and the preference for particular research designs. As noted earlier, large-survey data sets are hindered by

- problems of reliability and validity in measuring violence;
- differences in how they select, classify, and count violent acts;
- lack of information on the circumstances and people involved in violence; and
- data collection units defined by political, rather than cultural, boundaries.

The characteristics of large-survey data have also encouraged overreliance on certain research designs—in particular, quantitative analyses of official statistics from large samples of societies. The contributions of these studies are limited because they

- focus on homicide to the exclusion of nonlethal and noncriminal violence;
- treat societies as collections of scores on variables, rather than as coherent entities with particular cultural contexts for violence; and
- assume the equivalence of behaviors and reactions that are combined into officially-designated categories.

These criticisms of data and method imply two conclusions. To minimize the deficiencies listed above, we need to develop both new sources of cross-cultural data on violence and new analytical approaches to the cross-cultural study of violence.

## ALTERNATIVE SOURCES OF CROSS-CULTURAL DATA ON VIOLENCE

Proposals for alternative systems of cross-cultural data collection on violence (especially criminal violence) are not new. Wolfgang (1967), Robinson (1978), and Wilkins (1980), among others, have argued for systems that would redress the drawbacks of existing data sets. Of particular promise are alterations in two features of the data collection process: changes in sampling units and changes in the phenomena measured.

National sampling units have a number of advantages, both practical (e.g., official organizations presently collect data at the national level, reducing costs to researchers) and conceptual (e.g., most laws and policies that define and react to violence are formulated at the national level). But data collected at the national level are deficient in several respects. They obscure sub-national (and hence subcultural) variation in violence and its social correlates, they are distant from the violent acts and reactions to them that they are intended to measure, and they discourage examination of the processes by which acts become part of an official or unofficial record. Moreover, nations vary tremendously in their capacity and willingness to collect reliable data on violent acts and actors.

One solution is to coordinate data collection efforts in sub-national jurisdictions. A strong case can be made for initiating such efforts in cities or urban areas (Robinson, 1978; Wilkins, 1980), but regional data collection should also be considered. Using cities as sampling units could take advantage of existing administrative units (e.g., police agencies, hospitals, etc.) to increase the efficiency and accuracy of data collection, while avoiding many of the problems associated with national sampling units. The clustering of violence within nations (i.e., in urban areas and in particular regions) would both increase the efficiency of data collection and permit more precise measurement of the relevant contexts for violence (and nonviolence).

Independent researchers working with the cooperation of local officials could minimize many of the deficiencies associated with existing survey data sets. First, a wider range of violent events and the range of reactions to them could be documented in greater detail. Noncriminal forms of violence, criminal forms of violence that are grossly under-reported in official statistics, and official forms of violence could be more fully documented. With more detailed data, violence could also be grouped into categories with greater conceptual consistency (e.g., robbery homicides could be grouped with robberies; homicides resulting from domestic disputes could be grouped with nonlethal domestic assaults; etc.). By limiting data collection to an urban area, it would also be feasible to document the various stages of official response to cases of criminal violence, as well as unofficial, community reactions to violence.

Second, urban- or regional-based data collection would permit measurement of the more immediate contextual factors that affect violence and form the intervening links between individual behaviors and macro-social contexts. In particular, in nations with strong, diverse cultural groups, data from sub-national sampling units would permit examination of the symbolic role that violence plays in different cultures. But other aspects of local contexts could also be elaborated. Large urban areas are crosscut by communities that vary widely in their economic, political, and demographic features—all of which shape more local, subcultural contexts for violence.

Third, researchers more intimately involved in data collection can impose greater control over data quality and develop methods to assess data reliability and validity. This would permit expanding research to include more nonlethal forms of violence. Moreover, to the extent the sources of error in, and the domains tapped by, official statistics on violence could be elaborated in more local research, existing national-level data on nonlethal forms of violence could be used with greater confidence. No data source can hope to portray some objectively true picture of violence in a society; but researcher-collected, local data can help document the ways violence is socially constructed in various measurement processes and inform interpretation of data from official sources.

The value of such a data collection program would depend on several factors. To make a significant and continuing contribution to cross-cultural violence research would require data collection in a sufficient number of cities to permit statistical analysis and comparison, time-series data to adequately model reciprocal causal relationships and social change, and comparable measures of violence and its correlates. Coordination of such an effort could be done through a group of native scholars working independently but regularly interacting. This would necessitate considerable investment of time and money, but is not infeasible. Similar models of data collection, albeit with more limited scope, are already underway: for example, the Homicide Research Working Group includes members from the United States, Canada, Australia, Finland, Sweden, and Israel (Block & Block, 1992). One lesson emerging from these coordinated efforts is that, at present, there is probably more to be learned about violence from gathering detailed data on a smaller number of cases than from continuing to analyze the highly aggregated data generated by national organizations.

## Alternative Analytic Approaches for Cross-Cultural Research on Violence

Data with these characteristics would enormously expand the possibilities for both basic (e.g., theory development and testing) and applied (e.g., policy development and evaluation) cross-cultural research on violence. To fully exploit these possibilities, new analytical approaches are necessary. Fortunately, recent developments in social science methods offer opportunities to preserve the advantages of conventional approaches while compensating for their deficiencies.

Comparative sociologists, in struggling with the ever-present tension in cross-cultural research between generality and particularity, are developing methods that allow systematic attention to both. Ragin and colleagues (1991), for example, have applied his Qualitative Comparative Analysis (QCA) method to cross-cultural data on a number of substantive topics. This innovative method, which uses Boolean algebra as a data reduction technique, combines strengths of quantitative and qualitative research strategies. Its appeal to researchers accustomed to traditional quantitative techniques is its analytically formal and causal orientation; it can also yield delimited theoretical generalizations and be used with a relatively large number of cases. At the same time, QCA allows researchers to treat societies holistically, integrate external (i.e., between-society) analysis with internal (i.e., within-society) analysis, and attend to deviant cases.

One of the major limitations of research based on large-survey data on violence is its failure to examine intervening mechanisms linking the macro-social factors it measures to micro-social factors that produce violence. Recent progress has been made in developing multilevel methods that would explicitly model such linkages (e.g., Bryk & Raudenbush, 1992), which researchers agree is critical for understanding and explaining violence (Reiss & Roth, 1993). Because these methods can be applied to time-series data, they are particularly valuable for investigating the causes and consequences of violence, and the reciprocal relationships between violent acts and reactions to them.

Without doubt, an analytic strategy built around multilevel (e.g., urban, regional, and national levels) survey data would be fraught with problems. Its ideal outcome would be a balance between intensive scrutiny of violence and its control within particular nations and extensive analysis of the sociocultural correlates of violence across many nations. But its actual application would be enormously complex. One way to proceed is by beginning such a project in a small number of strategically selected nations—such as a sample of nations similar in some structural or cultural factors associated with violence but different in their levels or forms of violence.[9]

## CONCLUSION

Notwithstanding actual and potential difficulties, some type of coordinated, cross-cultural research program on violence is sorely needed. An ultimate goal of this program should be the collection of survey data from as many different cultural entities as feasible. Existing large-survey data will continue to be important for describing and explaining very general patterns of serious violence that distinguish societies and change over time. But new types of survey data are also needed—data that capture more diverse forms of violence and portray the sociocultural contexts within which they occur.

A cross-cultural research program should not be limited to survey data, however. Understanding and preventing violence requires multiple sources and types of data—historical, archival data; systematic observational data; ethnographic analysis; and so forth. A cross-cultural approach provides the unique opportunity to separate the effects of macro-social and micro-social factors on violence, but adequately modeling these effects cannot be done with large-survey data alone.

The scope of such a research program has benefits, as well as obvious costs. It would require considerable cooperation among scholars from different nations, cultures, and disciplines. By itself, this cooperation would begin to break down barriers that have pushed research on violence to the periphery and allowed it to be conducted largely by isolated specialists within various disciplines. We can hope that a cooperative research program would raise recognition of the central importance of violence research not only for scholarly purposes, but for community and global interests as well.

## NOTES

1. Nevertheless, I use the term "cross-cultural" instead of "cross-national" throughout this chapter, for the sake of consistency and because cross-cultural research can encompass (but is not limited to) cross-national research.

2. There may be reasons to take exception to this general conclusion. Some argue that cross-cultural differences in definitions of murder render homicide data unusable for most types of cross-cultural comparisons (e.g., Wilkins, 1980). Furthermore, official homicide data reported by some nations for some years appear to be highly unreliable (e.g., Gartner, 1991).

3. The nations participating in the survey were Australia, Belgium, Canada, England and Wales, Federal Republic of Germany, Finland, France, the Netherlands, Northern Ireland, Norway, Scotland, Spain, Switzerland, and the United States.

4. My review only considers works that include data from at least two countries or cultures, because single-nation or single-culture studies are not, strictly speaking, cross-cultural.

5. See Kohn (1987) for a discussion of the distinctions among cross-national analyses that treat nations as the object of study, the context of study, and the unit of analysis.

6. Some findings are also consistent with results from within-country analyses of homicide rates, including the findings regarding income inequality and cultural support for violence. See, for example, Williams and Flewelling (1988).

7. See Ragin (1987; 1991) for a discussion of these problems in comparative research generally, and Beirne (1983), Newman (1977), and Robertson and Taylor (1973) for discussions relevant to comparative crime research.

8. This is known as "Galton's problem" and has perplexed researchers using cross-cultural data for decades. Although the implications of Galton's problem have not been ignored in the literature on comparative violence and crime (e.g., Robertson & Taylor, 1973), attempts to deal with it in large-*n* cross-cultural research are notably lacking. One solution is to test and correct for spatial auto-correlation among geographic units of analysis (Doreian, 1980).

9. Kohn (1987), in his assessment of the prospects for cross-national sociological research, argues for a strategy of selecting a small number of nations that provide the maximum leverage for testing theory or evaluating policy. As he notes, this strategy reduces problems of interpretation that arise when research results differ among nations.

## REFERENCES

Adler, F. (1983). *Nations not obsessed with crime*. Littleton, CO: Rothman.

Archer, D. (In Press). Cultural scripts for violence: Evidence from different societies. In N. A. Weiner & B. Ruback (Eds.), *Socio-cultural aspects of violence behavior*. New York: Springer-Verlag.

Archer, D., & Gartner, R. (1984). *Violence and crime in cross-national perspective*. New Haven: Yale University Press.

Archer, D., & McDaniel, P. (1989). Violence and gender: Differences and similarities across societies. Paper presented at the American Sociological Association Annual Meeting, San Francisco.

Avison, W. R., & Loring, P. L. (1986). Population diversity and cross-national homi-
    cide: The effects of inequality and heterogeneity. *Criminology, 24,* 733-749.

Bailey, D. H. (1976). Learning about crime—the Japanese experience. *Public Inter-
    est, 44,* 55-68.

Beirne, P. (1983). Generalizations and its discontents: The comparative study of crime.
    In E. Johnson, & I. L. Barak-Glantz (Eds.), *Comparative criminology* (pp. 19-38).
    Beverly Hills: Sage.

Bennett, R. R., & Lynch, J. P. (1990). Does a difference make a difference? Compar-
    ing cross-national crime indicators. *Criminology, 28,* 153-182.

Block, C. R., & Block, R. (1992). Homicide Research Working Group: Synopsis of
    proceedings of the charter meeting. *American Society of Criminology, November*
    1991.

Block, R. (1984a). The impact of victimization, rates and patterns: A comparison of
    the Netherlands and the United States. In R. Block (Ed.), *Victimization and fear of
    crime: World perspectives* (pp. 23-28). Washington D.C.: U.S. Department of Jus-
    tice.

Block, R. (Ed.). (1984b). *Victimization and fear of crime: World perspectives.* Washing-
    ton D.C.: U.S. Department of Justice.

Braithwaite, J. (1989). *Crime, shame, and reintegration.* Cambridge: Cambridge
    University Press.

Braithwaite, J., & Braithwaite, V. (1980). The effect of income inequality and social
    democracy on homicide. *British Journal of Criminology, 20,* 45-53.

Brenner, H. M. (1976). Effects of the economy on criminal behavior and the administra-
    tion of justice in the United States, Canada, England and Wales, and Scotland.
    *Economic crisis and crime.* New York: United Nations Social Defence Research
    Institute.

Bryk, A., & Raudenbush, S. (1992). *Hierarchical linear models.* Newbury Park, CA:
    Sage.

Christie, N. (1970). Comparative criminology. *Canadian Journal of Corrections, 12,*
    40-46.

Clinard, M. B. (1978). *Cities with little crime.* Cambridge: Cambridge University Press.

Clinard, M. B., & Abbott, D. J. (1973). *Crime in developing countries: A comparative
    perspective.* New York: Wiley.

Corsaro, W. A. (1992). Cross-cultural analysis. In E. F. Borgatta, & M. L. Borgatta
    (Eds.), *Encyclopedia of sociology* (pp. 391-395). New York: Macmillan.

Currie, E. (1985). *Confronting crime: An American challenge.* New York: Pantheon.

Doreian, P. (1980). Linear models with spatially distributed data: Spatial disturbances
    or spatial effects. *Sociological Methods and Research, 9,* 29-60.

Fiala, R., & LaFree, G. D. (1988). Cross-national determinants of child homicide.
    *American Sociological Review, 53,* 432-445.

Gartner, R. (1990). The victims of homicide: A temporal and cross-national compari-
    son. *American Sociological Review, 55,* 92-106.

Gartner, R. (1991). Family structure, welfare spending, and child homicide in devel-
    oped democracies. *Journal of Marriage and the Family, 53,* 231-240.

Gartner, R., Baker, K., & Pampel, F. C. (1990). Gender stratification and the gender
    gap in homicide victimization. *Social Problems, 37,* 593-612.

Gartner, R., & Parker, R. N. (1990). Cross-national evidence on homicide and age
    structure of the population. *Social Forces, 69,* 351-371.

Groves, W. B., McCleary, R., & Newman, G. R. (1985). Religion, modernization, and
    world crime. *Comparative Social Research, 8,* 59-78.

Gurr, T. R. (1989). Historical trends in violent crime: Europe and the United States. In T. R. Gurr (Ed.), *Violence in America*, Vol. 1 (pp. 21-54). Newbury Park, CA: Sage.

Gurr, T. R., Grabosky, P. N., & Hula, R. C. (1977). *The politics of crime and conflict: A comparative history of four cities.* Beverly Hills: Sage.

Gurr, T. R., & Gurr, E. (n.d.). *Crime in western societies, 1945-1974.* (ICPSR 7769) Ann Arbor: Inter-University Consortium for Political and Social Research.

Hagan, J. (1989). Comparing crime and criminalization in Canada and the U.S.A. *Canadian Journal of Sociology, 14,* 361-371.

Hartnagel, T. F. (1982). Modernization, female social roles, and female crime: A cross-national investigation. *Sociological Quarterly, 23,* 477-490.

Heiland, H-G., Shelley, L. I., & Katoh, H. (Eds.). (1992). *Crime and control in comparative perspectives.* New York: Walter de Gruyter.

Horwitz, A. V. (1990). *The logic of social control.* New York: Plenum.

Huang, W. S. W., & Wellford, C. F. (1989). Assessing indicators of crime among international crime data series. *Criminal Justice Policy Review, 3,* 28-48.

International Criminal Police Organization. (1986). *International crime statistics for 1984-1985.* Paris: INTERPOL General Secretariat.

Kalish, C. B. (1988). *International crime rates.* Washington DC: Bureau of Justice Statistics.

Kick, E. L., & LaFree, G. D. (1985). Development and the social context of murder and theft. *Comparative Social Research, 8,* 37-58.

Kohn, M. L. (1987). Cross-national research as an analytic strategy. *American Sociological Review, 52,* 713-731.

Kohn, M. L. (Ed.). (1989). *Cross-national research in sociology.* Newbury Park, CA: Sage.

Krahn, H., Hartnagel, T. F., & Gartrell, J. W. (1986). Income inequality and homicide rates: Cross-national data and criminological theories. *Criminology, 24,* 269-295.

Kumagai, R., & Straus, M. A. (1983). Conflict resolution tactics in Japan, India, and the USA. *Journal of Comparative Family Studies, 14,* 377-392.

LaFree, G. D., & Birkbeck, C. (1991). The neglected situation: A cross-national study of the situational characteristics of crime. *Criminology, 29,* 73-98.

LaFree, G. D., & Kick, E. (1986). Cross-national effects of developmental, distributional, and demographic variables on crime: A review and analysis. International Annals of *Criminology, 24,* 213-235.

Lenton, R. (1989). Homicide in Canada and the U.S.A.: A critique of the Hagan thesis. *Canadian Journal of Sociology, 14,* 163-178.

Marshall, I. H. (1982). Women, work, and crime: An international test of the emancipation hypothesis. *International Journal of Comparative and Applied Criminal Justice, 6,* 25-37.

McDonald, L. (1976). *The sociology of law and order.* Montreal: The Book Centre.

Messner, S. (1980). Income inequality and murder rates: Some cross-national evidence. *Comparative Social Research, 3,* 185-198.

Messner, S. (1982). Societal development, social equality, and homicide: A cross-national test of a Durkheimian model. *Social Forces, 61,* 225-240.

Messner, S. (1985). Sex differences in arrest rates for homicide: An application of the general theory of structural strain. *Comparative Social Research, 8,* 187-201.

Messner, S. (1989). Economic discrimination and societal homicide rates: Further evidence on the cost of inequality. *American Sociological Review, 54,* 597-611.

Neuman, W. L., & Berger, R. J. (1988). Competing perspectives on cross-national crime. *Sociological Quarterly, 29,* 281-313.

Newman, G. (1976). *Comparative deviance: Perception and law in six cultures.* New York: Elsevier.

Newman, G. (1977). Problems of method in comparative criminology. *International Journal of Comparative and Applied Criminal Justice, 1,* 17-31.

Ragin, C. C. (1987). *The comparative method.* Berkeley: University of California Press.

Ragin, C. C. (Ed.). (1991). *Issues and alternatives in comparative social research.* New York: E. J. Brill.

Redo, S. M. (1986). The United Nations Crime Trends Surveys: Comparative criminology in a global context. *International Annals of Criminology, 24,* 163-179.

Reiss, A. J., & Roth, J. A. (1993). *Understanding and preventing violence.* Washington D.C.: National Academy Press.

Robertson, I., & Taylor, L. (1973). *Deviance, crime, and socio-legal control: Comparative perspectives.* London: Martin Robertson.

Robinson, R. W. (1978). A model system for world crime statistics. *International Journal of Comparative and Applied Criminal Justice, 2,* 61-69.

Shelley, L. I. (1981a). *Crime and modernization: The impact of industrialization and modernization on crime.* Carbondale: Southern Illinois University Press.

Shelley, L. I. (Ed.). (1981b). *Readings in comparative criminology.* Carbondale: Southern Illinois University Press.

Steinmetz, S. K. (1981). A cross-cultural comparison of marital abuse. Journal of Sociology and Social Welfare, 8, 404-414.

Straus, M. A. (1979). Measuring intrafamily conflict and violence: The Conflict Tactics (CT) Scales. *Journal of Marriage and the Family, 41,* 75-88.

United Nations. (1985). *New dimensions of criminality and crime prevention in the context of development: Challenges for the future.* A/CONF.121/18. Report prepared for the Seventh U.N. Congress on the Prevention of Crime and the Treatment of Offenders. New York: U.N. General Secretariat.

van Dijk, J. J. M., Mayhew, P., & Killias, M. (1991). *Experiences of crime across the world.* Deventer, the Netherlands: Kluwer.

Vidgerhous, G. (1978). Methodological problems confronting cross-cultural criminological research using official data. *Human Relations, 31,* 229-247.

Weiner, N. A., & Zahn, M. A. (1989). Violence arrests in the city: The Philadelphia story, 1857-1980. In T. R. Gurr (Ed.), *Violence in America,* Vol. 1 (pp. 102-121). Newbury Park, CA: Sage.

Wikstrom, P-O. H. (1991). Cross-national comparisons and context-specific trends in criminal homicide. *Journal of Crime and Justice, 14,* 1-25.

Wilkins, L. T. (1980). World crime: To measure or not to measure. In G. R. Newman (Ed.) *Crime and deviance: A comparative perspective* (pp. 17-39). Beverly Hills: Sage.

Williams, K. R., & Flewelling, R. L. (1988). The social production of criminal homicide: A comparative study of disaggregated rates in American cities. *American Sociological Review, 53,* 432-445.

Wolfgang, M. (1967). International crime statistics: A proposal. *Journal of Criminal Law, Criminology, and Police Science,* 58, 65-69.

World Health Organization. (1989). *World health statistics annual.* Geneva: World Health Organization.

Zehr, H. (1981). The modernization of crime in Germany and France, 1830-1913. In L. I. Shelley (Ed.) *Readings in comparative criminology* (pp. 120-140). Carbondale: Southern Illinois University Press.

# 3

# Issues in Cross-Cultural Studies of Interpersonal Violence

**Carol R. Ember**
**Melvin Ember**

There are relatively few cross-cultural studies of interpersonal violence. In those studies, relatively few variables have been studied; and very few of those variables have been measured similarly. In addition, the methodology of these studies differs considerably from the methodology of cross-national studies. With all these limitations, the results of the cross-cultural studies are remarkably consistent with each other and with cross-national findings. We have two main purposes here—to compare the methods of cross-cultural and cross-national research on interpersonal violence (mainly focusing on homicide) and to discuss the achievements and promise of cross-cultural studies.

## CROSS-CULTURAL VS. CROSS-NATIONAL RESEARCH

Because the reader of this volume is probably not that familiar with cross-cultural research, we begin our discussion by comparing it in some detail with cross-national research.

Cross-cultural research is more broadly comparative than cross-national research. The cross-national study compares only relatively complex societies. The cross-cultural study compares all types of society, from small hunter-gatherer societies with bands of fewer than 75 people and total populations in the hundreds, to large societies dependent on intensive agriculture with cities and populations in the millions. To be sure, the typical cross-cultural sample contains few or no modern industrial societies; so cross-cultural research is typically not as broadly comparative as it could be. But, other things being equal, the cross-cultural type of study (which compares many if not all types of society) has a better chance than other kinds of comparison of coming close to the goal of knowing that an observed relationship has more or less universal validity, which is consistent with the general scientific effort to seek more and more comprehensive explanations.

Cross-national research typically uses data that are quantitative; they may not originate or be found in quantitative form, but they can be counted and measured using interval scales. Cross-cultural research typically uses data that are qualitative to begin with; the information in ethnographic texts[1] is therefore more likely to be measured ordinally. Data that are quantitative to begin with may or may not be freer of error than qualitative data. It is important to remember that court or police records do not provide direct measures of violence; all measures are indirect, whether they use raw data that are sentences or numbers. Still, it is often presumed that the coding of qualitative information is likely to introduce a good deal of error, because coding rules do not always fit ethnographic descriptions that are often ambiguous and rarely quantitative. In addition, acts of violence may occur infrequently, and therefore the ethnographer (who is there for only a relatively brief time) may not collect information on cases over a longer period of time. But error in a cross-cultural measure can be reduced by using various controls on data quality, as we discuss below. Another way to reduce error is to omit ethnographic cases that are not rated reliably (Ember & Ember, 1992b).

The two types of comparative research (cross-cultural and cross-national) also differ in their typical units of analysis. The type of unit usually compared in the cross-cultural study is the society, a population that more or less contiguously inhabits a particular area and speaks a language not normally understood by people in neighboring societies. Cross-national research typically compares countries or nation-states, each of which is politically unified at least in some formal respects (e.g., there is a national parliament and/or some other centralized authority). Thus, in the modern world there are many nations that contain more than one society in the anthropological sense. Nigeria contains scores of societies (e.g., Hausa, Yoruba, Ibo); the former Yugoslavia and Soviet Union also contained many societies, as did most empires in world history.

The United States of America is often considered a multicultural society, but (except for Native American groups which are separate "nations") it does not contain more than one society in the anthropological sense. Ethnic groups here are not distributed mostly as distinct territorial populations, and most members of most ethnic groups no longer speak their original languages. For example, Italian-Americans do not just live in New Haven, and few still speak Italian.

The coding of variables for a society in a cross-cultural study is generally based on the ethnographic information that is available for at least one community or locality in the society. Thus, most cross-cultural studies are really comparisons of localities in different cultures, as John Whiting (1954) noted years ago. Most anthropologists conduct their field work in a single community. It is about that group that they write about mostly, despite the titles of books and articles referring to the society. This would be a problem if cross-culturalists were interested in establishing the typical values (on variables) for a society. But cross-cultural researchers are usually interested in discovering a relationship between or among variables, rather than inferring what is characteristic of a particular society in the sample, and so the fact that the community in the ethnography may or may not be representative of the society is not a problem for statistical inference about cross-cultural relationships. (For further discussion of sampling in cross-cultural studies, see Ember & Otterbein 1991.)

Once it is understood that most of the data in cross-cultural studies come from ethnographic monographs and articles written by anthropologists, most of the other differences between cross-cultural and cross-national research become obvious. So, for example, because most anthropologists worked in non-

Western societies in the past, cross-cultural samples are usually weighted toward preindustrial societies. Not only did such societies lack industry, they were generally also self-sufficient, and either hardly or not at all involved (at least at first) in a world market economy. In addition, most fieldwork sites until recent times lacked complex centralized governments. In fact, in about half of the societies described in the ethnographic record, the effective political unit was no bigger than the community (percentage calculated from Murdock, 1967).

There are implications of this last fact for the study of violence such as homicide. Societies that are politically organized at only the local level tend to have informal leadership (there are no full-time officials), their rules tend to be understood and shared without codified or written law (there are no lawyers), and they generally lack formal mechanisms (police, judges, etc.) for dealing with interpersonal violence (Textor, 1967). Hence, the study of violence in the ethnographic record cannot rely on court or police records, which are generally nonexistent.

But the differences between cross-cultural and cross-national studies also provide advantages. One of the most important, as indicated above, is that the ethnographic record provides us with a broader scope of variation than cross-national records. For example, all nations we know of have class stratification. While nations may vary with regard to degree of inequality, none of them approach the degree of social equality that characterizes societies labelled "egalitarian" by anthropologists, where families and other kin groups have more or less equal access to resources and power. If it is hypothesized that interpersonal violence is related to social inequality, it is important to study egalitarian as well as stratified societies. The relationship might obtain only in some types of societies, not across the entire range of recorded cultural variation.

Beatrice Whiting (1965) also directed us to the need for the broadest possible comparative studies. Many studies in this and other nations suggest a link between "broken homes" (i.e., father-absence) and juvenile delinquency. But, as B. Whiting pointed out, other conditions that may cause delinquency are also associated with broken homes, conditions such as a low standard of living. Unless and until we look at societies where father-absence is "normal" and is not associated with those other conditions, we will not be able to see if father-absence by itself predicts more delinquency.

Despite the methodological difficulties involved in cross-cultural research, such research is not only possible; it is also quite informative about the possible causes of interpersonal violence, as we shall see.

If we are extolling the advantages of cross-cultural research here, we do not mean to imply that such research must rely only on traditional ethnography; indeed, as we make clear later, other types of comparative research might be conducted to study interpersonal violence as well as other aspects of cultural variation. Yet, even with the limitations of traditional ethnography, the cross-cultural results obtained thus far suggest some conclusions about the etiology of interpersonal violence that are clearly applicable to our own society.

In what follows, we first review some of the special problems of definition and measurements in cross-cultural studies of interpersonal violence. Then we turn to a review of the results of such studies. Finally, we discuss how cross-cultural studies of violence might be improved, and why some theoretical possibilities should be investigated further.

## ISSUES OF DEFINITION AND MEASUREMENT

The two main issues to contend with in studying violence cross-culturally are: how to define variables theoretically to fit cross-cultural variation, and how to construct operational measures that can be applied to most ethnographically described cases.

So far we have avoided the word "crime" in discussing interpersonal violence. As we make clear in our discussion below, we prefer a more behaviorist way of talking about violence, since definitions of crime vary so widely from one society to another. For example, in our society, killing an infant intentionally is called a "homicide." However, in many societies, infanticide is a fairly frequent and accepted practice. Minturn and Shashak (1982) report that infanticide occurs in 53% of their mostly nonindustrial sample societies. They suggest that infanticide is best interpreted as "terminal abortion," since the reasons given for infanticide are very similar to those given for abortion (e.g., illegitimacy, excess children) and an infanticide almost always occurs before the ceremony that socially marks or announces a birth (Minturn & Shashak 1982). It seems then that *when* a society socially recognizes a new person (before, at, or after birth) is related to whether or not infanticide is considered a crime. Consider how the debate over abortion rights in this country often hinges on when a fetus is considered human, and deserving of the right to live.

Similarly, the killing of an adult means different things in different societies, depending generally on where the adult comes from. For example, among the Kapauku of western New Guinea, punishment for killing another person (intention did not count) varied according to whether or not the killing occurred within the polity. Killing within the village and the confederacy (comprising a few villages) was punishable; outside those political units killing was not punishable because it was war (Pospisil, 1958). Given that the biggest political unit in many societies is the band or village, it is not surprising that killing a person is interpreted differently in different societies. In our society, we consider killing in the context of war to be legitimate because the killed belong to another country. Further, we may consider execution legitimate not just because of what the "criminals" did, or because justice is administered by constituted authority, but because murderers (and traitors also) put themselves "outside the law" (which would otherwise protect their right to live).

In most if not all societies known to anthropology, the killing of some people is considered wrong or a "crime." But some acts we call "crimes" may have no analogs in other cultures. In a society with no concept of private property in land, the concept of trespass may not have any meaning. In societies where physical punishment is considered an appropriate form of discipline, severe beatings within the family will not be considered assault if they are administered by a person who is considered to have the right to beat someone. For example, wife-beating was not considered a crime by the Serbs (as in a large number of other societies); people believed that a husband had the right to beat his wife for any reason (Levinson, 1989, citing Erlich, 1966).

When cultural meanings vary, it is difficult to use a concept like crime in a cross-cultural study. In anthropological discourse, the cultural meaning is the "emic" meaning (as in the linguistic term "phonemic"). But that meaning is too particular or too difficult to discover reliably in ethnography to provide an easy basis for cross-cultural comparison. So cross-culturalists usually define their variables in "etic" or observable terms (from "phonetic")—the frequency of killing another person, the frequency of wife-beating, rather than the meaning or acceptability of murder and assault. For example, in his study of family violence, Levinson (1989) explicitly says he is looking at the relative frequency of wife-beating (measured ordinally), whether or not a society considers it appropriate or inappropriate.

With regard to wife-beating, the cross-cultural researcher knows to focus on the husband-wife dyad. But what level of social unit should we focus on if we are interested in estimating the relative frequency of homicide? As we discussed above, in many societies the killing of people in another community might be war, not homicide.

So in our own cross-cultural research on war and aggression, we define war as socially organized armed combat between local communities (bands, villages) or larger territorial units (Ember & Ember 1992a, 1992b). We made this decision largely for the reason already mentioned—as of the time of earliest description, half the societies in the ethnographic record had no political organization beyond the community. Given this definition of war, we chose to focus on the face-to-face community to assess the frequency of homicide too. We distinguish between individual homicide and socially organized homicide (e.g., homicide perpetrated by members of a kin group—see Ember & Ember 1992b). While most societies may appear to insist on peace within the community, a killing within the community may not be considered a crime if the community consists of a number of different kin groups that feud with each other periodically. (Many anthropologists consider feuding to be a special type of socially organized aggression.) We also chose to exclude infanticide from our definition of homicide because infanticide is so commonly accepted cross-culturally.

Notice that the measurement decisions we made in our research were in large part driven by the empirical realities of cross-cultural variation and description. If all societies had large political entities (multilocal chiefdoms, states), our definition of homicide would likely have been different. Instead of restricting our purview to killings within the community, we would also consider killings within the larger polity to be homicides (not war). Similarly, if all or most societies considered infanticide a crime, we probably would not have excluded it. However, our decisions could have been otherwise. We could have chosen an "etic" definition that was close to our own culture's definition. Or, we could have focused on each society's largest political unit as the appropriate unit of analysis (compare our definition of war with those of Otterbein [1970] and Ross [1983]).

We decided to focus on the local face-to-face community, which may or may not have been the largest political unit, for three reasons. The first, already mentioned, is that the community was the most inclusive political unit in about half of the societies known to anthropology (as of the times they were first described). Second, just about all societies have a local multifamilial group of people who interact daily (it may be a band, village, or town, or a neighborhood in a city). If a person fears frequent violence within that unit, life might be quite different from what it is like in a safer place. The homicide rate in a city may be lower than in a small town, but the quality of life may be affected by the perception that violence occurs frequently. So, for example, if a city-dweller hears (from gossip or the media) about several murders every day, the level of anxiety may be high even though the homicide rate is lower than in a small town (where a murder occurs only once in 20 years). The third reason we focus on the community in our research is a more practical one, also already alluded to. Ethnographers tend to live most or all of their time in the field in a particular community, and they tend to describe life as particularly experienced in that community. Therefore, we thought it best to have the community as our unit of analysis for the purpose of coding war and interpersonal violence. Even if the ethnographer claims to describe the society as a whole, he or she is still likely to be talking about the area he or she knows best.

Anyone looking at our coding schemes (and those of other cross-cultural researchers) for the frequency of homicide, assault, etc. will almost invariably find ordinal scales at best. The scale might use words like "low," "moderate," and "high." Why do most cross-cultural researchers do this? The answer is relatively simple; most ethnographers do not tell us enough to allow a computation of rate per 100,000 because they rarely give us quantitative information. Indeed, they may not give us even a qualitative frequency statement (e.g., "homicide is rare"). Even if ethnographers mention a number of cases they observed in a specified time period, they usually do not give a denominator (the number of people living in the place described as of the time of observation). For example, with reference to the Lepcha who live in the Indian Himalayas, the ethnographer Geoffrey Gorer (who worked there in 1937) tells us that the only authenticated murder in the area (we are not told how large) occurred two centuries before (Gorer, 1938). Indeed, rates are reported so rarely in the ethnographic record that we did not plan for that possibility; our scale for frequency only allowed for ratings of "low," "moderate," and "high." (Incidentally, our assistants did reliably code the Lepcha as having a low rate of homicide; see Ember & Ember, 1992b.)

Still, even in the absence of qualitative statements about frequency, coders often draw reliable inferences about frequency from other kinds of information. For example, Colin Turnbull (1965), who studied the Mbuti Pygmies, describes numerous quarrels and disputes between individuals. Although individuals were often verbally abusive to each other and sometimes assaulted each other, none of the trouble cases resulted in a homicide. It seems reasonable to infer, given Turnbull's interest in quarrels and disputes, that homicides would have been mentioned if they had occurred. Hence our coders judged the frequency of homicide to be low. In the section below on how we might improve cross-cultural studies, we suggest how researchers could strengthen their results by omitting cases with more ambiguous information. We also discuss later how researchers can formulate rules for inferring absence or a low frequency of something.

Different researchers may have very different reactions to the qualitative nature of typical ethnographic information. Those who are used to working with rates of homicide, assault, etc. as expressed in numbers per 100,000 may find the lack of quantification in ethnography intolerable. Even many cross-culturalists, who are used to quantifying qualititative statements for other purposes, may shy away from studying violence because the "standard" way of measuring frequency is almost always impossible. We have obviously followed a different course. We acknowledge that our three-point ordinal scales are very crude. We believe, however, that such crudeness in measurement is generally likely to result in *weaker* correlations because of more random error. Therefore, we think that if we get a significant result, there must really be something there! Moreover, as we review later, our results *are* consistent with cross-national findings, which makes us feel more secure about our conclusions.

Yet, in retrospect, we do not believe that previous researchers (ourselves included) have gotten the most they could out of the qualitative information available in ethnographies. We return to this idea later when we discuss possible improvements in future research.

We alluded earlier to city-dwellers possibly perceiving that murders were common because they were an everyday occurrence. This brings up a methodological question. Might an ethnographer living in a very small community say that it has a "low" homicide rate just because no homicides occurred while the ethnographer was there? Consider the case of the Aymara of Bolivia and Peru. Two independent ethnographers, Weston La Barre and Harry Tschopik, both said that the homicide rate was low (as reported and discussed by Ralph Bolton, 1984.) In contrast, Bolton (who did his fieldwork 20-30 years later) was particularly interested in homicide and deliberately collected data from dozens of informants and genealogies as well as from police and litigation files. He calculated a rate of *20 prosecuted* homicides per 100,000 population. It may be that the earlier ethnographers mistakenly concluded that homicide was rare because they did not hear of any cases during the time they were there. Alternatively, the homicide rate calculated by Bolton may have been high because his fieldwork was more recent (after all, 20-30 years had passed) and he worked in a different community (cf. Ember, 1985).

If the homicide rate we code or calculate for a case in a cross-cultural study were a function of the size of the ethnographically described community, we would expect that larger communities would generally be judged as having higher rates of homicide. However, as we shall see in the next section, larger communities do not have significantly higher rates of homicide or assault cross-culturally. Therefore, the cross-cultural coding of homicide and other violence rates is not likely to be an artifact of community size.

## REVIEW OF CROSS-CULTURAL RESULTS ON INTERPERSONAL VIOLENCE

### Child Socialization and Violence

Many researchers have looked to customs of child-rearing for the origins of patterns of violence. We discuss three aspects of child-rearing here: (1) frustrating socialization; (2) conditions that may promote what has been called "protest masculinity" or *machismo*; and (3) socialization for aggression.

Following Ross's (1985) factor-analysis, we distinguish two orthogonal types of frustrating socialization—punitive (harsh)socialization and low need-satisfaction. There is some evidence linking both types of frustration to more violence. Two differenct studies using different samples found significant relationships between less need-satisfaction and more violence (Allen, 1972, Ember & Ember, n.d.). Three different studies found significant relationships between harsh socialization and higher rates of violence (Allen, 1972, Palmer, 1970, Ember & Ember, n.d.).

Nevertheless, since some researchers (e.g., Bacon, Child, & Barry, 1963; Lester, 1967) did not find significant relationships between frustrating socialization and violence, and because the different researchers used different measures of need-satisfaction and harsh socialization as well as different measures of violence, it is difficult to say anything conclusive about how a specific type of frustration in socialization is linked to a specific type of violence. With improvements in research methods (some of which are discussed below), the picture may become clearer in the future.

Also equivocal is the research suggesting that there will be higher rates of violence when there are conditions (particularly father-absence) that presumably produce "protest masculinity" in males. As we noted, B. Whiting pointed to the necessity of investigating the effect of father-absence in societies where father-absence is normal and not associated with poverty and social stigma. Using comparative data from field studies in six cultures, B. Whiting (1965) did find more interpersonal violence where fathers are relatively absent. The theory is that "father-absent" boys unconsciously identify with their mothers early in life, because mothers are perceived to control access to resources. Later the boys want to be like men, because they eventually realize that males (not females) actually control resources in their patrilocal, patrilineal societies. According to Whiting, such boys should have a conflict in sex-identity that may be defensively expressed in "protest masculinity" or hyper-masculine behavior (including violence).

In a study comparing more than 100 societies, Bacon, Child, and Barry (1963) present evidence apparently consistent with this theory. Polygynous mother-child households (where the father lives separately from mother and child) and exclusive mother-child sleeping (early in the child's life) are both significantly associated with higher rates of interpersonal violence. Unfortunately, since the investigator's measure of the latter includes murder, assault, rape, and suicide, as well as sorcery and false accusations, it is difficult to know whether all or just some of the particular types of violence are predicted by father-absence. In our own study (Ember & Ember; 1993, n.d.), which looked at some different types of violence separately, the results are equivocal. We looked at ten child-rearing customs that have been presumed (by previous researchers) to lead to identity conflict in males, but found only one (mother sleeps closer to baby than to father) to be significantly linked to more homicide and assault.

Another possible explanation of more interpersonal violence is socialization for (and societal encouragement of) aggression in boys. We think socialization for aggression may be the most important cause of high rates of interpersonal violence. Not only is it significantly related in our own research to our measures of homicide and assault rates; socialization for aggression is also the only socialization variable that remains a significant predictor of high homicide in a multiple regression analysis that includes some of the kinds of variables discussed above (parental warmth, parental hostility, and mother sleeping closer to the baby than to the husband—see Ember & Ember [1993; n.d.] for details of the multiple regression analysis).

Even if future studies replicate that socialization for aggression is the main proximate cause of high rates of interpersonal violence, we still need to answer an important question: Why should parents unconsciously or consciously want to train their children (boys in particular) to be physically aggressive? We think that parents so motivated are trying to produce unambivalent, more effective warriors. Why else would pacified societies be significantly lower on socialization for aggression (Ember & Ember, 1993; n.d.)? That finding suggests that parents stop encouraging aggression when they no longer need warriors. It would seem then that high rates of homicide and assault are unintended (not necessarily desired) consequences of socialization for aggression in boys.

In short, the results of our multiple regression and path analyses suggest the following theory of interpersonal violence: more war causes people to encourage more aggressiveness in their boys (to make them more capable warriors), and more socialization for aggression inadvertently causes more interpersonal violence (homicide and assault); in addition, war also has a direct effect on interpersonal violence, perhaps because war legitimizes violence (see Ember & Ember [1993; n.d.] for details of the evidence supporting the theory that more war may be the ultimate cause of more homicide and assault).

## War and Violence

Whatever may explain the linkage between war and interpersonal violence, that relationship is one of the clearest and most replicated cross-cultural findings. Textor (1967) provided the scholarly community with a large set of intercorrelations for a large number of societies. Referring to those data, Eckhardt (1973) noted that four different measures of "militarism" were significantly linked to frequency of interpersonal violence. (The violence ratings were from Bacon, Child, & Barry [1963]; the data on militarism were from Simmons [1945], who measured frequency of war, and Slater [1964] who measured military glory, bellicosity, and killing and torturing the enemy.) Russell (1972), who factor-analyzed these same data, noted that a "war factor" emerged with high loadings for warfare as well as interpersonal violence. In our own study, using newly coded data and a different sample, we also found significant associations between the frequency of war in nonpacified societies and the separate measures of homicide and assault (Ember & Ember, 1993; n.d.).

In addition to being consistent with each other, the various cross-cultural findings linking interpersonal violence to war are also consistent with cross-national findings. In their extensive cross-national study, Dane Archer and Rosemary Gartner (1984) compared changes in homicide rates of nations before and after major wars. Whether a nation was defeated or victorious, homicide rates tended to increase following a war. These results, and the cross-cultural results, suggest that a society or nation legitimizes violence during wartime. During hostilities societies approve of killing the enemy; afterward, homicide rates may go up because inhibitions against killing have been relaxed (Archer & Gartner, 1984). Needless to say, these results do not necessarily mean that war legitimizes violence; they are certainly consistent with that interpretation, but they are also consistent with other possible interpretations. For example, family structure and social control may be weakened following a war as large numbers of young men at high risk of violence are reintegrated into society.

The idea that war legitimizes violence is echoed in data provided by the political scientist Ted Gurr. Although there seems to be a long-term downtrend in crime in Western societies, which is consistent with an increasing emphasis on humanistic values and nonviolent achievement of goals, such goals may be temporarily suspended during (and immediately after) wartime. In the United States, for example, surges in violent crime rates occurred during the 1860s and 1870s (during and after the Civil War), after World War I, after World War II, and during the Vietnam War (Gurr, 1989).

## Cultural Pattern of Violence

Is there a cultural pattern of violence? Are some cultures more violent generally than others? Because different cross-cultural studies have looked at different things and used different measures, it is difficult to tell if *all* forms of violence co-vary. However, there does appear to be a general pattern.

More often than not, societies with one type of violence have others. Societies with more war tend to have warlike sports (Sipes, 1973), beliefs in malevolent magic (Sipes & Robertson, 1975), and severe punishment for crimes (Sipes & Robertson 1975; Palmer, 1965). High murder rates are associated with a high general aggression index (Palmer, 1970). Feuding is associated with war between polities (Otterbein & Otterbein, 1965). Internal war (within the society) is associated with external war (Ember & Ember, unpublished data). Family violence is associated with violent resolution of conflict (Levinson, 1989). Finally, Ross's (1985) factor-analytic results suggest that societies high in some types of violence tend to be high in others.

## Social Structure and Violence

A few studies have suggested a link between more crime and more complex social systems. Allen (1972), using his own coding of crime (undefined), found that it was more frequent in societies with larger communities, class stratification, and more levels of political integration beyond the community (data on those correlates from the "Ethnographic Atlas," installments of which appeared periodically in the journal *Ethnology* from January 1962 on—see Murdock, 1967).

We raised the issue earlier of whether an obtained association between violence and social complexity might be an artifact of ethnographers' tendency to underestimate rates of homicide and other violence in small communities (which are characteristic of less complex societies). We think that possibility is unlikely, judging by our own results. We used Murdock & Provost's (1973) ordinal scale for size of community (their scale 4) and our own codes for frequency of homicide and assault (Ember & Ember, 1992b, excluding those cases for which we had no reliability scores or whose reliability ratings were 7 or more—see ibid.). We find no significant associations between community size and homicide or assault. However, homicide seems to be related weakly to other aspects of social complexity (political integration, class stratification; ordinal data on the latter from Murdock & Provost [1973], their scales 9 and 10). At best, then, the available results in regard to complexity are equivocal. We return later to some possible links between complexity and child-rearing, which might clarify the nature of the situation.

We turn finally to the possible influence of another kind of socially structured inequality the inequality between men and women. In particular, it appears that violence against women may be linked to sexual inequality; wife-beating (Levinson, 1989) and rape (Sanday, 1981) both seem to be associated with sexual inequality (social and economic). Levinson (1989) finds that wife-beating is significantly more likely when men control the products of family labor and have the final say in household decision-making; and wife-beating is also related to the custom of polygyny and difficulty for a woman to obtain a divorce. Sanday (1981), focusing on rape frequency, found it significantly related to less female power and authority, less female decision-making, and contempt for women as decision-makers. Although Levinson did not took at rape and Sanday did not look at wife-beating, the similarity of their findings strongly suggests a common etiology.

## FUTURE CROSS-CULTURAL RESEARCH ON INTERPERSONAL VIOLENCE

### Suggested Improvements

While researchers may generally recognize the need for replication of results, the process is hindered in the kind of research discussed here by the fact that there are no standard cross-cultural measures of interpersonal violence. Thus, when findings differ from one study to another, they may be due solely to differences in the definition and measurement of violence. In the absence of standard definitions, we recommend that researchers try to measure the various types of violence separately. Separate measures can always be combined into summary measures later, but summary measures cannot be deconstructed.

In constructing "summary" kinds of measures of violence, cross-culturalists should expose their data to item analyses, factor analyses, optimal scaling, etc. to see whether different measures can justifiably be combined into more complex scales (Ember et al., 1991). Such analytic procedures may be standard practice in psychology and sociology, but they are not commonly employed in anthropology.

When cross-culturalists use data provided by previous researchers, they should take steps to ensure that the time and place foci (for the various measures) match for a particular culture. Not doing so will likely increase random measurement error and thereby lower correlations. (For further discussion of this point, see Ember et al., 1991; to match time and place foci across eight different cross-cultural samples, see Ember, 1992.)

Since ethnographies usually do not contain rates of homicide and other violence, and the qualitative information provided is very variable in clarity, we recommend that cross-culturalists develop codes to assess data quality on a case-by-variable basis (Ember et al., 1991; see also Ember & Ember, 1993). So, for example, the highest data quality score might go to a homicide rating based on a reported quantitative homicide rate; the next highest score might go to a homicide rating based on extrapolation from some but not all the necessary quantitative information (e.g., a certain number of homicides reported for a given time frame in a population whose size must be estimated). Lower data quality scores would be given to ethnographers' qualitative statements; where the ethnographer was more attentive to violence, the assigned data quality score might be higher than where an ethnographer described homicide only briefly without providing any evidence. With this kind of "data quality" code for each violence variable (for each society), researchers could reanalyze results with different gradations of data quality. If a finding is stronger in analyses with higher data quality, we would have more confidence that the finding is correct.

Finally, we could do other types of comparative study that could provide high-quality data on variables hardly (not generally) described in the ethnographic record. One thing we could do is compare those cultures for which homicide (and other violence) rates are available. (Bolton & Vadheim [1973] pioneered this strategy in their comparison of 34 cultures in East Africa for which homicide rates had already been published.) A second thing we could do is collect primary data from a limited number of field-sites to test hypotheses (see Munroe & Munroe, 1991a, 1991b; and Johnson, 1991 for discussions of comparisons using primary data). For example, if we want more precise data on rates of homicide and other kinds of violence than we can usually get from ethnographies, comparative field researchers could ask a sample of informants in each of a series of field sites about the frequency of various kinds of violence in the recent past. You do not have to stay in a place 20 years to collect precise information of this sort from memories. In addition, in collecting genealogies you could ask for the causes of death. Not only might comparative field studies provide more and better data on violence; they could also be designed at the outset to allow for intra-cultural as well as cross-cultural testing of hypotheses.

## Theoretical Possibilities to Be Investigated Further

*Protest Masculinity*.  As we have seen, the cross-cultural findings regarding the possible influence of father-absence (and cross-sex identification) on violence are somewhat equivocal. We think this line of research is worth pursuing, but we also think that it is essential to try to disentangle the possibly relevant variables.

One variable that needs to be distinguished is how strongly the society considers aggression to be a component of the male role as compared with the female role. After all, "protest masculinity" or trying to act super-masculine may be likely to involve violence only if aggression is an important part of that role. Consider a culture in which men were expected to be sensitive, caring, and nonviolent. Boys in such a culture who grew up without fathers might try to be super-sensitive and super-nonviolent (Ember & Ember, 1993).

Many researchers have suggested that aloof or antagonistic husband-wife relations may be partially caused by (and possibly also an effect of) conflict in boys about their sexual identification (Whiting, 1965); such conflict has been called an "exaggerated Oedipus complex" (Stephens, 1962; Ember, 1978). Thus, the nature of the husband-wife relationship (for example, whether antagonistic or not) may be critical to an understanding of violent behavior in boys. Indeed, we suspect that the more antagonistic the husband-wife relationship, the more likely mother-child sleeping arrangements and other aspects of mother-child closeness may increase the likelihood of protest masculinity of all kinds, including violent behavior (assuming that violence is part of the conventional male role). If a boy initially wishes to be like his mother, but then perceives that males consider women dangerous, polluting, or inferior, he may feel a much stronger need to reject any or all feminine behaviors in himself (and a stronger need to be violent). If, on the other hand, his father and mother sleep apart, but do not otherwise reject each other, his need to reject femininity in himself and prove that he is "male" may not be as strong.[2]

When mothers bring up their children more or less alone, we also need to try to untangle father-absence *per se* from the mother's view of that absence. We suggest that different reasons for father-absence might differentially affect the mother's behavior toward the child, which in turn may affect the child's behavior (Ember, 1970). Mothers who perceive themselves to be rejected by their husbands (and perhaps by men generally) may displace their anger onto their children, particularly their male children, leading boys to feel rejected by their mothers. Under these circumstances, when boys later wish to be like males, they may have a stronger need to reject female behavior in themselves as well as in others. But raising a child alone because of death or work-related absence may have different consequences because the mother may not be angry with males *per se*.

Regardless of the mother's attitude toward the father, raising a child alone does apparently have consequences for how the child is treated. Rohner (1975) reports that mothers who have no or little help in child care are likely cross-culturally to be more rejecting of children; as such they may provide an aggressive model for the child. So we need to consider the degree to which others help the mother care for the child, in father-absent as well as other families.

We have discussed the possibility that father-absence may have differential effects on aggressive behavior depending on the degree to which society considers aggression to be part of the male role, the degree of husband-wife antagonism, the degree to which mothers reject men, and the degree to which the mother has help in child rearing. With the possible exception of mothers' attitudes toward men, information on these conditions may be found fairly often in ethnographies. But field studies, particularly comparative ones, may be necessary to discover maternal attitudes (after all, most ethnographies have thus far been written by men).

***Socialization: the Role of Modelling versus the Direct Encouragement of Aggression.*** Societies that employ physical punishment (and other harsh treatment of children) are likely to socialize for aggression (Ross, 1985). It seems important to us here to disentangle two different theoretical possibilities. One is that an aggressive role model, regardless of what the model is trying to communicate, will produce children who are more prone to violence. The child may learn from the behavior of the model, regardless of what is taught. If this is so, any parent who severely punishes a child for being too aggressive, or even for not being nurturing, may produce an aggressive child.

A second possible way to produce an aggressive child is for the parent to communicate explicitly that aggression is good. If this is the communication, the child may grow up prone to violence whether a parent rewards or merely does not punish aggressive behavior. To date, the different ways aggression might be encouraged have not been systematically investigated cross-culturally, but they could be.

But what does it mean to encourage aggression? There are a variety of ways to do so—some more obvious than others. Some societies may rely on subtle ways. In our society, parents deny that they encourage boys to be more aggressive than girls (Maccoby & Jacklin, 1974). Nevertheless, they may handle boys more roughly and thereby unconsciously encourage rough and tumble play later in childhood (Ember, 1981). They may give boys toy guns and GI Joe uniforms, but give girls dolls. They may encourage their boys to go out for sports, which in our society are often either directly or symbolically combative, (e.g., football, hockey, wrestling, chess, and many computer games).[3] In some societies, parents may directly encourage aggressive behavior, as when Yanomamo (of the Brazilian-Venezualan border) encourage a four-year old boy to give his father a smack on the face when something displeases the boy (Chagnon, 1968). Do all of these methods work? Are all associated with more homicide and other kinds of violence? Only future research, particularly multivariate studies that can tease out the relative influence of different factors, will possibly tell.

***Frustrating Socialization and Social Complexity.*** As we indicated above, some socialization practices—low need-satisfaction and harsh socialization—are cross-culturally linked in a few studies to higher levels of violence. Many social scientists tend to think that socialization is cause and adult behavior (such as violence) is effect; it is believed that socialization practices change first and, later, adult behavior changes. But the correlation between socialization and adult behavior may be caused in the reverse way. That is, the conditions of life and adult behavior may change first, and then adults begin to socialize differently. For example, it seems that schools and parents have recently been encouraging children to be more afraid of strangers. Why? Might parents and schools be influenced by the real (or perceived) increase in kidnappings, rapes, and other violence, so that they are now starting to teach children to mistrust others more? Or might the increase in perceived violence create more anxiety and stress in parents and lead them to treat their children more harshly? Both are possibilities. After all, as LeVine (1973) suggested, most parents consciously and unconsciously wish their children to be successful in whatever environment they live in. If parents perceive that the environment is changing to a harsher one, they may alter their child rearing practices so that their children can adapt to the new environment.

Another possibility is that higher rates of interpersonal violence and harsher socialization are both spurious products of social inequality and complexity. Levinson (1989), summarizing his own and others' research, reports a link between the physical punishment of children and greater social complexity (cf. also Ross, 1981). Why? Levinson cites a possible explanation by Petersen, Lee, and Ellis (1982): they suggest that in societies with supervised complex work teams and political hierarchy, conformity is highly valued, and parents may be likely therefore to use physical punishment to teach their children to conform.

But why should training for conformity require physical punishment? Is it more efficient than relying on reward? (Physical punishment by an adult who is larger and more powerful can be quite intimidating to a child.) Or is it that the child identifies with the aggressor (who is perceived as also conforming)? Training for conformity by punishment may be more likely in societies that have authoritarian political as well as family systems. Possibly relevant is the suggestion by Barry, Child, and Bacon (1959) that nonindustrial agricultural societies may encourage conformity or compliance because it is too risky for adults to depart from tried and true agricultural methods. Such societies may be likely to be authoritarian.[4] As we have seen, some cross-cultural studies have linked aspects of complexity (particularly social stratification and political hierarchy) to higher rates of some types of violence. So it is possible that the link between frustrating socialization and violence is spurious, that a stratified society selects for frustrating socialization because of organizational requirements and generates interpersonal violence because of frustration and inequities.

What can be done about untangling the causality? Cross-culturalists do not readily have the option of doing time-series analyses, since we rarely have all the variables we need for a series of time periods, much less one time period. A variety of causal scenarios, however, can usually be evaluated for plausibility by contingency control analyses, partial correlations with ordinal or interval data, or multiple regression and path analyses. Researchers need to test for the alternative causal possibilities. Such research still mostly remains to be done. When it is, we should understand more about what produces interpersonal violence, and how to reduce it.

## CONCLUSION

Interpersonal violence is a serious social problem. We believe, as do many other researchers, that solutions to social problems require understanding of their probable causes. If we can discover the causes, we may be able to reduce or eliminate them and thereby solve the problem. What is the role of cross-cultural research in our quest for understanding? As we have discussed in this paper, the major advantage of cross-cultural studies is their potentially universal validity. If results have less than universal validity, the solutions suggested by them may be less effective. An explanation that seems to fit our own society, or a few societies like our own, may be spurious (capitalizing on a historically accidental combination of circumstances). Such an explanation is not likely to suggest effective solutions to a problem. Cross-cultural research is good protection against parochial understanding.

We believe that the validity and power of social science will be enhanced by "triangulation" across the different disciplines. It is essential to try to improve the research strategies of each, but they all have their weaknesses and strengths. If the same or related predictors of interpersonal violence emerge from various kinds of studies—comparisons of individuals within societies, cross-regional comparisons within societies, cross-national comparisons, and cross-cultural comparisons— our understanding will be most trustworthy and most useful.

## NOTES

1. Retrieving and coding information from the ethnographic record is facilitated immeasurably by the annually growing full-text database known as the Human Relations Area Files (HRAF). Complete and incomplete copies of this database, which currently covers more than 350 societies past and present, are located in more than 300 institutions in the United States, Canada, and 24 other nations. Now usually available in microfiche format, the HRAF database will be converted to electronic format (particularly CD-ROM) over the next decade. (See Ember, 1988 for more about HRAF.)

2. We agree with Broude (1990) in principle that researchers should try to measure the relationship between father and infant separately from the relationship between mother and infant. But we do not think that her use of Barry and Paxson's (1971) code for the role of the father in infancy is an adequate measure of "father-absence." According to the Barry and Paxson code, fathers in many cultures have "frequent, close proximity" to their infants. However, on the basis of actual time-allocation data on infant care in a number of societies, Johnson and Behrens (1989, including data from Hames, 1981) suggest that fathers rarely spend more than 10 minutes a day in child

care. Thus, the Barry and Paxson code probably does not pick up much variance in the quantity of time the father spends with the infant.

3. Sipes (1973) defines combative sports as involving two opponents and at least one of the following two features: "(1) There is actual or potential body contact between opponents, either direct or through real or simulated weapons. One of the objectives of the sport appears to be inflicting real or symbolic bodily harm on the opponent or gaining playing field territory from the opponent...;" or "(2) There is no body contact, harm, or territorial gain but there is patently warlike activity ... must include use of actual or simulated combat weapons against an actual or simulated human being." Many computer games that came into widespread use after Sipes's article was published do not apparently fit his definition of combative sports, inasmuch as one of the two opponents is a computer program, but such programs often do simulate an enemy (e.g. aliens from outer space) with whom the player engages in combat.

4. Hendrix (1985), who factor-analyzed the Barry, Child, and Bacon (1959) data, suggests that a number of socialization variables (including positive and negative pressure to be obedient, and punishment for failing to be nurturant and responsible) cluster on a dimension he labels "authoritarianism."

## REFERENCES

Allen, M. G. (1972). A cross-cultural study of aggression and crime. *Journal of Cross-Cultural Psychology*, *3*, 259-271.

Archer, D., & Gartner, R. (1984). *Violence and crime in cross-national perspective.* New Haven: Yale University Press.

Bacon, M. K., Child, I. L., & Barry, H. III. (1963). A cross-cultural study of correlates of crime. *Journal of Abnormal and Social Psychology*, *66*, 291-300.

Barry, H. III, Child, I. L., & Bacon, M. K. (1959). Relation of child training to subsistence economy. *American Anthropologist*, *61*, 51-63.

Barry, H. B. III, & Paxson, L. M. (1971). Infancy and early childhood: Cross-cultural codes 2. *Ethnology*, *10*, 466-508.

Bolton, R. (1984). The hypoglycemia-aggression hypothesis: Debate versus research. *Current Anthropology*, *25*, 1-53.

Bolton, R., & Vadheim, C. (1973). The ecology of East African homicide. *Behavior Science Notes*, *8*, 319-342.

Broude, G. J. (1990). Protest masculinity: A further look at the causes and the concept. *Ethos*, *18*, 103-122.

Chagnon, N. A. (1968). *Yanomamö: The fierce people*. New York: Holt, Rinehart.

Eckhardt, W. (1973). Anthropological correlates of primitive militarism. *Peace Research*, *5*, 5-10.

Ember, C. R. (1970). *Effects of feminine task-assignment on the social behavior of boys.* Ph.D. dissertation, Harvard University.

Ember, C. R. (1978). Men's fear of sex with women: A cross-cultural study. *Sex Roles*, *4*, 657-678.

Ember, C. R. (1981). A cross-cultural perspective on sex differences. In Ruth H. Munroe, Robert L. Munroe, & Beatrice B. Whiting (Eds.), *Handbook of cross-cultural human development* (pp. 531-580). New York: Garland Press.

Ember, C. R. (with the assistance of Hugh Page, Jr., Timothy O'Leary, & M. Marlene Martin) (1992). *Computerized concordance of cross-cultural samples*. New Haven: Human Relations Area Files.

Ember, C. R., & Ember, M. (1992a). Resource unpredictability, mistrust, and war: A cross-cultural study. *Journal of Conflict Resolution, 36,* 242-262.

Ember, C. R., & Ember, M. (1992b). Warfare, aggression, and resource problems: Cross-cultural codes. *Behavior Science Research, 26,* 169-226.

Ember, C. R., & Ember, M. (1993). *War, socialization, and violent crime.* Paper presented at the annual meeting of the Society for Cross-Cultural Research, Washington, D. C.

Ember, C. R., & Ember, M. (n.d.). *War, socialization, and interpersonal violence: A cross-cultural study.* Manuscript submitted for publication.

Ember, C. R., Ross, M. H., Burton, M. L., & Bradley, C. (1991). Problems of measurement in cross-cultural research using secondary data. *Behavior Science Research* (Special issue, Cross-cultural and comparative research: Theory and method), 25, 187-216.

Ember, M. (1985). Evidence and science in ethnography: reflections on the Freeman-Mead controversy. *American Anthropologist, 87,* 906-910.

Ember, M. (1988). The Human Relations Area Files: Past and future. *Behavior Science Research, 22,* 97-104.

Ember, M., & Otterbein, K. F. (1991). Sampling in cross-cultural research. *Behavior Science Research.* (Special issue, Cross-cultural and comparative research: Theory and method), *25,* 217-233.

Erlich, V. (1966). *Family in transition: A study of 300 Yugoslav villages.* Princeton: Princeton University Press.

Gorer, G. (1938). *Himalayan village: An account of the Lepchas of Sikkim.* London: M. Joseph.

Gurr, T. R. (1989). Historical trends in violent crime: Europe and the United States. In Ted R. Gurr (Ed.), *Violence in America, vol. 1: The history of crime* (pp. 21-49). Newbury Park: CA: Sage.

Hames, R. B. (1981). The allocation of parental care among the Ye'kwana. In L. Betzig, M. B. Mulder, & P. Turke (Eds.), *Human reproductive behavior* (pp. 237-254). New York: Cambridge University Press.

Hendrix, L. (1985). Economy and child training reexamined. *Ethos, 13,* 246-261.

Johnson, A. (1991). Regional comparative field research. *Behavior Science Research* (Special issue, Cross-cultural and comparative research: Theory and method), *25,* 3-22.

Johnson, A., & Behrens, C. (1989) Time allocation research and aspects of method in cross-cultural comparison. *Journal of Quantitative Anthropology, 1,* 313-334.

Lester, D. (1967). Suicide, homicide, and the effects of socialization. *Journal of Personality and Social Psychology, 5,* 466-468.

LeVine, R. A. (1973). *Culture, behavior, and personality.* Chicago: Aldine Publishing.

Levinson, D. (1989). *Family violence in cross-cultural perspective.* Newbury Park, CA: Sage Publications.

Maccoby, E. E., & Jacklin, C. N. (1974). *The psychology of sex differences.* Stanford, CA: Stanford University Press.

Minturn, L., & Shashak, J. (1982). Infanticide as a terminal abortion procedure. *Behavior Science Research, 17,* 70-90.

Munroe, R. L., & Munroe, R. H. (1991a). Comparative field studies: Methodological issues and future possibilities. *Behavior Science Research* (Special issue, Cross-cultural and comparative research: Theory and method), *25,* 155-185.

Munroe, R. L., & Munroe, R. H. (1991b). Results of comparative field studies. *Behavior Science Research* (Special issue, Cross-cultural and comparative research: Theory and method), *25*, 23-54.

Murdock, G. P. (1967). Ethnographic atlas: A summary. *Ethnology, 6*, 109-236.

Murdock, G. P., & Provost, C. (1973). Measurement of cultural complexity. *Ethnology, 12*, 379-392.

Otterbein, K. (1970). *The evolution of war*. New Haven: HRAF Press.

Otterbein, K., & Otterbein, C. S. (1965). An eye for an eye, a tooth for a tooth: A cross-cultural study of feuding. *American Anthropologist, 67*, 1470-1482.

Palmer, S. (1965). Murder and suicide in forty non-literate societies. *Journal of Criminal Law, Criminology and Police Science, 56*, 320-324.

Palmer, S. (1970). Aggression in fifty-eight non-literate societies: An exploratory analysis. *Annales Internationales de Criminologie, 9*, 57-69.

Petersen, L. R., Lee, G. R., & Ellis, G. J. (1982). Social structure, socialization values, and disciplinary techniques: A cross-cultural analysis. *Journal of Marriage and the Family, 44*, 131-142.

Pospisil, L. (1958). *Kapauku Papuans and their Law*. New Haven: Yale University Publications in Anthropology, No. 54.

Rohner R. P. (1975). *They love me, they love me not: A worldwide study of the effects of parental acceptance and rejection*. New Haven: HRAF Press.

Ross, M. H. (1981). Socioeconomic complexity, socialization, and political differentiation: A cross-cultural study. *Ethos, 9*, 217-247.

Ross, M. H. (1983). Political decision-making and conflict: Additional cross-cultural codes and scales. *Ethnology, 22*, 169-192.

Ross, M. H. (1985). Internal and external conflict and violence: Cross-cultural evidence and a new analysis. *Journal of Conflict Resolution, 29*, 547-579.

Russell, E. W. (1972). Factors of human aggression: A cross-cultural factor analysis of characteristics related to warfare and crime. *Behavior Science Notes, 7*, 275-312.

Sanday, P. (1981). The sociocultural context of rape: A cross-cultural study. *Journal of social issues, 37*, 5-27.

Simmons, L. W. (1945) *The role of the aged in primitive society*. New Haven: Yale University Press.

Sipes, R. G. (1973). War, sports, and aggression: An empirical test of two rival theories. *American Anthropologist, 75*, 64-86.

Sipes, R. G., & Robertson, B. A. (1975). *Malevolent magic, mutilation, punishment, and aggression*. Paper presented at the annual meeting of the American Anthropological Association, San Francisco.

Slater, P. E. (1964). Unpublished coding guide for the cross-cultural study of narcissism. Waltham, MA: Brandeis University.

Stephens, W. N. (1962). *The Oedipus complex: Cross-cultural evidence*. Glencoe, IL: Free Press.

Textor, R. B., comp. (1967). *A cross-cultural summary*. New Haven: HRAF Press.

Turnbull, C. M. (1965). *Wayward servants: The two worlds of the African Pygmies*. Garden City, NY: The Natural History Press.

Whiting, B. B. (1965). Sex identity conflict and physical violence. *American Anthropologist, 67*, 123-40.

Whiting, J. W. M. (1954). The cross-cultural method. In G. Lindzey (Ed.), *Handbook of social psychology, vol. 1* (pp. 523-531). Cambridge, MA: Addison-Wesley.

# 4

# Violent Criminal Behavior over the Life Course: A Review of the Longitudinal and Comparative Research

John H. Laub
Janet L. Lauritsen

Thirty years ago, Sheldon Glueck (1964, p. 304) pointed out the need for a "Comparative Criminology—a project designed to uncover etiologic *universals* operative as causal agents irrespective of cultural differences among different countries" (emphasis in original).[1] Despite Glueck's recommendation, most extant criminological research overlooks a comparative perspective. Indeed, the recently released National Academy Report, *Understanding and Preventing Violence* (Reiss & Roth, 1993), does not discuss in any detail similarities and differences in violence between countries exhibiting cultural variation.

A similar situation exists in research on human development. For example, Munroe, Munroe, and Whiting (1981, p. ix) note that "findings ... are presented as relevant to the human race." Furthermore, Munroe and colleagues (1981) argue that many variables are assumed to be normative and universal so that their unique contextual effect is not recognized. In a similar vein, Rogoff and Morelli (1989, p. 343) contend that without cross-cultural research, "very basic assumptions regarding developmental goals, the skills that are learned, and the contexts of development" are not examined. As a result, "the generality of theories of development that have been based on Western children" is not known (p. 344).

In this chapter, we restate the concerns of Sheldon Glueck and other researchers by arguing for more comparative research in the study of crime, especially violent criminal behavior. Moreover, we are especially interested in longitudinal research from a comparative perspective. Longitudinal research is required in order to identify the developmental patterns of aggression and violence over the life course.[2] This research strategy also allows us to assess the extent to which these developmental patterns are universal and to investigate the role of sociocultural context in these unfolding processes.

The purpose of this chapter is to review the existing longitudinal research on violent behavior, including whenever appropriate research relating to aggressive behavior. Our primary focus is on long-term longitudinal studies; that is, those studies that have followed individuals from childhood and adolescence to adulthood. Although we will review the extant comparative research on this topic, virtually all of the longitudinal research studies we found comprised individuals from Western societies. As articulated by Sheldon Glueck above, the key issue remains: Are there universal patterns of violent behavior over the life course? Interestingly, Gottfredson and Hirschi (1990, pp. 174-175) argue that "cultural variability is not important in the causation of crime ... and that a single theory of crime can encompass the reality of cross-cultural differences in crime rates." Moreover, Gottfredson and Hirschi (1990, p. 179) state that "culture-dependent" correlates of crime primarily reflect differences in opportunity structures. Given Gottfredson and Hirschi's statements, the examination of potentially unique sociocultural effects in longitudinal research seems especially timely.

## A DEVELOPMENTAL PERSPECTIVE ON AGGRESSION AND VIOLENCE

In general, a developmental perspective focuses on intraindividual behavioral changes from birth until death. Although there are several aspects of development (e.g., biological, cognitive, and emotional), our specific focus in this chapter is on social development over the full life course; specifically, developmental processes from childhood and adolescence through adulthood (see Rutter & Rutter, 1993).

Recently, Sampson and Laub (1993) developed an age-graded theory of informal social control to explain crime and deviance over the life span. Following Elder (1975, 1985), they differentiate the life course of individuals on the basis of age and argue that the important institutions of both formal and informal social control vary across the life span. However, they emphasize the role of age-graded informal social control as reflected in the structure of interpersonal bonds linking members of society to one another and to wider social institutions such as work, family, and school. Unlike formal sanctions that originate in purposeful efforts to control crime, informal social controls "emerge as by-products of role relationships established for other purposes and are components of role reciprocities" (Kornhauser, 1978, p. 24).

Sampson and Laub's developmental framework contains three main components, all of which are useful for our review here. The first is that structural context is mediated by informal social controls, which in turn explain delinquency in childhood and adolescence. In the case of the United States, informal social controls in family and school are found to play a mediating role. The second is that there is strong continuity in antisocial behavior from childhood through adulthood in a variety of life domains. The third component is that social ties to the adult institutions of informal social control (e.g., family, community, work) explain changes in criminal behavior over the life course, regardless of prior individual differences in criminal propensity. A key point in this model is the transition to adulthood and, in turn, the new role demands from full-time employment and marriage. By identifying the transitions embedded in individual trajectories that relate to adult informal social control,

Sampson and Laub (1993) argue that childhood pathways to crime or conformity can be significantly modified by adult social bonds.

We find Sampson and Laub's framework useful in both guiding our review
and for interpreting the findings from longitudinal research on aggression and
violence. Theoretically, this work directs our attention to sociocultural differences in the links between structural and cultural factors, age-graded role transitions, social bonds, and informal social control. Analytically, the strategy of
examining both between-individual differences and intraindividual change is
essential to understanding patterns of aggression and violence over the life course
(Sampson & Laub, 1993). Thus, we keep this approach in mind as we review
the literature, and our subsequent interpretations and recommendations are
guided by the general theoretical framework outlined above.

This chapter organizes the longitudinal research on aggression and violent
behavior along three dimensions: (1) the precursors of aggression and violence
among individuals; (2) the continuity of aggression and violent behavior over
the life course; and (3) patterns of change in individual's propensity for aggression and violence. Although each of these areas have been reviewed in part
elsewhere (see, e.g., Blumstein, Cohen, Roth, & Visher, 1986; Farrington, Ohlin,
& Wilson, 1986; Farrington, 1979; 1987; 1988; Pepler & Rubin, 1991; Reiss &
Roth, 1993; Weiner, 1989), our goal here is to summarize these findings and
illustrate the extent to which life course patterns of aggression and violence
may vary across sociocultural contexts.

It should be noted that nearly all longitudinal studies of individual patterns
of violence are based on samples from the United States or northern European
countries (or their descendants) (Farrington, 1988). Thus, the extent of variation in sociocultural context is relatively limited and as a result, the direct and
indirect effects of context on the development of an individual propensity for
violence are necessarily difficult to ascertain. In addition, sociocultural variation within samples is also limited, since many of the samples are drawn solely
from urban areas, or specific race or gender groups. Definitions of violence are
also predetermined by the available data and consist primarily of behaviors
such as physical assaults, robberies, sexual assaults, and homicides. In other
words, "behaviors by individuals that intentionally threaten, attempt, or inflict
physical harm on others" (Reiss & Roth, 1993, p. 2) and that would be classified as a crime within each society. Intentionally harmful acts that are not in
violation of the law (e.g., warfare, collective violence, aggression by social
control agents) are excluded by the domain assumptions of all available longitudinal studies. Furthermore, a considerable portion of the data on violence
consists of official arrest records for violent offenses. The potential limitations
of such operationalizations of violence are discussed in more detail below.

## Precursors of Aggression and Violence

Longitudinal research conducted in Western societies indicates that the precursors of violent behavior include individual, family, school, and peer factors.
Individual characteristics that can be measured very early in childhood have
been found to be related to later violence either directly or through their association with childhood aggressive behaviors. Such factors include perinatal difficulties for children raised in unstable homes (Kandel & Mednick, 1991; Reiss
& Roth, 1993) and childhood temperament (Loeber & Dishion, 1983; White,

Moffitt, Robins, & Silva, 1990). Children who in the preschool years tend to be fearless, restless, or difficult to manage are more likely to have antisocial behavioral problems in later childhood and early adolescence. Children with low IQ scores have also been found to be more impulsive and aggressive as children and adolescents (Farrington, 1989; Huesmann & Eron, 1984); however, Huesmann and Eron (1984) found that IQ does not significantly predict adult aggression once childhood aggression is taken into account.

Family characteristics, particularly poor family functioning and childrearing, are significantly associated with later violent offending (see, e.g., Farrington, 1979; Loeber & Stouthamer-Loeber, 1986; Widom, 1989). In a meta-analysis of the literature on family and juvenile conduct problems, Loeber and Stouthamer-Loeber (1986) show that four dimensions of family functioning (neglect, conflict, disruption, and parental deviance) are significant predictors of juvenile aggressiveness and delinquency. School factors such as academic failure and truancy are also associated with juvenile aggression (Farrington, 1991), as is rejection by peers (Cairns & Cairns, 1992).

While temperamental, family, school, and peer factors predict between-individual differences in the onset of childhood aggression and violent adult offending, limitations in existing studies prevent a complete test of the causal role of these factors in the etiology of violent offending in the United States and Europe (see Farrington, 1988). Given the lack of detailed time-sequencing information causal inferences remain unclear. For example, it has been argued that difficult children may elicit less effective childrearing techniques (e.g., Lytton, 1990), and that children's aggressiveness leads to rejection by peers (see Coie, Underwood, & Lochman, 1991). Moreover, many of these behaviors in longitudinal studies are measured over fairly long recall periods, also making causal inferences less certain.

Even though each of the above factors have been found to be significant among North American and European samples, it seems unlikely that the predictors of the onset of aggression would be the same across all sociocultural contexts. There is strong anthropological evidence that perceptions of and responses to individual temperament are socioculturally and historically bound, and also vary according to the age and gender of the child and caregiver (see, e.g., Whiting & Edwards, 1988). Family functioning concepts like "neglect" or "disruption" that may predict the onset of aggression in industrialized societies are difficult to operationalize in cultures with different beliefs about children and parenting.

For example, cross-cultural studies of childhood socialization show substantial variation in factors such as the amount of time mothers and fathers spend with young children, the age at which children are assigned responsibilities, the degree to which infants are cared for by child nurse siblings, and the average distance children are away from home when playing (Whiting & Edwards, 1988). High scores on each of these factors might be considered evidence of neglect among U.S. and European researchers, yet there appears to be no clear relationship between these parenting factors and the level of aggression found among children across these diverse cultures (Whiting & Edwards, 1988).[3] Thus, while the precursors of aggression and violence appear to be fairly consistent, additional comparisons to individuals living in dissimilar sociocultural contexts may uncover unique predictors (see Ember & Ember, this volume).[4]

**Continuity of Aggressive and Violent Behavior Over the Life Span**

Are those who display aggressive and violent behavior as children and adolescents more likely to display such behaviors in adulthood? In the United States, Canada, and northern Europe the answer appears to be yes. The stability of aggressive behavior patterns throughout the life course is one of the most consistently documented patterns found in longitudinal research (Caspi, Elder, & Bem, 1987; Gottfredson & Hirschi, 1990; Eron & Huesmann, 1990; Jessor, Donovan, & Costa, 1991; Loeber, 1982; Olweus, 1979; and Robins, 1966; 1978). When using the term stability, researchers are typically referring to the relative position of individuals in the population over time. Individuals who are aggressive in childhood are more likely to engage in violence as adolescents or adults than are persons who did not behave aggressively as children (see Reiss & Roth, 1993: Appendix A for a review).

The stability of aggressive behavior over time is defined as *homotypic continuity*, which refers to the tendency of individuals to exhibit similar behaviors or phenotypic attributes over time (Caspi & Bem, 1990). For example, in a study of the aggressiveness of 600 subjects, their parents, and their children over a 22-year period, Huesmann, Eron, Lefkowitz, and Walder (1984) found that early aggressiveness predicted later aggression and criminal violence. They concluded that "aggression can be viewed as a persistent trait that ... possesses substantial cross-situational constancy" (p. 1120).

More generally, Olweus's (1979) comprehensive review of over 16 studies on aggressive behavior revealed "substantial" stability—the correlation between early aggressive behavior and later criminality averaged .68 for the studies reviewed (pp. 854-855). Loeber (1982) completed a similar review of the extant literature in many disciplines and concluded that a "consensus" has been reached in favor of a general stability hypothesis: "children who initially display high rates of antisocial behavior are more likely to persist in this behavior than children who initially show lower rates of antisocial behavior" (p. 1433). Recent empirical studies documenting stability in criminal and deviant behavior across the life course covered a range of locales and countries including Philadelphia (Wolfgang, Thornberry, & Figlio, 1987); Boston (McCord, 1983; Sampson & Laub, 1993); a Rocky Mountain State in the U.S. (Jessor, Donovan, & Costa, 1991); Kauai (Werner & Smith, 1992); Montreal (LeBlanc & Frechette, 1989); London (Farrington, 1990); Sweden (Magnusson, Stattin, & Duner, 1983; Andersson, 1990); Finland (Pulkkinen, 1982); and Norway (Olweus, 1984). This pattern of continuity thus maintains across different places, historical periods, and methods of reporting, as well as among subgroups within Western societies (e.g. males and females).[5]

Even more intriguing is the empirical evidence suggesting that the linkage between childhood misbehavior and adult outcomes can be found across life domains that go well beyond the legal concept of crime or violence. This phenomenon is defined as *heterotypic continuity*—continuity of an inferred genotypic attribute presumed to underlie diverse phenotypic behaviors (Caspi & Bem, 1990). A specific behavior in childhood might not be predictive of the exact same behavior in later adulthood, but may still be associated with behaviors that are conceptually consistent with that earlier behavior (Caspi & Moffitt, 1993). Although not always criminal per se, adult behaviors falling in this category might include excessive drinking, traffic violations, marital conflict or abuse, and harsh discipline of children.

Evidence for the behavioral coherence implied by heterotypic continuity is found in the Huesmann, Eron, Lefkowitz, and Walder (1984) study, where they report that aggression in childhood was related not just to adult crime but spouse abuse, drunk driving, moving violations, and severe punishment of offspring. Other studies that report a similar coalescence of deviant and criminal acts over time include West and Farrington (1977), Robins (1966), and Jessor, Donovan, and Costa (1991). It is interesting that the findings of heterotypic continuity are consistent with criminological research showing little specialization in crime (Wolfgang, Figlio, & Sellin, 1972; Blumstein et al., 1986; Elliott et al., 1989). We return to this point below.

Highlighting another dimension of heterotypic continuity, Caspi (1987) has argued that personality characteristics in childhood (e.g., ill-tempered behavior) will not only appear across time but will be manifested in a number of diverse situations. Specifically, Caspi (1987) found that the tendency toward explosive, under-controlled behavior in childhood was recreated over time, especially in problems with subordination (e.g., in education, military, and work settings) and in situations that required negotiating interpersonal conflicts (e.g., marriage and parenting). For example, children who display temper tantrums in childhood are more likely to abort their involvement with education, which in turn is related to a wide-ranging number of adult outcomes such as unemployment, job instability, and low income. Robins (1966) also found strong relations between childhood antisocial behavior and adult employment status, occupational status, job stability, income, and mobility. In a similar vein, Sampson and Laub's (1993) reanalysis of the Gluecks' longitudinal data also found that childhood antisocial behavior strongly predicted not just adult criminality but outcomes as diverse as divorce, joblessness, and welfare dependence—independent of age, ethnicity, IQ, and neighborhood socioeconomic status. Overall, there is evidence that individual differences in both antisocial and aggressive behavior remain relatively stable across stages of the life course, regardless of traditional sociological variables like stratification. As Caspi and Moffitt (1993) conclude, robust continuities have been revealed over the past 50 years, in different nations, and with multiple methods of assessment (e.g., official records, teacher ratings, parent reports, and peer nominations of aggressive behavior).

While these studies across time and space yield a set of consistent findings that is rare in social science research, to our knowledge, no comparable research exists among countries or subgroups with vastly different economic or political structures than those found in Western cultures. While it certainly seems plausible that individual stability exists in non-Western countries, one should also expect stability coefficients to be attenuated among those groups for whom violence is very rare. This is because stability coefficients are in part a function of the amount of variation in the measure of aggression or violence. Relatedly, it is also true that stability coefficients are sensitive to definitions of aggression and violence used in the calculations. For example, among societies experiencing collective unrest and rioting, variation in the measure of adult aggression could be at a minimum as nearly all members of a group might be rated high on this index. In other words, measures of the stability of aggressive behaviors are to a certain extent dependent on the operating definition of the phenomenon and the overall level of occurrence of the particular behaviors. This, along with the fact that existing evidence is based on data collected from persons living in relatively similar societies, suggests to us that it may be premature to state that between individual stability is a *universal* phenomenon.

Nonetheless, even with this caution the apparent consistency of between-individual differences in North America and Western Europe requires interpretation. Offering an explanation for continuity over the life course, Sampson and Laub's theory of informal social control incorporates a causal role of prior delinquency in facilitating adult crime by integrating the concept of *state dependence* (Nagin & Paternoster, 1991) with that of *cumulative continuity* (Moffitt, 1993). This work emphasizes a developmental model where delinquent behavior has a systematic attenuating effect on the social and institutional bonds linking adults to society (e.g., labor force attachment, marital cohesion). The idea of cumulative continuity posits that delinquency incrementally mortgages the future by generating negative consequences for the life chances of stigmatized and institutionalized youth. For example, arrest and incarceration may spark failure in school, unemployment, and weak community bonds, in turn increasing adult crime. Serious delinquency in particular leads to the "knifing off" (Caspi & Moffitt, 1993; Moffitt, 1993) of future opportunities such that participants have fewer options for a conventional life. The cumulative continuity of disadvantage is thus not only a result of stable individual differences in criminal propensity, but a dynamic process whereby childhood antisocial behavior and adolescent delinquency foster adult crime through the severance of adult social bonds. In this view, weak social bonding serves as a mediating and hence causal sequential link in a chain of adversity between childhood delinquency and adult criminal behavior (see Laub & Sampson, 1993).

The thesis of cumulative continuity suggests that sociocultural context plays a potentially important role in generating continuity in antisocial behavior (including violence) over the life span. For example, Sampson and Laub (1993) found that social bonds to employment were directly influenced by State sanctions, so that, incarceration as a juvenile and as a young adult appeared to have a negative effect on later job stability, which in turn was negatively related to continued involvement in crime over the life course. Recent studies using data from Sweden and London support the idea that arrest and incarceration negatively influence future employment chances (see Bondeson, 1989; Nagin and Waldfogel, 1992). In contrast, societies (e.g., Japan) that rely on Braithwaite's (1989) notion of "reintegrative shaming" whereby parents (and by extension other key institutions) punish in a consistent manner and within the context of love, respect, and acceptance of the child may well have less continuity in antisocial behavior over the life course. Without comparative research on this issue, it is difficult to say how structural and cultural variations in formal or informal social control contribute to cumulative continuity.

## Change in Violent and Aggressive Behavior Over the Life Span

Dannefer (1984) sharply critiques existing models of adult development, drawn primarily from the fields of biology and psychology, for their exclusive "ontogenetic" focus and their failure to recognize the "profoundly interactive nature of self-society relations" and the "variability of social environments" (p. 100).

He further argues that "the contributions of sociological research and theory provide the basis for understanding human development as socially organized and socially produced, not only by what happens in early life, but also by the effects of social structure, social interaction, and their effects on life chances throughout the life course" (p. 106). Is there is evidence in the criminological literature to support Dannefer's (1984) general observations regarding change over the life course and the importance of sociocultural interactions?

We begin to answer this question with an apparent paradox. While studies reviewed earlier do show that antisocial behavior in children is one of the best predictors of antisocial behavior in adults, "most antisocial children do not become antisocial as adults" (Gove, 1985, p. 123). Robins (1978) found identical results in her review of four longitudinal studies, also stating that most antisocial children do not become antisocial adults. Relatedly, in a follow-up of the subjects of the Cambridge-Somerville Youth study, McCord found that "a majority of adult criminals had no history as juvenile delinquents" (1980, p. 158). Loeber and LeBlanc make a similar point: "Against the backdrop of continuity, studies also show large within-individual changes in offending, a point understressed by Gottfredson and Hirschi" (1990, p. 390).

Caspi and Moffitt's (1993) review reaches a similar conclusion when they discover large variations in the stability of antisocial behavior over time. In particular, antisocial behavior appears to be persistent for a subgroup of males who exhibit extreme behavior problems. Loeber's (1982) review also found that stability is contingent on prior behavior, with extremes in antisocial conduct linked to persistent stability. Moffitt (1993) builds on this information to argue that stability is a trait among those she terms "life-course-persistent" delinquents. In other words, whereas change is the norm for the majority of adolescents, individual-level stability is overwhelming among those at the extremes of the antisocial conduct distribution. This conceptualization points out the dangers of relying on measures of central tendency and aggregate stability correlations which mask divergent subgroups.

Moffitt's (1993) review further suggests that social factors may work to modify childhood trajectories, especially for the majority of youth who are not "life-course persistent." In support of this idea recent criminological research suggests that salient life events influence behavior and modify trajectories—a key thesis of the life course model. Sampson and Laub find support for this notion in their reanalyses of the Gluecks' data. Consistent with the Gluecks' earlier reports (see Glueck & Glueck, 1968), they report that marked differences in adolescent delinquency are relatively stable over the life course (1993). For example, not one of the nondelinquent control group subjects was arrested for a crime of violence as an adult. In contrast, 33% of the delinquent subjects were arrested for a crime of violence between the ages of 17-25, and 18% were arrested for violence at 25-32 years.

At the same time, however, Sampson and Laub find that job stability and marital attachment in adulthood are significantly related to changes in adult crime—the stronger the adult ties to work and family, the less crime and deviance among both delinquents and controls. For example, using event history analyses, they show that job stability at ages 17-25 has a significant negative effect on the hazard rate of arrest for a violent crime at ages 25-32 (pp. 173–178). This suggests that social ties embedded in adult transitions (e.g., marital attachment, job stability) explain variations in crime unaccounted for by childhood propensities toward antisocial behavior.

The prediction of aggression, crime, and violence from childhood to adulthood is problematic—errors in prediction are made even though the relative rank ordering of persons over time appears to be stable. This literature suggests that we need to examine both stability and change in the course of human development. While it is true that there is longitudinal consistency, research has established that variations in later adolescent and adult criminal behavior are not simply accounted for by childhood propensities. Furthermore, changes in adult criminality appear to be systematically structured by social transitions and adult life events in the life course, underscoring the utility of a life-course perspective. Whether this finding holds across a variety of cultural settings is a crucial question for future research.[6]

## DIRECTIONS FOR FUTURE RESEARCH

As indicated above, there is very little longitudinal research on crime and violence that is derived from non-Western, non-industrialized societies. Moreover, if the objective is to understand "how social structures and cultures interact with individuals' psychosocial development to influence their potentials for violent behavior" (Reiss & Roth, 1993, p. 157), it is not altogether clear what conclusions can be drawn from the existing base of cross-cultural, longitudinal research. The difficulties in interpreting findings on individual patterns of aggression and violence across different countries parallel those that exist when the sociocultural context is defined as a neighborhood, community, or city (see Sampson & Lauritsen, 1993). We simply do not know the extent to which similarities in findings reflect common measurement error (e.g., in data sources and operationalization of key concepts), universal continuity in individuals, or similarities in the social structure, culture, or opportunities of different environments.

Future research should not artificially divorce individuals from the larger sociocultural context in which they develop. In the following sections, we outline a research agenda for studying the sociocultural processes underlying development of antisocial behavior, especially aggression and violence. This research agenda builds upon the existing longitudinal research base and furthers the advancement of our knowledge in this perplexing area of research. We recognize that this research agenda is ambitious, however, the examination of the role of sociocultural context on violent behavior is an extraordinarily complex and challenging enterprise.

### The Need for a Comparative, Longitudinal, Ethnographic Approach

We believe that the best strategy to understand the development of crime and violence is a combined approach consisting of comparative longitudinal and ethnographic methods (Corsaro, 1993). This research would have two aims: (a) to use sociocultural variation to study the processes of becoming antisocial and violent and (b) to study the interaction between social structure, culture, and behavior (Taft, 1987).[7]

This approach assumes that human development is the result of interactions between individuals and their sociocultural environment and looks for the variations in these interactions. A comparative study of diverse cultural contexts will allow us to isolate variations in family structure and socialization processes, especially child-rearing practices regarding the use of discipline and the quality of parent–child relations, that appear important in the development of antisocial and violent behavior. In particular, longitudinal data on key developmental transition stages throughout the life course is needed to identify continuities and discontinuities in antisocial and violent behavior as they unfold over time.

A longitudinal and ethnographic approach is recommended as the best technique to capture the underlying developmental processes of stability and change. The ethnographic method has the greatest potential for gathering details of the environments in which children grow up and the child's experiences in these environments (Whiting, 1976). Ethnographic studies which are able to link children's socialization across culturally bound settings (e.g., home, school, and peer group) and levels (e.g., structural and situational) are believed to be the most fruitful (see Corsaro, 1993). In this approach, "individual development is seen as embedded in children's collective weaving of their places in the 'webs of significance' that constitute their culture. The collective weaving is the product of children's interactions with adults and other children in the various institutional locales or fields making up their culture" (Corsaro, 1993, p. 36).

## The Need for a Life-Course Framework

Along with gathering data across a divergent set of contexts, we need to develop a coherent analytical framework in which to understand these data. We offer the life course as such an organizing framework. The life course has been defined as a "sequence of culturally defined age-graded roles and social transitions that are enacted over time" (Caspi, Elder, & Herbener, 1990, p. 15). Age-graded transitions are embedded in social institutions and subject to historical change (Elder, 1975, 1992).

Two central concepts underlie the analysis of life-course dynamics. A *trajectory* is a pathway or line of development over the life span such as worklife, parenthood, and criminal behavior. Trajectories refer to long-term patterns of behavior and are marked by a sequence of transitions. *Transitions* are marked by life events (e.g., first job or first marriage) that are embedded in trajectories and evolve over shorter time spans (Elder, 1985). The interlocking nature of trajectories and transitions may generate turning points or a change in life course (Elder, 1985). Adaptation to life events is crucial because the same event or transition followed by different adaptations can lead to different trajectories (Elder, 1985). The long-term view embodied by the life-course focus on trajectories implies a strong connection between childhood events and experiences in adulthood. Nevertheless, the simultaneous shorter-term view implies that transitions or turning points can modify life trajectories—they can "redirect paths."

As pointed out by Hogan (1991), life course studies have neglected the cultural context, or more specifically, the meaning of life course transitions in individual lives. The work by Modell (1989) and others illustrates how culturally defined age and gender roles have changed in the United States since 1920. Specifically, Modell (1989) identifies the cultural cues for appropriate developmental transitions throughout an individual's life course and he discusses how these roles have been influenced over time by cultural and structural forces.

More research is needed in order to help uncover underlying social processes of stability and change in individuals' lives across different cultural settings because it is likely that social transitions (e.g., marriage, parenthood, work) do not have the same organization and meaning across different structural and cultural settings (see Whiting, 1976; Valsiner, 1989). It is difficult to talk about variables like social class, family, or marriage as if they were "transcultural terms" (Whiting, 1976). It also seems likely that explanations of individual change must vary across societies because change is tied to the type, timing, and ease of transition across the major roles available in society. In some societies certain roles are rigidly age-graded, whereas in others they are not. For example, Whiting and Edwards (1988) describe children in agricultural communities who tend their younger sibs and work in the home and fields as early as 4 to 6 years of age. Thus, the transition from childhood to adulthood varies by culture (see Valsiner, 1989). Also, it should be noted that the social institution of marriage has taken four forms—monogamy, polygyny, polyandry, and polygynandry—when considering all cultural settings (see Valsiner, 1989). Thus, there is a need to "unpack" key developmental, transition periods like marriage, and understand how "cultural meanings guide the developmental process" (Valsiner, 1989, p. 384). A key issue for future research then is to explore the social developmental processes across a wide range of cultural contexts to better understand patterns of stability and change of criminal behavior including violence.[8]

## The Need to Study a Wide Range of Antisocial Behavior

Much of the longitudinal research suggests that violent offending is part of a larger syndrome of antisocial behavior. Focusing exclusively on violence and violent offenders seems contrary to the existing longitudinal research. Indeed, Farrington has found that *"violent offenders and nonviolent offenders are virtually identical in childhood, adolescent, and adult features"* (1991, p. 24, emphasis in original). West and Farrington (1977) have contended that violence is better explained by an antisocial personality that arises in childhood and persists across the life course manifesting itself in a variety of different types of deviant and antisocial behavior. Similarly, Robins and Ratcliff (1980, p. 248) have argued that "there exists a single syndrome made up of a broad variety of antisocial behaviors arising in childhood and continuing into adulthood" (see also Gottfredson & Hirschi, 1990). It is simply not the case that one type of behavior in childhood (such as aggression) predicts one specific type of behavior in adulthood (such as violence), and it appears that *"the causes of aggression and violence must be essentially the same as the causes of persistent and extreme antisocial, delinquent, and criminal behavior"* (Farrington, 1991, p. 25, emphasis in original).

Moreover, the available research suggests that efforts to prevent antisocial behavior generally will also serve to reduce violent behavior. The available research shows that potential offenders can be identified at a young age, and special attention should be directed to child-rearing behaviors—parental supervision, parental affection, and parental conflict (e.g., McCord, 1979). As Farrington (1990) has argued:

> Because of the link between crime and numerous other social problems, any measure that succeeds in reducing crime will probably have benefits that go far beyond this. Early prevention efforts that reduce crime will probably also reduce alcohol abuse, drunk driving, drug abuse, sexual promiscuity, and family violence, and probably also school failure, unemployment, marital disharmony, and divorce. It is clear from this research that problem children tend to grow up into problem adults, and that problem adults tend to produce problem children. (p. 110)

Future research and policy should consider a broad array of antisocial, criminal, and deviant behaviors, and not just limit the focus to one subgroup or crime type.

## The Need to Examine Sociocultural Context Within the U.S.

While Americans may share a system of formal social control, substantial variations exist both across and within groups in the ability to informally regulate individuals' behavior. As stated earlier, informal social controls are a consequence of role relationships and reciprocities, and in the U.S., family, school, and work constitute the most important institutions guiding such affiliations. It follows then, that variation in social ties to family, school, and work are pivotal to the understanding of group differences in aggression and violence throughout the life course. Such variations in social institutions must be understood in the context of structural and cultural variation. Ethnographic approaches, such as Burton's and Jarrett's on African-American teenagers and their families, show the promise of such research strategies.

For example, Burton (1993) shows that while schools and parents provide guidelines concerning the social expectations and behaviors of adolescents, the adolescent experiences for economically disadvantaged, urban, African-American teens is quite different from wider normative expectations. On the contrary, many teens in the study moved from childhood directly to adulthood without experiencing adolescence as a clearly delineated developmental life stage (Burton, 1993). In the families studied by Burton (1993), teens often assumed adult roles in the family, competed for the same jobs as adults, lived in age-condensed families, and possessed a truncated life course view of the world. Furthermore, Burton (1993) pointed out that perceptions of successful developmental outcomes were heavily influenced by cultural norms within their environment.

Similarly, Jarrett (1990) examined socialization patterns among low-income African-American, Chicano, Puerto Rican, and white families and her work illustrates the importance of cultural context by race. For instance, Jarrett uncovered different definitions of family (e.g., use of surrogate parents and what she calls "informal fosterage") as well as important differences as to how kinship groups are organized. To illustrate, an extended network of kin including mothers, grandmothers, paternal and maternal kin, and older siblings, often exist in African-American families. This leads to a multiplicity of socialization agents across a variety of geographic settings (Jarrett, 1990). While ethnographic studies of sociocultural differences in family functioning are more common, they should not be the only focal point of future comparative research. Variations in social ties to education and work institutions must be considered as well.

Thus, in addition to focusing on life-course variations across groups or countries, we recommend examining within-group variation and within-country variation as well. Research in the United States that examines life-course patterns, antisocial behavior, and structural location (class and race) seem especially important (see Laub & Sampson, 1993). A comparative longitudinal approach involving a variety of contexts both within and outside of the U.S. would allow researchers to begin to separate individual from group effects, irrespective of how the group is defined (e.g., family, ethnicity or race, neighborhood, country). A longitudinal component would permit an examination of individual developmental patterns within the context of either stable or changing sociocultural conditions. Of course, these are precisely the concerns of recent calls for a multi-community longitudinal research program (see Reiss & Roth, 1993). Given that this appears to be the direction of new research in the United States, the time seems ripe for coordinating longitudinal ethnographic projects across a variety of sociocultural contexts.

## CONCLUSION

The focus of this chapter was on the sociocultural sources of violent behavior over the life course. We were especially interested in longitudinal and comparative research on this topic, although we found that virtually all of the longitudinal studies were comprised of individuals from Western societies. Therefore, we cannot answer the key issue posed at the onset of this chapter: Are there universal patterns of violent behavior over the life course? Based on the existing evidence, our best guess is that such universal patterns do not exist. However, to what extent sociocultural differences primarily reflect differences in opportunity structures (Gottfredson & Hirschi, 1990) or reflect differences in the developmental trajectories and transitions over the life course cannot be answered definitively with the extant research. Given the intriguing similarities and differences found across cultures, we believe the examination of the sociocultural context, both within countries and cross-nationally, is an important area for future research on human development and criminal behavior.

## NOTES

1. It is ironic that in calling for comparative research the quote by Glueck assumes that universals exist. The question arises: Why do comparative research then? We support Glueck's call for a comparative criminology, but do not assume a priori that universals, in fact, exist.

2. Since a large portion of the longitudinal research we review includes measures of aggression as well as violence, we have expanded our focus to include both concepts. For purposes of this paper, aggression is defined as hostile or destructive behavior or actions; violence is defined as physical force exerted for the purpose of violat-

ing, damaging, or abusing; and antisocial behavior is defined as destructive actions that violate generally accepted norms of society. For a discussion of the problems of defining these terms see Krebs and Miller (1985).

3. In their study of six diverse cultures (Africa, India, the Philippines, Okinawa, Mexico, and the United States), Whiting and Edwards (1988) find that assaultive behavior is generally rare, especially among girls. Physical assaults among children were lowest in the more egalitarian societies, and highest among those cultures "in which boys have a particularly strong need to prove that they are not women and not like their sisters" (p. 261). Interestingly, these cultures also have the smallest sex differentials in aggression (see also Ember & Ember, this volume).

4. One area of cognitive development that has received some attention in the research literature concerns moral development. Unfortunately, the specific links between structures of moral reasoning and aggression and violent criminal behavior have not been well articulated (Kreps & Miller, 1985, p. 25). Moreover, a large portion of this research has been cross-sectional in design. With respect to cross-cultural research on moral development, in his review of 45 studies of moral development covering 27 cultural areas, Snarey (1985) found universal support for stages 1 through 4 in Kohlberg's theory of moral development. Note that the longitudinal studies were conducted in the following countries: Bahamas, Canada (French), India, Indonesia, Israel (kibbutz), Turkey, and the United States (Snarey, 1985, p. 207).

5. Although focusing only on children aged 6 to 11, Eron and Huesmann (1987) designed a comparative, three year longitudinal study of television and aggression. (For a complete description of this study see Huesmann & Eron, 1986). Eron and Huesmann (1987) report stability coefficients for aggression over a three year period to be between .57 and .82 for girls and boys respectively. What is significant is that these coefficients held among subjects in countries not often examined—Australia, Poland, and an Israeli city and kibbutz. In addition, Eron and Huesmann (1987) found that more aggressive children watch more television, but the results were weak for Israeli Kibbutz and Australian children. Only in the U.S. did less popular children watch more television than their more popular counterparts, leading the authors to conclude that the link between unpopularity, television viewing, and violence/aggression is only plausible in the U.S. This suggests that the effects of television have to be considered in a specific sociocultural context.

6. It is possible that massive sociocultural changes at the macro-level can lead to increases in the prevalence and incidence of violence. In other words, macro-level influences may account for the onset of violence over the full life course. For example, there is evidence that crime has become more violent and pervasive in Russia over the last two years as totalitarian institutions in that society have been totally restructured (Bohlen, 1993). The same situation seems to be taking place in other Eastern European countries that are currently experiencing dramatic sociocultural changes in key institutions.

7. Valsiner (1989, p. 48, 384) has identified two dimensions of culture—the *collective culture* of a society as reflected in shared meanings and norms and the *personal culture* which is each individual's internalized version of the collective culture. Thus, culture itself is a dynamic entity that is constructed and reconstructed over time.

8. Of course, it may be that cultural differences have been overstated. For instance, there is evidence that differences in informal social control account for the variation in crime and violence among four ethnic groups in the Netherlands (Junger & Polder, 1992; see also Junger-Tas, 1992; and Torstensson, 1990). Therefore, while there may

be cultural variation in the level and type of crime, and in the forms of social control, given a sufficient level of abstraction, the explanations of criminal behavior including violence may indeed, not vary significantly across cultures (Gottfredson & Hirschi, 1990).

## REFERENCES

Andersson, J. (1990). Continuity in crime: Sex and age differences. *Journal of Quantitative Criminology, 6*, 85-100.

Blumstein, A., Cohen, J., Roth, J. A., & Visher, C. A. (Eds.). (1986). *Criminal careers and "career criminals"* (Vol. 1). Washington, DC: National Academy Press.

Bohlen, C. (1993). Russia mobsters grow more violent and pervasive. *New York Times*, August 16, A1, A4.

Bondeson, U. V. (1989). *Prisoners in prison societies*. New Brunswick, NJ: Transaction Books.

Braithwaite, J. (1989). *Crime, shame, and reintegration*. Cambridge: Cambridge University Press.

Burton, L. M. (1993). *Conceptual issues in the study of development among economically disadvantaged inner-city African-American teens: Lessons learned from an ethnographic study*. Paper prepared for the Conference on Ethnographic Approaches to the Study of Human Development.

Cairns, R. B., & Cairns, B. D. (1992). The sociogenesis of aggressive and antisocial behavior. In J. McCord (Ed.) *Facts, frameworks, and forecasts* (pp. 157-191). New Brunswick, NJ: Transaction Publishers.

Caspi, A. (1987). Personality in the life course. *Journal of Personality and Social Psychology, 53*, 1203-1213.

Caspi, A., & Bem, D. (1990). Personality continuity and change across the life course. In L. Pervin (Ed.), *Handbook of personality: Theory and research* (pp. 549-575). New York: Guilford.

Caspi, A., & Moffitt, T. E. (1993). The continuity of maladaptive behavior: From description to understanding in the study of antisocial behavior. In D. Cicchetti & D. Cohen (Eds.), *Manual of developmental psychopathology* (in press). New York: Wiley.

Caspi, A., Elder, G. H., Jr., & Bem, D. J. (1987). Moving against the world: Life-course patterns of explosive children. *Developmental Psychology, 23*, 308-313.

Caspi, A., Elder, G. H., Jr., & Herbener, E. S. (1990). Childhood personality and the prediction of life-course patterns. In L. Robins & M. Rutter (Eds.), *Straight and devious pathways from childhood to adulthood* (pp. 13-35). Cambridge: Cambridge University Press.

Coie, J. D., Underwood, M., & Lochman, J. E. (1991). Programmatic intervention with aggressive children in the school setting. In D. J. Pepler & K. H. Rubin (Eds.), *The development and treatment of childhood aggression* (pp. 389-410). Hillsdale, NJ: Erlbaum.

Corsaro, W. A. (1993). *Transition in early childhood: The promise of comparative, longitudinal ethnography*. Paper prepared for the Conference on Ethnographic Approaches to the Study of Human Development.

Dannefer, D. (1984). Adult development and social theory: A paradigmatic reappraisal. *American Sociological Review, 49*, 100-116.

Elder, G. H., Jr. (1975). Age differentiation and the life course. *Annual Review of Sociology*, *1*, 165-190.

Elder, G. H., Jr. (1985). Perspectives on the life course. In G. H. Elder Jr. (Ed.), *Life course dynamics* (pp. 23-49). Ithaca: Cornell University Press.

Elder, G. H., Jr. (1992). The life course. In E. F. Borgatta & M. L. Borgatta (Eds.), *The encyclopedia of sociology*. (pp. 1120-1130). New York: Macmillan.

Elliott, D., Huizinga, D. & Menard, S. (1989). *Multiple problem youth: Delinquency, substance use, and mental health problems*. New York: Springer-Verlag.

Ember, C. & Ember, M. (1993). Methodological issues in cross-cultural studies of violent crime. *Violence and Victims*, 8(3), 217-234.

Eron, L. D., & Huesmann, L. R. (1987). The stability of aggressive behavior in cross-national comparison. In C. Kagitcibasi (Ed.), *Growth and progress in cross-cultural psychology* (pp. 207-217). Lisse, Switzerland: Swets & Zeitlinger B. V.

Eron, L. D., & Huesmann, L. R. (1990). The stability of aggressive behavior—even unto the third Generation. In M. Lewis & S. M. Miller (Eds.), *Handbook of developmental psychopathology* (pp. 147-156). New York: Plenum Press.

Farrington, D. P. (1979). Longitudinal research on crime and delinquency. In N. Morris & M. Tonry (Eds.), *Crime and justice* (pp. 289-348). Chicago: University of Chicago Press.

Farrington, D. P. (1987). Early precursors of frequent offending. In J. Q. Wilson, & G. C. Loury (eds.), *From children to citizens* (pp. 27-50). New York: Springer-Verlag.

Farrington, D. P. (1988). Advancing knowledge about delinquency and crime: The need for a coordinated program of longitudinal research. *Behavioral Sciences & the Law*, 6, 307-331.

Farrington, D. P. (1989). Early predictors of adolescent aggression and adult violence. *Violence and Victims 4*, 79-100.

Farrington, D. P. (1990). Implications of criminal career research for the prevention of offending. *Journal of Adolescence 13*, 93-113.

Farrington, D. P. (1991). Childhood aggression and adult violence: Early precursors and later-life outcomes. In D. J. Pepler & K. H. Rubin (Eds.), *The development and treatment of childhood aggression* (pp. 5-29). Hillsdale, NJ: Erlbaum.

Farrington, D. P., Ohlin, L. E., & Wilson, J. Q. (1986). *Understanding and controlling crime*. New York: SpringerVerlag.

Glueck, S. (1964). Wanted: A comparative criminology. In S. Glueck & E. Glueck (Eds.), *Ventures in criminology* (pp. 304-322). Cambridge, MA: Harvard University Press.

Glueck, S., & Glueck, E. (1968). *Delinquents and nondelinquents in perspective*. Cambridge: Harvard University Press.

Gottfredson, M. R., & Hirschi, T. (1990). *A general theory of crime*. Stanford, CA: Stanford University Press.

Gove, W. R. (1985). The effect of age and gender on deviant behavior: A biopsychosocial perspective. In A. S. Rossi (Ed.), *Gender and the life course* (pp. 115-144). New York: Aldine.

Hogan, D. P. (1991). Reintroducing culture in life course research. *Contemporary Sociology*, *20*, 1-4.

Huesmann, L. R., & Eron, L. D. (1984). Cognitive processes and the persistence of aggressive behavior. *Aggressive Behavior*, *10*, 243-251.

Huesmann, L. R., & Eron, L. D., (Eds.) (1986). *Television and the aggressive child: A cross-national comparison*. Hillsdale, NJ: Lawrence Erlbaum Associates.

Huesmann, R., Eron, L., Lefkowitz, M., & Walder, L. (1984). Stability of aggression over time and generations. *Developmental Psychology, 20,* 1120-1134.

Jarrett, R. L. (1990). *A comparative examination of socialization patterns among low-income African-Americans, Chicanos, Puerto Ricans, and whites: A review of the ethnographic literature.* Working paper, Social Science Research Council, New York.

Jessor, R., Donovan, J. E., & Costa, F. M. (1991). *Beyond adolescence: Problem behavior and young adult development.* Cambridge: Cambridge University Press.

Junger, M., & Polder, W. (1992). Some explanations of crime among four ethnic groups in the Netherlands. *Journal of Quantitative Criminology, 8,* 51-78.

Junger-Tas, J. (1992). An empirical test of social control theory. *Journal of Quantitative Criminology, 8,* 9-28.

Kandel, E., & Mednick, S. (1991). Perinatal complications predict violent offending. *Criminology, 29,* 519-530.

Kornhauser, R. (1978). *Social sources of delinquency.* Chicago: University of Chicago Press.

Kreps, D. L., & Miller, D. T. (1985). Altruism and aggression. In G. Lindzey & E. Aronson (Eds.), *Handbook of social psychology Volume II* (pp. 1-71). New York: Random House.

Laub, J. H., & Sampson, R. J. (1993). Turning points in the life course: Why change matters to the study of crime. *Criminology, 31,* 301-325.

LeBlanc, M., & Frechette, M. (1989). *Male criminality activity from childhood through youth: Multilevel and developmental perspectives.* New York: Springer-Verlag.

Loeber, R. (1982). The stability of antisocial child behavior: A review. *Child development, 53,* 1431-1446.

Loeber, R., & Dishion, T. (1983). Early predictors of male adolescent delinquency: A review. *Psychological Bulletin, 94,* 68-99.

Loeber, R., & Stouthamer-Loeber, M. (1986). Family factors as correlates and predictors of juvenile conduct problems and delinquency. In N. Morris & M. Tonry (Eds.), *Crime and justice* (pp. 29-149). Chicago: University of Chicago Press.

Loeber, R., & LeBlanc, M. (1990). Toward a developmental criminology. In M. Tonry & N. Morris (Eds.), *Crime and justice* (pp. 375-437). Chicago: University of Chicago Press.

Lytton, H. (1990). Child and parent effects in boys' conduct disorder: A reinterpretation. *Developmental Psychology, 26,* 683-697.

Magnusson, D., Stattin, H., & Duner, A. (1983). Aggression and criminality in a longitudinal perspective. In K. Teillman Van Dusen, & S. A. Mednick (Eds.), *Prospective studies of crime and delinquency* (pp. 277-301). Boston: Kluwer-Nijhoff Publishing.

McCord, J. (1979). Some child-rearing antecedents of criminal behavior in adult men. *Journal of Personality and Social Psychology 37,* 1477-1486.

McCord, J. (1980). Patterns of deviance. In S. B. Sells, R. Crandall, M. Roff, J. S. Strauss, & W. Pollin (Eds.), *Human functioning in longitudinal perspective* (pp. 157-165). Baltimore: Williams and Wilkins.

McCord, J. (1983). A study of aggression and antisocial behavior. In K. Teillman Van Dusen & S. A. Mednick (Eds.), *Prospective studies of crime and delinquency* (pp. 269-275). Boston: Kluwer-Nijhoff Publishing.

Modell, J. (1989). *Into one's own: From youth to adulthood in the United States 1920-1975.* Berkeley: University of California Press.

Moffitt, T. E. (1993). Adolescent-limited and life-course persistent antisocial behavior: A developmental taxonomy. *Psychological Review*, in press.

Munroe, R. H., Munroe, R. L, & Whiting, B. B. (Eds.) (1981). *Handbook of cross-cultural human development*. New York: Garland Press.

Nagin, D., & Paternoster, R. (1991). On the relationship of past and future participation in delinquency. *Criminology, 29*, 163-190.

Nagin, D., & Waldfogel, J. (1992). The effects of criminality and conviction on the labour market status of young British offenders. Unpublished manuscript. Pittsburgh: Carnegie Mellon University.

Olweus, D. (1979). Stability of aggressive reaction patterns in males: A review. *Psychological Bulletin, 86*, 852-875.

Olweus, D. (1984). Development of stable aggressive reaction patterns in males. In R. J. Blanchard & D. C. Blanchard (Eds.), *Advances in the study of aggression* (pp. 103-138). Orlando: Academic Press, Inc.

Pepler, D. J., & Rubin, K. H. (Eds). (1991). *The development and treatment of childhood aggression*. Hillsdale, NJ: Erlbaum.

Pulkkinen, L. (1982). Self-control and continuity from childhood to late adolescence. In P. B. Baltes & O. G. Brim, Jr. (Eds.), *Life-span development and behavior* (pp. 63-105). New York: Academic Press.

Reiss, A. J., Jr. & Roth, J. A. (1993). Understanding and preventing violence. Washington, DC: National Academy Press.

Robins, L. (1966). *Deviant children grown up*. Baltimore: Williams & Wilkins.

Robins, L. (1978) Sturdy childhood predictors of adult antisocial behavior: Replications from longitudinal studies. *Psychological Medicine, 8*, 611-622.

Robins, L., & Ratcliff, K. (1980). Childhood conduct disorders and later arrest. In L. Robins, P. J. Clayton, & J. K. Wing (Eds.), *The social consequences of psychiatric illness* (pp. 248-263). New York: Brunner/Mazel.

Rogoff, B., & Morelli, G. (1989). Perspectives on children's development from cultural psychology. *American Psychologist, 44*, 343-348.

Rutter, M. & Rutter, M. (1993). *Developing minds: Challenge and continuity across the life span*. New York: Basic Books.

Sampson, R. J., & Laub, J. H. (1993). *Crime in the making: Pathways and turning points through life*. Cambridge, MA: Harvard University Press.

Sampson, R. J., & Lauritsen, J. L. (1993). Violent victimization and offending: Individual, situational, and community-level risk factors. In *Understanding and preventing violent behavior*, Volume 3. Washington, DC: National Academy Press.

Snarey, J. R. (1985). Cross-cultural universality of social-moral development: A critical review of Kohlbergian research. *Psychological Bulletin, 97*, 202-232.

Taft, R. (1987). Cross-cultural psychology as psychological science. In C. Kagitcibasi (Ed.), *Growth and progress in cross-cultural psychology* (pp. 3-9). Lisse, Switzerland: Swets & Zeitlinger B. V.

Torstensson, M. (1990). Female delinquents in a birth cohort: Tests of some aspects of control theory. *Journal of Quantitative Criminology, 6*, 101-115.

Valsiner, J. (1989). *Human development and culture: The social nature of personality and its study*. Lexington, MA: Lexington Books.

Weiner, N. A. (1989). Violent criminal careers and "violent career criminal": An overview of the research literature. In N. A. Weiner, & M. E. Wolfgang (Eds.), *Violent crime, violent criminals* (pp. 35-138). Newbury Park, CA: Sage Publications.

Werner, E., & Smith, R. (1992). *Overcoming the odds: High risk children from birth to adulthood*. Ithaca, NY: Cornell University Press.

West, D. J., & Farrington, D. P. (1977). *The delinquent way of life*. London: Heinemann.

White, J. L., Moffitt, T. E., Earls, F., Robins, L., & Silva, P. (1990). How early can we tell?: Predictors of childhood conduct disorder and adolescent delinquency. *Criminology, 28,* 507-534.

Whiting, B. B. (1976). The problem of the packaged variable. In K. F. Riegel, & J. A. Meacham (Eds.), *The developing individual in a changing world* (pp. 303-309). Chicago: Aldine.

Whiting, B. B., & Edwards, C. P. (1988). *Children of different worlds: The formation of social behavior*. Cambridge, MA: Harvard University Press.

Widom, C. S. (1989). The cycle of violence. *Science, 244,* 160-166.

Wolfgang, M. E., Figlio, R., & Sellin, T. (1972). *Delinquency in a birth cohort*. Chicago: University of Chicago Press.

Wolfgang, M. E., Thornberry, T. P., & Figlio, R. (1987). *From boy to man: From delinquency to crime*. Chicago: University of Chicago Press.

# 5

# Violence and Gender:
# Differences and Similarities Across Societies

**Dane Archer**
**Patricia McDaniel**

Although various arguments have been proposed to explain gender differences in aggression, the subject remains in dispute. In part, this is because different theoretical perspectives and empirical studies draw on very different disciplinary traditions. Some studies utilize laboratory experiments that center on a participant's willingness to administer electric shocks to another person; others attempt to generalize from animal experiments to human populations; others rely on field research focused, for example, on play behavior among children; others examine gender differences in aggregate data such as rates of violent crime; and finally, still others use psychological studies that measure levels of some form of aggression in the presence or absence of violent media. These different approaches employ not only different methodologies but also different definitions of aggression and violence. As a result, cumulative evidence in this area is elusive, and no study or method focused on a single form of violence can hope to resolve all dispute.

What is possible, perhaps, is to indicate different theoretical models that can be adduced to explain the relationship between gender and violence. Four such models are indicated below, illustrated briefly with research examples. We will discuss these theoretical models as pure types, so disclaimers are in order. Each theoretical model will be presented as if it operated alone, independent of other influences. It is for this reason that we will use the term "determinism" (e.g., biological determinism, cultural determinism, etc.). This involves obvious hyperbole and requires immediate qualification. By the word "determinism," we intend to imply only a simple question: Does this factor affect the probability of violence, and if it does, what sort of data pattern would one expect to see?

In reality, of course, no single factor operates alone. All important human behaviors are probably determined by a confluence of different factors acting in concert, or even acting in contradiction. No single factor governs complex behavior; thus, determinism of any sort is impossible. For example, biological factors—to the extent that they impact violence at all—can only operate in concert with social, cultural, and other factors. The human life course is never studied in a factorial design, with individuals randomly assigned to various levels of biology, society, and culture. In the absence of such experimental control, we are left to ponder probabilistic correlations in search of patterns that implicate the presence of biological, social, cultural, or other causal forces. If the reader prefers, he or she should feel free to substitute the word "influence" where we have, for the sake of argument alone, used the word "determinism."

The first of our theoretical, pure type models, biological determinism, is clearly distinct from the other three: social determinism, environmental determinism, and cultural determinism. These three theoretical models overlap somewhat but are sufficiently distinct that a separate discussion of each may be useful. We have tried to derive expectations or predictions from each—that is, what does each model lead one to expect about the nature and extent of the relationship between gender and violence? Finally, data from a new cross-cultural study are examined for evidence consistent (or inconsistent) with these four general theoretical models.

## THEORETICAL MODEL 1: BIOLOGICAL DETERMINISM

Although inherently controversial among social scientists, the potential contributions of biological factors (genetic, endocrinological, biochemical, and other differences) have figured prominently in thinking about gender and violence. For example, the over-representation of men in rates of violent crime is sometimes cited as evidence for the role of male hormones (or some correlated biological entity) in elevating the probabilities of violent behavior. According to this view, "maleness" (or at least the possession of testosterone and other innately "male" qualities) is biologically linked to a potential for aggressiveness, if not actual aggression and violence.

This perspective tends toward gross over-prediction (i.e., the "false positive" problem), since only small numbers of males ever commit serious acts of violence. Nevertheless, the persistence and attraction of this model remain strong. Indeed, one writer goes so far as to end her work on the evolution of the "violent sex" with practical advice for potential parents on how to avoid perpetuating inevitable violence—by trying to ensure the birth of a girl (Holliday, 1978). Serious research on potential biological links between gender and violence tends to fall into one of four domains: (1) correlational studies of hormones and aggression, (2) criminal populations, (3) human prenatal exposure to hormones, and (4) animal studies. The nature of these lines of research is indicated in turn.

### Correlational Studies of Hormones and Aggression

Observations of the relationship between hormones and aggression in humans and animals provide grist for the biological view. Studies of "normal" (i.e., noncriminal) adults form one branch of the study of testosterone and aggression in humans.[1] Persky, Smith, and Basu (1971) measured testosterone production (by taking blood samples) and administered a number of psychological tests, including the Buss-Durkee Hostility Inventory to two groups of normal men, 18 between the ages of 17 and 28 and 15 between the ages of 31 and 66. They found a correlation between a high aggression score and testosterone production for the younger men only. (Four independent psychological measures of aggression and hostility were significantly related to plasma testosterone levels; $n = 18$, multiple $R^2 = .82$). This finding remains controversial since subsequent researchers failed to replicate it (Doering, Brodie, Kraemer, Becker, & Hamburg, 1974; Meyer-Bahlburg, Nat, Boon, Sharma, & Edwards, 1974), even when the sample size was increased ($n = 100$) (Monti, Brown, & Corriveau, 1977); however, a more recent attempt, also using a large sample ($n = 117$), did find testosterone to be positively correlated to self-ratings of spontaneous aggression (six psychological measures of aggression showed a small positive correlation with serum testosterone; median *rho* = .13) (Christiansen & Knussman, 1987).

Other researchers find that testosterone levels may be related only to *certain* aggressive behaviors rather than to aggression in general. Olweus, Mattsson, Schalling, and Low (1980) examined aggression, impulsiveness, lack of frustration tolerance, extraversion, anxiety, and testosterone levels in 58 16-year-old boys and found that the boys' reaction to provocation and threat were the only two aggressive behaviors associated with testosterone levels. Scaramella and Brown (1978) examined the relationship between testosterone levels and types of aggressive behavior in 14 male college hockey players. Two coaches were asked to rate each player for leadership qualities, competitiveness, frustration tolerance, body contact, and response to threat; only response to threat significantly correlated to testosterone levels.

A study of women found a correlation between testosterone levels[2] and different types of occupations, with students and professional, managerial, and technical workers having higher levels of testosterone than clerical workers and homemakers (Purifoy & Koopmans, 1979). The authors concluded that although increased testosterone levels may lead to nontraditional career choices for women, the effect of stress on testosterone production cannot be ruled out as a contributing factor, because negative stress, such as fear and anxiety, associated with traditional women's jobs lowers testosterone production.

## Criminal Populations

Studies of criminal populations constitute another approach to this question. Kreuz and Rose (1972) administered psychological tests, including the Buss-Durkee Hostility Inventory and the IPAT Anxiety Scale, and compared testosterone levels in 10 criminals who had been in more than one fight to testosterone levels in 11 prisoners who had been in one or no fights during their imprisonment. They found no correlation between fighting behavior or test scores and testosterone levels; however, they did find a relationship between high testosterone levels and violent offenses committed during adolescence, leading them to hypothesize that levels of testosterone could be a factor influencing men subject to adverse social conditions to commit aggressive crimes in adolescence.

Ehrenkranz, Bliss, and Sheard (1974) performed a similar study on 36 prisoners, 12 categorized as very aggressive, 12 categorized as not aggressive but dominant in the prison hierarchy, and 12 categorized as neither aggressive nor dominant. They found that the very aggressive males had higher mean levels of testosterone than the other subjects, but there was no correlation between high aggression scores on the psychological tests and testosterone levels.

Rada, Laws, and Kellner (1976) measured testosterone levels and administered psychological tests to 52 incarcerated rapists, and a control group of 12 incarcerated "nonviolent" child molesters. They classified the rapists according to the degree of violence (over and above the rape itself) committed during the rape, ranging from verbal threats only to brutal violence resulting in physical injury to the victim. They found no significant difference in mean testosterone levels between the groups except for the most violent types of rapists, who had significantly higher levels. Once again, there was no correlation between testosterone levels and psychological test scores.

## Human Prenatal Exposure to Hormones

The effects of prenatal exposure to hormones are often cited as evidence for a biological role in gender differences in aggression. Money and Ehrhardt (1972) interviewed 10 mothers who had been given progestin, a synthetic male hormone, to prevent miscarriage. This had the unexpected side effect of masculinizing their daughters' genitalia. The researchers also interviewed the mothers of 15 girls with "androgenital syndrome," a condition caused by the secretion of excessive male hormones that results, in females, in the masculinization of external genitalia. By comparing these 25 girls to a group of "normal" control girls (matched in terms of age, IQ, class, and race), Money and Ehrhardt concluded that the androgenized girls exhibited "masculinized" behavior as a result of exposure to male hormones. These girls preferred male playmates, outdoor sports, and traditional male toys (such as cars, trucks, and guns), were more often identified as "tomboys," and had less interest in dolls, weddings, or infants.

Critics charge that Money and Ehrhardt (1972) failed to consider emotional and social aspects of the girls' medical condition. Fried (1979) argues that the parents' perceptions and expectations may have been influenced by knowledge of the girls' medical history, resulting in a tendency to label their daughters' behavior as "tomboyism." Bleier (1984) points out that the girls' attitudes and behaviors could have been influenced by "the intense medical, surgical and psychological scrutiny and interventions that the girls had undergone since birth, all centered on their genitalia."

Focusing specifically on aggression, rather than the more ambiguous term "tomboyism," Reinish (1981) studied 17 female and 18 male children of mothers treated with progestin during pregnancy, comparing them to at least 1 unexposed sibling. The children were evaluated using the Leifer-Roberts Response Hierarchy, a measure designed to estimate the potential for physical and verbal aggressive behavior by eliciting verbal responses to a series of common conflict situations. Overall, the males scored higher on physical aggression than the females, and the progestin-exposed children, both male and female, scored higher on physical aggression measures than their same-sex sibling.

Fausto-Sterling (1985) points out that the effect of exposure to progestin on children is unclear, because a pregnant woman produces increased amounts of progesterone naturally. The average daily dose of progestin taken by the women in Reinish's (1981) study was much lower than the woman's own natural levels (25 mg of progestin vs. 300 mg of progesterone), so the synthetic hormone "may have only been a drop in an already filled bucket" (p. 140). She also points out that there could be a relationship between stress during pregnancy (women who are given synthetic hormones are at high risk for miscarriage) and the postnatal development of aggression.

In an examination of the effects of female hormones on boys, Yalom, Green, and Fisk (1973) examined two groups of boys, 20 aged 6 and 20 aged 16, who had been exposed prenatally to estrogen and progesterone and compared them to a matched control group. The researchers administered questionnaires; conducted interviews with the boys, their parents, and their teachers; and observed them directly. The 16-year-olds prenatally exposed to female hormones rated lower on general "masculinity," assertiveness, and athletic ability than the unexposed matched controls. The 6-year-olds who had been exposed rated lower on aggressiveness and athletic ability. One important consideration that the authors note is the fact that the test group had mothers with diabetes, a chronic illness, which may have caused the boys to be over-protective or anxious toward their mothers, thus interfering with "aggressive masculine development."

## Animal Studies

Studies of the relationship between hormones and aggression in animals seem to parallel findings with human populations. In a laboratory experiment with monkeys (Young, Goy, & Phoenix, 1964), two females given testosterone while pregnant gave birth to two "pseudohermaphroditic" or "androgenized" females (genetic females with male genitalia). After observing interactions between the androgenized females and two normal females, the researchers concluded that the androgenized females exhibited behavior more commonly found in male monkeys: threat behavior and rough-and-tumble play. Similarly, Connor and Levine (1969) found that castration of newborn male rats reduces their aggressive behavior in adulthood, with the deprivation of androgens presumably resulting in the "feminization" (and therefore reduced aggressiveness) of the rats.

One study of the social behavior of rhesus monkeys suggests, however, that even primates are not governed entirely by biology. Mitchell and Brandt (1970) studied 16 female rhesus monkeys and their infants and observed that mothers of males threatened and bit them more than did mothers of females. They also observed that mothers of females restrained and retrieved their infants more than did mothers of males, concluding that "the mother plays a role in prompting greater independence and activity that is typical of males." The mothers of the androgenized females in the study by Young et al. (1964) may have treated their female infants more like males, because they were born with malelike genitalia, thus causing them to behave more like male monkeys.

As a result of these four lines of research, the biological perspective on gender and aggression remains influential. For example, in their ambitious work on gender differences, Maccoby and Jacklin (1974) argued that greater male aggression is always the norm and that these differences are observed too early in life (approximately age 2 to 2°) to be attributed to differential socialization. There are, however, contrary perspectives. Condry and Condry (1976) raised questions about researcher bias in the labeling of "feminine" and "masculine" behavior in their study of male and female observers' responses to the same infant labeled as a boy or girl. They found that the sex of the infant significantly affected the behavior-labeling process: observers who thought the infant was a boy were more likely to label "his" response to an object as pleasure, whereas observers who thought the infant was a girl were more likely to label "her" response as fear. Research on parents' attitudes toward newborns also suggests that sex-role socialization begins at birth. Rubin and Provenzano (1974) found that among parents of physically similar (in terms of height, weight, and health) newborns, daughters are more likely to be labeled as significantly "softer," "finer featured," "littler," and "more inattentive" than are sons. As the children grow, gender presumably continues to influence parental perceptions of (and responses to) a wide range of behaviors, including aggression. In addition, Fausto-Sterling (1985) points out that Maccoby and Jacklin's (1974) dismissal of socialization practices as a factor in the aggression equation ignores their own findings that parents mete out more physical punishment to boys, stimulate gross motor behavior more often in male infants than in female infants, and are more concerned about appropriate sex-typing behavior in boys than in girls; such differential treatment could certainly result in the development of gender differences in aggression.

In its most sweeping form, the biological determinism model leads to the expectation that gender differences govern. *The predictions of this model are that male-female differences in violence and aggression will be substantial and consistent across societies.* In addition, since the driving force is thought to be endocrinology or other physiology, one would expect males in different societies to be equally disposed toward violence, just as one would expect females in different societies to be equally indisposed. Male rates of violence should therefore be relatively invariant across societies just as, at a lower level, female rates should also be invariant. In terms of this model, the principal forces have to do with biological heritage; the effects of society and culture are therefore predicted to be relatively inconsequential.

## THEORETICAL MODEL 2: SOCIAL DETERMINISM

A strong tradition in the social sciences argues for the power of nurture over nature. Many social scientists argue that learning and socialization account for whatever gender differences are observed. This view posits that males (and not females) are consistently reinforced for aggressive behavior throughout the socialization process. Parents and other socializing agents (teachers, media, etc.) tend to regard some aggression as a natural, even desirable aspect of male personality while discouraging aggressive behavior in females (Sears, Maccoby, & Levin, 1957). Boys are more often encouraged to fight back if another child starts a fight, and they are allowed to be more aggressive in interactions with parents than are girls (Sears et al., 1957). Girls' aggressive behavior is also more likely to be ignored by peers and adults, effectively extinguishing such aggression because it fails to produce desired results (Fagot & Hagan, 1985).

As a result of these socialization patterns, girls are inhibited from expressing aggression, at least in its more direct, physical forms. When girls are given assurances that aggressive behavior is acceptable, however, these inhibitions disappear, and girls may display as much aggression as boys (Bandura, 1973). Other researchers have suggested that socialization practices encourage males and females to use different *types* of aggression, resulting in gender differences not in the amount of aggression but in its form. Mischel (1966) states that "prosocial" aggression, "the stating of rules with threats of punishment for breaking them" is encouraged for girls, whereas physical aggression is rewarded in boys. Bardwick (1971) adds that girls are more likely to engage in verbal aggression, "subtle interpersonal rejection," manipulation of others, and passive aggression (e.g., getting a powerful adult to intervene on their behalf) than are boys. Bardwick suggests that researchers who have studied gender differences have a tendency to view the male model of direct physical aggression as the only one.

Despite the central status of the concept of socialization throughout the social sciences, the implications of the social determinism model for cross-cultural comparisons are not intuitively obvious. For example, because it seems improbable that socialization of boys and girls would be the same everywhere, one might expect that male–female differences in aggression would be large in some societies, small or negligible in others, and perhaps even reversed in still other societies. If socialization processes construct gender from the newborn's tabula rasa, then one would not expect *consistent* male–female differences in violence and aggression across societies. Even here, however, there is a caveat. If socialization turns out to pursue parallel courses across societies (e.g., valuing male aggression because of real, imagined, or anachronistic needs for hunting and combat), then it could be argued that socialization would act independently in every society to produce higher levels of male aggressiveness. *The predictions of the social determinism model are therefore either (a) that different societies will show no consistent male–female differences in violence and aggression, or (b) that such consistencies only can occur if male–female socialization differences are everywhere consistent with respect to violence and aggression.*

## Theoretical Model 3: Environmental Determinism

The environmental model of human aggression conceived by Leonard Berkowitz (1962, 1964, 1965, 1978; Berkowitz & LePage, 1967) suggests that aggression occurs in response to external, aggression-associated cues, such as violent movies or weapons. Anger may increase the likelihood of aggression by sensitizing the individual to the presence of environmental cues, but it is not a necessary ingredient for aggressive behavior. The strength of an individual's inhibitions against aggression also plays an important role in determining whether or not aggression is displayed. If the individual anticipates punishment for aggressive behavior or believes that such behavior is morally wrong or will result in disapproval from others, aggression will be inhibited.

Berkowitz (1962) attributes gender differences in aggression to differential learning processes that condition men and women (a) to respond differently to aggression-provoking cues and also (b) to create differences in the strength of inhibitions against aggression. Due to greater parental reinforcement of aggression in boys, males develop stronger "aggressiveness habits" than do females, causing men to respond to aggression-provoking cues with greater hostility. Girls develop stronger inhibitions against aggression than boys due to parental discouragement. In the presence of similar environmental cues, these inhibitions prevent women from acting as aggressively as men, whose weaker inhibitions and childhood training encourage a more hostile response.

There are clearly areas of overlap between the social and environmental models. Both involve learning processes, although the environmental hypothesis draws greater attention to stimuli, images, and influences external to the parent–child relationship: weapons, television, movies, news stories, etc. The environmental model, unlike the social model, draws attention to the material and informational nature of the societies in which socialization takes place. Nonexperimental support for the environmental model includes the finding that postwar societies are characterized by higher homicide rates than are prewar societies (Archer & Gartner, 1976, 1984). Although this model offers a generic explanation for male–female differences, its principal contribution concerns the societal *context* in which these differences occur. *Specifically, the environmental model leads to the expectation that individuals, male and female, raised in societies high in violent imagery will differ from individuals raised in societies lower in violent imagery.*

## Theoretical Model 4: Cultural Determinism

Although it clearly shares elements with the social and environmental models, the cultural model is firmly embedded in the anthropological tradition. For this reason, the cultural model alone is constructed with cross-cultural variation in mind. Several researchers explain gender differences in aggression within the larger context of cultural differences. Mead (1935) argues: "Differences between individuals who are members of different cultures, like differences between individuals within cultures, are entirely to be laid to differences in conditioning, especially during early childhood, and the form of this conditioning is culturally determined."

Although it is frequently difficult to specify the content of "culture," societies obviously differ in more than material terms, and significant *cultural* differences exist. Cultures are thought to value aggression in both sexes to varying degrees, and although most cultures may prefer greater aggression in males, there is clearly room in this model for variation across societies.

Rohner (1976) studied verbal and physical aggressiveness in children aged 2 to 6 in 14 traditional societies. Using a 9-point scale, Rohner coded published ethnographic accounts and found that boys were more aggressive than girls *within* the cultures in these accounts but that large differences existed *between* cultures. In more aggressive cultures (such as the Colombian Mestizo and the Chamorros), both men and women were described as more aggressive than both men and women in less violent cultures (such as the Potawatomi and the Malekula). Rohner's findings suggest that cultural ideals regarding aggression differ, so what is considered an acceptable level of aggressive behavior for females in one society may exceed the acceptable level of aggressive behavior for males in a different society.

Cultural theorists have attempted to address the tendency in many cultures to socialize for greater aggression in men. One explanation involves the sexual division of labor (D'Andrade, 1966; Segall, 1983; Tieger, 1980). Because the adult roles that boys and girls eventually play require different traits, with the male role allegedly requiring more aggressiveness, children may be socialized accordingly. Girls are encouraged to engage in domestic tasks that require little aggression, whereas boys are encouraged to engage in independent and group activities that facilitate aggressive behavior. Whiting and Edward's (1973) six-culture analysis supports this hypothesis, finding that when task assignments are changed and boys are required to perform domestic tasks, gender differences in aggression are reduced, with the boys displaying less aggressive behavior. A similar reduction in gender differences is found when girls are freed from domestic chores and allowed to engage in more "masculine" activities.

The cultural model recasts familiar variables (socialization, reinforcement, parenting, adult development, etc.) in societal terms. This model emphasizes the consistencies shared *across* families within the same society, rather than the idiosyncratic patterns that differentiate families within the same society. According to the cultural model, each society is characterized by its own unique patterns of socialization that determine the course and likelihood of aggression in that society. *The cultural model therefore leads to the prediction of substantial differences in overall levels of aggression and violence across societies.* This prediction is empirically supported by cross-national research on levels of violent crime—for example, the United States has a homicide rate 50 times as high as that in New Zealand, 30 times as high as that in Great Britain (Archer & Gartner, 1984). The predictions of the cultural model for male–female differences are somewhat less clear, but may predict greater aggressiveness for males as a function of preparation for differing adult roles.

## THEORETICAL MODEL 5: INTERACTIONISM

It is quite possible that more than one of these models has merit and that, in fact, the relationship between gender and violence may be best explained by a hybrid or "interactionist" theoretical model. For example, a provocative interactionist model hypothesizes the existence of *both* biological *and* social–environmental–cultural effects. Rather than an eclectic lack of specificity, this "bio-social interactionist model" should ideally search for unambiguous evidence of *both* of these theoretical traditions, rather than conclude weakly that the data are merely indeterminate. In other words, for a bio-social interactionist model to be supported, the evidence would need to indicate *independent* evidence for both of these theoretical forces.

## A METHODOLOGICAL NOTE ON MALE–FEMALE DIFFERENCES

Recent empirical research has been oriented toward assessing with greater precision the extent of male–female differences. Frodi, Macaulay, and Thome's (1977) review of the experimental literature on gender and aggression challenges the common belief that men are always more physically aggressive. They identify several factors that influence whether experimental subjects are likely to behave aggressively (guilt, empathy with the victim, "aggression anxiety," etc.), and they conclude that "if empathy-arousing factors are controlled and if arousal of aggression anxiety is avoided by justification of aggression, women may act as aggressively as men." This argument is supported in later work by White (1983).

Recent research has also examined the actual magnitude of reported gender differences. For example, "meta-analyses" by Hyde (1984, 1986) and Eagley and Steffen (1986) both conclude that although gender differences exist throughout the research literature, with males exhibiting more aggression, the magnitude of the differences involves "medium" effect sizes (Cohen, 1977). Hyde found a mean sex-of-subject effect size of .50 in both of her analyses, whereas Eagley and Steffen found an effect size of .29—indicating that average levels of aggression (however measured in various studies) for males and females are roughly a third to a half standard deviation apart. Researchers have also attempted to identify the kinds of empirical studies most or least likely to find male-female differences in violence and aggression. For example, laboratory studies may be more likely than field studies to find male–female differences, studies of children produce larger differences than do studies of adults, and studies using direct observation report larger differences than studies using self-reports or reports from parents and teachers.

## NEW CROSS-CULTURAL RESEARCH

During the past 6 years, we have begun a program of work to try to illuminate cultural aspects of violence. The catalyst for this work was the finding by Archer and Gartner (1984) of large, problematic, and intriguing differences in the levels of violence across societies. This new work complements their use of aggregate statistics on national rates of violent crime by examining social psychological differences across cultures. The basic method used in this new research presents individuals aged 16–18 with a series of 12 standardized "problem-solving" tasks. Each task involves a different conflict or problem (an unfaithful spouse, a romantic triangle, disciplining a child, a public dispute, a rejected lover, conflict at work, a quarrel between two nations, etc.). The individual is asked to write an imaginative story about how characters in these situations will respond to the conflict.

In each case, potential solutions range from nonviolent to violent. The research focus is on the *quantities and qualities of violence in the stories as a reflection of attitudes toward, expectations about, and justifications for violence as a means of solving conflicts*. The approach can be illustrated by 2 of the 12 conflict situations. Both involve an unfaithful spouse. In one case, the husband (William) is unfaithful; the other problem is identical but involves an unfaithful wife (Mary). Participants are given the following problem, and they are asked to write a story about how the characters would respond:

> William and Mary have been married for two years. They both leave the house during the day, but they have different schedules. A friend of Mary's tells her that her husband has been seen with another woman while Mary is away from the house. Mary decides to see for herself. After pretending to leave the house as usual, Mary parks her car half a block from her house. Twenty minutes later, Mary sees a woman drive up to the house. Mary sees William come out of the house. He gives the woman a long, intimate kiss, and they go inside the house together. What will Mary do?

The 12 problem-solving situations used in the study are:

Unfaithful Mary—a husband discovers his wife is unfaithful.
Unfaithful William—a wife discovers her husband is unfaithful.
Unhappy Ann—a depressed young woman confronts school failure.
Demonstrators—an extended protest occurs at a factory.

Catherine Leaves James—a young woman tells boyfriend she loves another.
James Leaves Catherine—a young man tells girlfriend he loves another.

Co-Worker Dispute—a person steals work and credit from a co-worker.
Mark the Policeman—a policeman confronts two thieves.

Roger and His Son—a father disciplines five-year-old son.
Big and Small Nation—two nations are in conflict.
Mary Denies Richard—a woman refuses the sexual advances of a male friend.
John in the Pub—a man is confronted by an aggressive drunk.

For each of 3 of these 12 conflicts (4 different test booklets are used, each containing 3 problems), participants in the study generate an imaginative story about how the characters will respond to or attempt to solve the conflict described. In every case, the problem can be solved by either nonviolent or violent means. For example, the problem presented above ("Unfaithful William") generates a wide variety of solutions, including the two examples presented here. The first was written by a Swedish high school student; the second by an American high school student. The reader is cautioned that the American example contains a graphic description of violence.

*Swedish Example*: Mary runs into the house and catches them red-handed. Mary is very unhappy. She yells at William and runs out of the house. William runs after her. Mary calms down. They decide to talk about it in peace and quiet. The other woman drives home. William and Mary take a seat on the sofa. William explains that he loves the other woman and wants a divorce. Mary says that she agrees. She will not live with a man who does not love her. (female, 23095)

*American Example*: Mary feels a sudden surge of anger deep from within her inner-most self. Mary vows revenge. She slams the car into gear and races out to the hardware store where she purchases a 33-inch McCulloch chainsaw. When she arrives at the house most of the lights are out, so she creeps around back only to discover that William and his mistress are in back on the deck, dining with fine food over candle light. Seeing this, Mary pulls the rip cord on her chainsaw. The chainsaw whines to life as William jumps up and screams, "What the fuck is going on?" Mary springs up on to the deck and buries the chainsaw deep into the other woman's head. Her body convulses as blood, flesh, gray matter, and bone fragments fly everywhere. William screams with terror as Mary cuts the motor and pulls the chainsaw out of the shaking lump of flesh which used to be a human. William is cornered as Mary fires up the saw. "Don't Mary, I can explain, please wait, don't!" Mary's eyes are glazed over and she seems possessed. She screams, "Rot in hell you stinking motherfucker!" as she slams the roaring chainsaw into William's mouth. (male, 01128)

By themselves, of course, two isolated stories tell us little. The important questions involve the possibility of *general* and *systematic* differences in large samples obtained from different societies. Stories written in response to the 12 problem-solving stimuli were obtained from secondary-level schools in several societies. Data were collected from 11 nations. In general, no sampling frame of the world's nations exists, and a cross-national study such as this is perhaps best served by ensuring diversity with respect to the dependent variable. In this case, this means ensuring that the sample of nations varies with respect to the prevalence of violence, with some nations characterized by low rates of violent crime and others by high rates of violent crime.

Within each of the societies included in the study, efforts were made to identify secondary schools diverse in parental social class, academic ability, and
probable educational future. Secondary schools were chosen, rather than col-
leges and universities, because secondary schools are much more likely to be
representative of all levels of class and ability. In most societies, tertiary education is highly stratified, drawing overwhelmingly from the highest financial
and ability strata. In each case, a knowledgeable local scholar was asked to
identify schools that were likely to draw from populations diverse in social
class. In each national sample, approximately 600 to 750 stories were obtained
from 200 to 250 individuals—that is, each individual wrote three stories. The
general instructions were as follows:

> SOLVING PROBLEMS. In each of the following situations, a specific problem is de-
> scribed. After reading each description, make up a *detailed* story about how the
> characters in the story will try to solve this problem. In your story, describe what
> the characters do and what happens as a result. PLEASE MAKE YOUR STORIES AS
> *DETAILED* AS POSSIBLE.

Although many of the samples tested were English-speaking, some were not.
In the latter case, the instrument was converted by using "back-translation"—
one native-speaking translator creates a foreign language version of the English original, and a second independently translates this version back into English. In this way, subtleties and nuances that are lost (or gained) in translation
can be identified and remedied. Translation is repeated until the foreign version
can "return" from back-translation essentially unchanged from the English language original.

A "Violence Code" was created using the method of content analysis to summarize the quantities of violence in the stories from each national sample.[3] This
Violence Code was developed to summarize systematically the *quantities* of
violence in the resulting stories and also capture specific characteristics and
outcomes of the violence. Content analysis obviously requires a definition of
"violence," something once referred to as "an invitation for a stroll through a
semantic jungle" (Bandura, 1973). Although a great many definitions are possible, the following definition of violence was developed:

> Violence is behavior that willfully or impulsively causes physical damage, harm,
> or injury to a person. This definition is intended to *exclude* "accidents" (e.g.,
> simple vehicle fatalities), unintentional injuries, rites of passage, most types of
> surgery, and purely psychological harm. Some examples of behaviors that are
> *included* in this definition are virtually all homicides, assault, physical struggle,
> rape, suicide, negligent injury (e.g., as a result of drunk driving or corporate
> malfeasance), injury or killing caused by police and other authorities (including
> executions), military actions, and all acts of war.

Individual sections of the Violence Code address different facets of the violence in each story—whether fatal violence occurs and (if so) how many fatal-
ities occur, the seriousness of any nonfatal violence, whether sexual violence
occurs, whether weapons are used and (if so) the types of weapons, which character commits the violence, and so on. The code variables are designed to tap
different facets of any acts of violence that may occur in a story, and there are
too many variables to reproduce the entire code here. It may, however, be of

interest to reproduce one key variable here, a seven-level code for whether violence occurs in the story being coded:

> PRESENCE: The goal of the "Presence" section is to identify the most serious act of violence, if any, present in the sample. If several different acts are present, code the highest possible number of the seven numbers in this "Presence" code. All acts of violence can be coded, but there is a coding priority: (1) First priority is for any *actual* violence (a fight, a knifing); (2) second priority is for any *attempted* violence (pointing a weapon); (3) third priority is for any *contemplated* violence (planning a homicide); (4) fourth priority is for all *other* violence (a negligent accident, etc.).

For example, an actual fist fight takes precedence over a contemplated homicide. The "Presence" variable has seven levels:

1. No physical violence—includes unspecified "punishment"
2. Physical restraint or coercion—e.g., peaceful handcuffing, apprehending, "busting," arresting, etc. No physical violence is mentioned. Use if arrest and no weapon is mentioned.
3. Unintentional injury or death occurs—e.g., most car accidents, falls, or other misfortunes.
4. Violence may or may not occur (e.g., "If . . . then," "Either . . . or" statements). Actual violence is one of the possibilities; more than just a threat.
5. Violence (homicide, injury, or suicide) is contemplated by a character but does not occur. (Code as if it occurred)
6. Violence is threatened or attempted, but no violence occurs—e.g., weapon is pointed or brandished; character says, "Stop, or I'll shoot," etc. Use for "attempted rape" unless additional violence occurs. Use if arrest occurs with a weapon. Includes shooting and missing.
7. Violence occurs (injury or death occurs).

Following the "Presence" variable, the other variables in the Violence Code tap the relationships among the people involved in any act of violence, any weapons involved, consequences, and the like. The code also records background data for the person writing the story: age, gender, and parental social class—using four variables (father's education and occupation, mother's education and occupation). In the case of stories written in languages other than English, bilingual coders were used.

Although the Violence Code permits the systematic enumeration of the *quantities* of violence in the stories, qualitative differences between the national samples are also extremely important, since these differences are often subtle and elude simple tabulation. The two methods, quantitative and qualitative, are complementary rather than redundant since they tap very different facets of the data set.

## Results: Quantitative Data

A comparison of 11 national data sets reveals that large differences occur in terms of the quantities of violence contained in the stories, and these differences are indicated in Table 5.1. These data are for all 12 problem-solving stories combined. The overall incidence of violence shows low values for the

**Table 5.1. Levels of Violence in Imaginative Stories from Different Societies**

| Violence Type | National Sample (*n*) | | | | | | | | | | | Max/Min[a] |
|---|---|---|---|---|---|---|---|---|---|---|---|---|
| | Australia (596) | Canada (767) | England (728) | France (561) | Japan (693) | Korea (742) | Mexico (417) | New Zealand (489) | Northern Ireland (258) | Sweden (729) | U.S. (1728) | |
| Any violence | 37.8% | 27.2% | 28.7% | 24.2% | 29.0% | 18.6% | 19.9% | 38.7% | 32.6% | 19.3% | 30.2% | 2.1 |
| Homicide | 12.9 | 5.7 | 5.9 | 4.5 | 4.0 | 3.1 | 4.1 | 14.4 | 6.2 | 5.9 | 8.7 | 4.6 |
| 2 or more dead | 4.8 | 1.1 | 0.9 | 0.6 | 1.4 | 0.9 | 1.7 | 4.8 | 2.7 | 1.2 | 3.3 | 8.0 |
| Suicide | 4.9 | 4.6 | 3.4 | 3.1 | 3.8 | 2.5 | 1.9 | 5.9 | 3.9 | 2.7 | 4.3 | 3.1 |
| Rape | 3.5 | 0.3 | 2.1 | 0.4 | 2.8 | 3.0 | 1.7 | 3.2 | 3.6 | 1.0 | 1.7 | 12.0 |
| War | 4.0 | 4.1 | 2.5 | 5.0 | 4.6 | 1.9 | 1.4 | 2.9 | 2.3 | 3.0 | 4.6 | 3.6 |
| Weapon present | 16.2 | 7.2 | 7.3 | 8.4 | 2.6 | 2.7 | 4.3 | 16.4 | 7.5 | 6.6 | 12.4 | 6.3 |
| Firearms | 8.7 | 5.4 | 3.0 | 6.6 | 1.6 | 2.0 | 3.3 | 7.4 | 2.0 | 4.2 | 7.5 | 5.4 |
| Handgun | 1.0 | 0.1 | 0.3 | 0.0 | 0.1 | 0.0 | 0.7 | 1.2 | 0.4 | 0.1 | 0.6 | 12.0 |
| Nuclear weapon | 1.5 | 0.3 | 0.1 | 0.0 | 0.3 | 0.0 | 0.0 | 1.2 | 0.4 | 0.3 | 0.8 | 15.0 |

[a] The Max/Min Index is the simple ratio of the maximum value to the minimum value. When the minimum is zero, a minimum value of 0.1 is used.

Korean (18.6%), Swedish (19.3%), and Mexican samples (19.9%); much higher values occur for the New Zealand (38.7%), Australian (37.8%), and American (30.2%) samples. Differences among the 11 samples are even larger for several specific forms of violence, and the 11-sample range for the incidence of each form of violence is shown by the "maximum/minimum" ratio in Table 5.1. For example, homicide is more than four times as common in the New Zealand and Australian samples as it is in the Korean sample, weapon use varies by a factor of 6, and the ratio for rape varies by a factor of 12.

The 11 national samples can be ranked from high to low in the following order in terms of the frequency of any form of violence in the stories: New Zealand, Australia, Northern Ireland, United States, Japan, England, Canada, France, Mexico, Sweden, and Korea. If one ranks the 11 samples on the other outcomes shown in Table 5.1, most of the rankings correspond closely to this same order. There are a few cases, however, where a nation's ranking changes by two or more ranks from the overall violence ranking. For example, this is reflected in relatively low incidences of rape in the Canadian stories; relatively high levels of rape in the Korean stories; relatively low levels of war in the New Zealand and Australian stories; and relatively low levels of firearm use in New Zealand. With these exceptions, rankings of the 11 samples generally persist across the different types of violence indicated in Table 5.1.

## Gender Differences

Stories written by men are more likely to contain violence than are stories written by women. This pattern is consistent (1) across all 11 societies and (2) across all 12 problem-solving situations. These gender differences are shown in Table 5.2. A higher proportion of male stories (35% overall) contained violence than did female stories (22.5%) for all 11 national samples. This indicates that male stories were 1.56 times as likely to contain violence as female stories (Cohen's $d$ = roughly .33).

The differential for stories containing homicides was even greater; compared to women's stories, men's stories were 2.40 times more likely to contain a homicide. The differential for stories containing firearms was roughly 2.13. It should be noted that these male–female differences were not found in only one or two societies. Consistent male–female differences occurred for 35 of the 36 comparisons (97.2%) and for 28 of the 28 significant differences (100%) shown in Table 5.2. Independent of the nation studied, therefore, men were more likely than women to write violent stories.

In addition to global levels of violence in male and female stories, it is interesting to ask whether the gender differences summarized in Table 5.2 result from only one or two types of stories, for example, stories that involve male–female conflict ("Mary Denies Richard") or sexual jealousy ("Unfaithful Mary" and "Catherine Leaves James"). The answer to this question is obtained by presenting gender differences disaggregated across all 12 conflicts, and these results are given in Table 5.3.

As shown in Table 5.3, gender differences in violence are not found in only a few specific conflicts. In general, all 12 stimuli prompt more violent stories from men in most of the national samples. The tendency for male stories to be more violent can be summarized in three ways. Male stories are more likely

**Table 5.2. Who Writes More Violent Stories: Men or Women? (% of Stories with Specified Content)**

| Content by Gender of Author | National Sample (*n*) | | | | | | | | | | | |
|---|---|---|---|---|---|---|---|---|---|---|---|---|
| | Australia (596) | Canada (767) | England (728) | France (561) | Japan (693) | Korea (742) | Mexico (417) | New Zealand (489) | Northern Ireland (258) | Sweden (729) | U.S. (1728) | Mean |
| **Violence** | | | | | | | | | | | | |
| Male | 47.4 | 31.8 | 35.9 | 34.0 | 32.8 | 25.5 | 23.6 | 43.4 | 44.6 | 27.9 | 37.8 | 35.0% |
| Female | 28.3 | 23.0 | 20.5 | 18.5 | 25.0 | 11.6 | 18.3 | 34.3 | 28.6 | 15.3 | 23.9 | 22.5% |
| | *** | * | *** | *** | * | *** | | * | ** | *** | *** | *** |
| Difference | 19.1 | 8.8 | 15.4 | 15.5 | 7.8 | 13.9 | 5.3 | 9.1 | 16.0 | 12.6 | 13.9 | 12.5% |
| **Homicides** | | | | | | | | | | | | |
| Male | 20.8 | 8.1 | 7.8 | 9.9 | 5.6 | 4.6 | 6.3 | 18.1 | 7.7 | 10.2 | 12.4 | 10.1% |
| Female | 4.8 | 3.4 | 3.6 | 1.4 | 2.4 | 1.6 | 3.0 | 11.3 | 5.5 | 3.7 | 5.4 | 4.2% |
| | *** | ** | * | *** | * | * | | * | | *** | *** | *** |
| **Firearms** | | | | | | | | | | | | |
| Male | 11.6 | 6.8 | 5.9 | 7.9 | 3.1 | 3.5 | 4.7 | 9.6 | 1.5 | 8.2 | 9.3 | 6.6% |
| Female | 5.9 | 4.4 | 0.3 | 5.4 | 0.0 | 0.5 | 2.4 | 5.8 | 1.6 | 2.4 | 5.8 | 3.1% |
| | * | | *** | *** | ** | ** | | | | *** | ** | *** |

*** $p < .001$ (at least).
** $p < .01$.
* $p < .05$.

**Table 5.3. Gender Differences in Violence Levels on 12 Stories**

| | National Sample (n) | | | | | | | | | | | |
|---|---|---|---|---|---|---|---|---|---|---|---|---|
| Story | Australia (596) | Canada (767) | England (728) | France (561) | Japan (693) | Korea (742) | Mexico (417) | New Zealand (489) | Northern Ireland (258) | Sweden (729) | U.S. (1728) | Rank |
| Unfaithful Mary | .36** | .33* | .38** | .35** | .10 | .15 | .01 | .15 | .26 | .26* | .32*** | 1 |
| Unfaithful William | .44*** | .01 | .18 | .08 | .04 | -.14 | .07 | -.01 | .42* | .09 | .10 | 8 |
| Unhappy Ann | .28* | -.11 | .00 | .41** | .07 | .14 | .27 | -.37* | -.05 | -.04 | .03 | 9 |
| Demonstrators | .10 | .01 | .00 | .16 | -.05 | .31** | .01 | .06 | -.05 | .36** | .23** | 11 |
| Catherine Leaves James | .24* | .07 | .13 | .18 | .04 | .21 | -.08 | .41** | .26 | .07 | .27*** | 5 |
| James Leaves Catherine | .31* | .06 | .27* | .19 | -.01 | .25* | .17 | .23 | -.17 | .17 | .25** | 3.5 |
| Co-Worker Dispute | .34** | .30** | .23 | .13 | .21 | -.01 | .22 | .24 | .66** | .13 | .19* | 2 |
| Mark the Policeman | .03 | .06 | -.06 | .27* | .35** | -.10 | -.09 | .08 | -.41 | .25* | .20** | 11 |
| Roger and His Son | -.14 | .19 | .06 | .12 | .32** | .37** | -.39* | .00 | .50** | .06 | .00 | 11 |
| Big and Small Nation | .07 | .24* | .20 | .08 | .14 | .40*** | .02 | .20 | .33 | .18 | .19* | 3.5 |
| Mary Denies Richard | .28* | -.37* | .18 | .01 | .04 | .53*** | .30* | .16 | .09 | -.06 | .04 | 7 |
| John in the Pub | .32** | .28* | .26* | .26 | -.10 | -.03 | .17 | -.05 | .04 | .33** | .11 | 6 |

NOTE: Values shown are correlations between gender and the presence of violence in each story. Positive values indicate more violence in stories written by men; negative correlations indicate more violence in stories written by women. Ranks reflect the median correlation for each story—the story ranked number "1" is most likely to have male authors write more violent stories. The sample size is approximately 50 per correlation for most of the national samples, and approximately 140 per correlation for the U.S.

\*** p < .001 (at least).
\** p < .01.
\* p < .05.

than female stories to contain violence: (a) for 41 of the 44 (93.2%) significant correlations in Table 5.3;[4] (b) for 77 of the 87 (88.5%) correlations with absolute *r* values greater than plus or minus .10; (c) for 105 of the 128 (82%) non-zero correlations. No matter how one reads Table 5.3, therefore, it is clear that male stories are consistently more likely to contain violence than are female stories. There are only three (out of 132) cases in which female stories are significantly more violent than male stories ("Mary Denies Richard" for Canada, "Roger and His Son" for Mexico, and "Unhappy Ann" for New Zealand), and the general pattern in Table 5.3 is extremely clear. Independent of the conflict studied, therefore, men were more likely than women to write violent stories.

## Results: Qualitative Data

Because roughly 8,000 stories were collected and examined, enumeration such as the content analysis just described was indispensable to data reduction. Indeed, quantification provides the most comprehensive answer to questions about how much violence is reflected in these stories and whether there are gender differences. At the same time, even a casual perusal of the stories indicates that a close qualitative reading is essential to understanding the cultural differences contained in this archive of stories.

Only qualitative examples can provide a sense of the gulf that separates the data stories obtained from the 11 different nations in the study. The 11 national data sets vary dramatically, not only in the frequency of violent acts— something quantification does a reasonable job of summarizing—but also in the nuances that make the 11 data sets so dissimilar. These nuances defy quantification, and they reflect some of the most important qualities that make the Swedish stories unlike the American stories and that make both unlike the English stories, for example. Many of the themes, patterns, and outcomes found frequently in the stories from one nation were infrequent or even unknown in the stories from another society. Quantification therefore leaves unanswered many subtle questions regarding cultural differences, and a close reading of the stories is required.

With so many stories to choose from, it is possible here to illustrate only some of the diversity and cultural uniqueness in the stories. For the sake of simplicity, the examples given here are all from the "Unfaithful William" and "Unfaithful Mary" conflicts. In American stories written in response to these two problems, reactions generally involve anger and rage. In these stories, both love and marriage are seen as ended. When violence occurs in these stories, it is frequently fatal, occurs rapidly in hot blood, and often involves firearms. The following examples are from the American sample, with examples written by men presented first. There was a gender difference in the frequency of violence in American stories about "Unfaithful Mary" (36.8% of male stories contained violence; 9.6% of female stories contained violence) and, to a lesser degree, about "Unfaithful William" (22.6% of male stories; 14.6% of female stories). The reader is cautioned that these texts are sometimes violent and vary widely in literary merit.

> William waits for three hours. Then finally the man comes out of the house tucking his shirt. By this time, William is outraged so he starts up his car and drives casually over towards the man and parks right in the way of the man's car. Wil-

liam steps out very casually and reaches under the seat and pulls out his service 45 and chambers a round. In the meantime the man steps out of the car and is walking toward William. William sees him coming towards him so he just points it towards the man and pulls the trigger. The shock of the slug to the man's chest was so great it broke all his ribs and put a hole through him that you could stick a baseball through. (male, 01049)

First, William hit the dashboard as hard as he could and nearly broke his hand doing so. William starts to get an angry look on his face and all of a sudden, pulls out a .357 Magnum, the most powerful in the world. . . . When William began the third knock, the man answered the door. William asked if Mary was there, the man said that he doesn't know any Mary and so she wasn't there. William then blew off his head and took Mary home and romped on her. (male, 03102)

William is going to go kick some ass on this dude. First thing William does is wait 15 minutes so he can barge into the house and catch this man fucking the brains out of his wife. Then William fucks this dude up, beats his head in and gets a gun and shoots his ass. Then he goes and fucks Mary's pussy all the rest of the day to make sure she won't want any more Dick for a while. (male, 12180)

William should talk to Mary about what's going on. He should ask her what kind of problem is going on between them, and ask her if there is a problem (and) why she can't tell him instead of sleeping around with other guys. Maybe they should see a marriage counselor. (female, 12085)

At the door to the bedroom he stops and listens carefully. His blood is pounding so loudly through his ears that it is hard to hear. Taking a deep breath, he opens the door and stalks into the bedroom. Mary is undressed in bed with a man William has never seen before. She jumps up and the blood rushes from her face. "What the hell is going on here?!," William shouts. Mary breaks down and starts crying as the stranger hurriedly gets dressed and runs out the door. . . . Mary rambles on and on, not seeing what Will is doing, then out of nowhere William pulls out a gun and says, "If I can't have you neither can he!," and with that he proceeds to shoot Mary in the head and, only seconds later, to shoot himself. (female, 03106)

Mary will probably sit there and think "I want to kill them both." But obviously she won't hurt him. The other woman would yell at him for not getting rid of Mary and the two women will end up fighting and, at the end, the other woman will probably just give up and say something to William like, "You'll be sorry." (female, 11012)

The following stories are drawn from some of the other national samples. These examples vary in the quantities and qualities of violence they contain, and they also reflect some degree of cultural uniqueness; that is, they contain themes and solutions encountered rarely if at all in the American stories.

William, a bit sexually frustrated himself, is extremely jealous. He finds however that this jealousy provokes an erotic feeling. His loins tingled as he watched them kiss. His normal uncreative mind starts to burn with new and exciting ideas. He decides to cut loose from his inhibitions and join them. Once in the house, he can hear their laughter in the bathroom. He begins to unbutton his shirt as he approaches the door. As he turns the knob, he can hear the couple gasp. "It's OK," he whispers, "I've come to join you." The couple is noticeably apprehensive but, as he undresses, they begin to relax. Their innovative afternoon has begun. (Swedish male, 23194)

William will go into the house and call for an explanation, [and] ask what the other man is doing in his house with his wife and so on. If it just was a temporary romance, they can be friends again. Or perhaps William will sue for a divorce. (Swedish female, 23127)

After a very hard morning at work, she returns home. William by this time would have gone to work. Mary, in her hunt for evidence, finds an article of the woman's clothing under the bed. Later when her husband returns she confronts him. They don't argue about it but talk sensibly, deciding the best course of action calmly among the two of themselves. Agreeing eventually that she, Mary, is willing to give him a second chance if he gives his word to forget that woman. (English female, 28066)

William sat in his car trying to decide what to do. Should he burst in on them, should he kill them both, should he go to a lawyer or ignore what was happening? William drove up to his house, walked up to the door. He goes inside. Giggles can be heard upstairs. He goes up to the bedroom and Mary and her lover are lying on the bed, semi-naked. Both try to cover themselves up. Mary gets out of bed and tries to calm William down. William pushes her away over a chair. Her lover gets up to defend her and receives a fist in the face. William leaves the house and drives off at high speed to the nearest bar. (English male, 28015)

Mary pretends she knows nothing. Mary then, in the morning and at night, uses these times to see how William feels about her. . . . If William still does not show any affection, Mary will leave the house and will live alone. She will never go out with another man and will never change her feelings about her loving William. In short, she will not revenge, hate or hold a grudge against William loving somebody else. If she ever felt this way, she will condemn her feelings. On the other hand, she will try to understand why men behave in this manner. As a result, they will end in a divorce but she will love William more than she ever had during her marriage. (Japanese male, 27007)

William was angered but, having run to the front of the house, he tiptoed to peek into the window where Mary and the man were. He peeked for a while. Shocked by what Mary and the man were doing, William rushed into the house and shouted at Mary, "Who is this guy?" Mary told excuses but William smacks her. . . . (Japanese male, 27039)

Mary is stunned. Slowly she walks to her car and in a daze drives off. Images of the woman kissing her husband flash through her mind. Resolutely, she parks her car near a deserted beach and goes for a walk. She is in a turmoil. Should she confront her husband and demand an explanation or should she bide her time and hope that he tells her himself? Direct confrontation is best, so slowly Mary gets back into her car and drives back home. She is just in time to see the lady leaving. . . . Guilt is written all over William's face as he sees Mary. "It was nothing," he stutters desperately. Mary doesn't say anything. She walks determinedly to their bedroom, pulls out her suitcase and starts packing her belongings. For a moment her eyes fall upon their wedding picture, but she turns away. At the door, she turns one last time to take a look at what was her home and at the man she once loved. Then she turns and purposefully walks towards her car. (Australian female, 26018)

There were noises coming from the bedroom so she moved down the passage slowly and then she peered around the corner. Her friend was right. Then Mary quickly moved to the passage closet and pulled out a handgun. She then returned to the bedroom with the loaded gun, shooting her husband first and then his little playmate. Then turning the gun on herself, after shooting everybody. They had all died instantly. (Australian male, 26109)

Mary investigates their relationship with suspicion. She tries to find out whether their relationship is unclean or just friendship, or has to do with business. If the relationship turns out to be serious (unclean), Mary will suffer deeply from agony and anguish. Since Mary loves William very much, she will leave him for his happiness. Mary's life will be filled with joy thinking that William, the one whom she loves the most, is living a happy life by her sacrifice. (Korean female, 25043)

When William gets home, he asks Mary with a smiling face, "Did you have fun while I was gone?" Mary looks surprised, "How did you know?" If I were William, I'd go to the man and hit him a few times, then give my wife (Mary) to the man. (Korean male, 25149)

## AN ATTEMPT AT THEORETICAL SYNTHESIS

The large gender differences reported in this chapter have implications for the theoretical models with which the chapter began. These can be revisited briefly as follows.

**Biological Determinism**. Given the large and highly consistent gender differences obtained, the role of biological factors cannot in our view be discounted—males wrote more violent stories than women in every national sample and for virtually every conflict. In our view, this cross-national finding is apparently consistent with the proposition that gender differences in violence are influenced by biological factors.

**Social Determinism**. It seems improbable that socialization in all societies and on all conflicts would produce higher levels of violence for men. Unless one is willing to assume that the content of socialization is everywhere the same, favoring the production of greater violence and aggression in males, it is difficult to explain the gender differences observed. At the same time, it should be emphasized that—quite apart from gender—*national samples as a whole also differed strongly* in the levels of violence in the stories. This finding is consistent with the view that differences in violence are socially constructed.

**Environmental Determinism**. It seems difficult to explain the highly consistent gender differences obtained across societies in terms of the specific stimuli and images (movies, media, weapon availability, etc.) present in a given society. Again, however, it is critical to emphasize the aggregate differences (i.e., neglecting gender) across national samples—these could well result from environmental and other social factors.

**Cultural Determinism**. As with social and environmental perspectives, the simple version of the cultural model appears unable to account for the gender differences found. Given the diversity of cultural practices and variation in child-rearing in different societies, highly consistent gender differences in violence are somewhat unexpected. Again, however, the large aggregate differences across national samples are perfectly consistent with the notion that different cultures produce aggression and violence in different quantities.

## CONCLUSION

As noted earlier, there is clearly overlap in the predictions implied by social, environmental, and cultural theories; these perspectives could be referred to collectively as "social-cultural" explanations. While the surprisingly consistent gender differences in this study lend apparent credibility to biological explanations, the large aggregate differences across nations just as strongly support social-cultural explanations.

The gender differentials in Tables 5.2 and 5.3 are consistent with biological models. These are consistent gender differences *within* each of the national data sets, and it seems that biology—or at least universals that transcend national boundaries—may be implicated. However, the aggregate levels of violence across nations (Table 5.1) are difficult to explain without social-cultural models. The enormous differences *between* national data sets in terms of the prevalence of violence in the stories cannot be explained by biological factors and, instead, require consideration of social and cultural variables that vary across these societies. The precise nature of these social and cultural variables remains unknown at this point, but the huge cross-national differences reported here appear to provide a "smoking gun" proving that these variables exist.

The data reported here therefore provide support for the role of very different types of etiological explanations. *Both social-cultural and biological explanations can claim support in these data since both differences (the variation in aggregate violence levels across samples) and similarities (the almost universally higher levels of male violence) are found in this cross-cultural comparison.*

This is easily illustrated. Although males are more likely than females to write violent stories in every national sample, these differences are relative within samples, not absolute. In Table 5.2, for example, *women* from Australia and New Zealand were more likely to write violent stories (28.3% and 34.3%, respectively) than *men* from Sweden and Korea (27.9% and 25.5%, respectively).

This suggests that social-cultural factors anchor the overall or *absolute* quantities of attitudes, expectations, and values affecting violence in a society. Around this aggregate, however, our data suggest that biological factors may inflexibly determine *relative* gender differences—with men always more associated with violence than are women. A book-length analysis, now in progress, will address the national and cultural differences that affect the probability that a conflict will spark violence in one society but nonviolent conflict resolution in another.

## NOTES

1. Readers are cautioned that plasma testosterone is not a readily measured quantity like height; it is influenced by stress and other environmental conditions. The complexity of human hormonal systems also makes it difficult or impossible to prove a causal relationship between aggression and testosterone, which is only one of many human androgens.

2. Testosterone is not exclusive to males, nor is estrogen exclusive to females. As a group, however, males have higher mean concentrations of testosterone, whereas females have higher means levels of estrogen.

3. The Violence Code was created for the imaginative data collected for the present study, but the code is intended for general use in studies of thematic, fictional, imaginative, artistic, dramatic, or media violence. Any narrative, depiction, or account that describes what happens to one or more characters should be codable with the Violence Code. The code appears to be reliable. For example, using a 7-item code for the presence of violence in a story, interjudge reliabilities are .90 (C.R.).

4. The overall proportion of *significant* correlations in this table is of course affected by the power of each test (Cohen, 1977). In Table 5.3, unlike Table 5.2, gender comparisons are disaggregated for each of the 12 different problem-solving situations. The effective $n$ for each situation is roughly 50. Assuming a "medium" effect size (i.e., of $r = .30$), this yields a power of .57, and a sample of this size requires an absolute value of $r$ of roughly .27 to reach significance. The effective $n$ for the U.S. sample is roughly 140 per conflict situation, yielding a higher power of .95 and also requiring a lower absolute value of $r$ (roughly .17) to reach significance.

## REFERENCES

Archer, D., & Gartner, R. (1976). Violent acts and violent times: A comparative approach to postwar homicide rates. *American Sociological Review, 41*, 937–962.

Archer, D., & Gartner, R. (1984). *Violence and crime in cross-national perspective*. New Haven, CT: Yale University Press.

Bandura, A. (1973). *Aggression: A social learning analysis*. Englewood Cliffs, NJ: Prentice-Hall.

Bardwick, J. (1971). *The psychology of women: A study of bio-cultural conflicts*. New York: Harper and Row.

Berkowitz, L. (1962). *Aggression: A social psychological analysis*. New York: McGraw-Hill.

Berkowitz, L. (1964). Aggressive cues in aggressive behavior. *Psychological Review, 71*, 104–122.

Berkowitz, L. (1965). Some aspects of observed aggression. *Journal of Personality and Social Psychology, 2*, 359–369.

Berkowitz, L. (1978). External determinants of aggressive behavior. In W. W. Hartup & J. de Wit (Eds.), *Origins of aggression*. The Hague: Moriton Publishers.

Berkowitz, L., & LePage, A. (1967). Weapons as aggression-eliciting stimuli. *Journal of Personality and Social Psychology, 7*, 202–207.

Bleier, R. (1984). *Science and gender: A critique of biology and its theories on women.* New York: Pergamon Press.

Christiansen, K., & Knussman, R. (1987). Androgen levels and components of aggressive behavior in man. *Hormones and Behavior, 21,* 170–180.

Cohen, J. (1977). *Statistical power analysis for the behavioral sciences.* New York: Academic Press.

Condry, J., & Condry, S. (1976). Sex differences: A study of the eye of the beholder. *Child Development, 47,* 812–819.

Connor, R., & Levine, S. (1969). Hormonal influences on aggressive behavior. In S. Garattini & E. B. Sigg (Eds.), *Aggressive behavior.* New York: John Wiley and Sons.

D'Andrade, R. (1966). Sex differences and cultural institutions. In E. Maccoby (Ed.), *The development of sex differences.* Stanford, CA: Stanford University Press.

Doering, C., Brodie, H., Kraemer, H., Becker, H., & Hamburg, D. (1974). Plasma testosterone levels and psychologic measures in men over a two-month period. In R. C. Friedman, R. M. Richart, R. L. Van Wiele, & L. O. Stern (Eds.), *Sex differences in behavior.* New York: John Wiley and Sons.

Eagley, A., & Steffen, V. (1986). Gender and aggressive behavior: A meta-analytic review of the social psychological literature. *Psychological Bulletin, 100,* 309–330.

Ehrenkranz, J., Bliss, E., & Sheard, M. (1974). Plasma testosterone: Correlations with aggressive behavior and social dominance in man. *Psychosomatic Medicine, 36,* 469–475.

Fagot, B., & Hagan, R. (1985). Aggression in toddlers: Responses to the assertive acts of boys and girls. *Sex Roles, 12,* 341–351.

Fausto-Sterling, A. (1985). *Myths of gender.* New York: Basic Books.

Fried, B. (1979). Boys will be boys will be boys: The language of sex and gender. In R. Hubbard, M. Henifen, & B. Fried (Eds.), *Women look at biology looking at women: A collection of feminist critiques.* Boston: G. K. Hall and Co.

Frodi, A., Macaulay, J., & Thome, P. (1977). Are women always less aggressive than men? A review of the experimental literature. *Psychological Bulletin, 84,* 634–660.

Holliday, L. (1978). *The violent sex: Male psychobiology and the evolution of consciousness.* Guerneville, CA: Bluestocking Press.

Hyde, J. S. (1984). How large are gender differences in aggression? A developmental meta-analysis. *Developmental Psychology, 20,* 722–736.

Hyde, J. S. (1986). Gender differences in aggression. In J. S. Hyde & M. Linn (Eds.), *Psychology of gender: Advances through meta-analysis.* Baltimore: Johns Hopkins University Press.

Kreuz, L., & Rose, R. (1972). Assessment of aggressive behavior and plasma testosterone in a young criminal population. *Psychosomatic Medicine, 34,* 321–332.

Maccoby, E., & Jacklin, C. (1974). *The psychology of sex differences.* Stanford, CA: Stanford University Press.

Mead, M. (1935). *Sex and temperament in three primitive societies.* London: George Routledge and Sons.

Meyer-Bahlburg, H., Nat, R., Boon, D., Sharma, M., & Edwards, J. (1974). Aggressiveness and testosterone measures in man. *Psychosomatic Medicine, 36,* 269–274.

Mischel, W. (1966). A social learning view of sex differences in behavior. In E. Maccoby (Ed.), *Development of sex differences.* Stanford, CA: Stanford University Press.

Mitchell, G., & Brandt, E. M. (1970). Behavioral differences related to experience of mother and sex of infant in the rhesus monkey. *Developmental Psychiatry*, *3*, 149.

Money, J., & Ehrhardt, A. (1972). *Man and woman, boy and girl.* Baltimore: Johns Hopkins University Press.

Monti, P., Brown, W., & Corriveau, D. (1977). Testosterone and components of aggressive behavior in man. *American Journal of Psychiatry*, *34*, 692–694.

Olweus, D., Mattsson, A., Schalling, D., & Low, H. (1980). Testosterone, aggression, physical, and personality dimensions in normal adolescent males. *Psychosomatic Medicine*, *42*, 253–269.

Persky, H., Smith, K., & Basu, G. (1971). Relation of psychologic measures of aggression and hostility to testosterone production in man. *Psychosomatic Medicine*, *33*, 265–277.

Purifoy, F., & Koopmans, L. (1979). Androstenedione, testosterone and free testosterone production in women of various occupations. *Social Biology*, *26*, 79–188.

Rada, R., Laws, D., & Kellner, R. (1976). Plasma testosterone levels in the rapist. *Psychosomatic Medicine*, *38*, 257–268.

Reinish, J. (1981). Prenatal exposure to synthetic progestins increases potential for aggression in humans. *Science*, *211*, 1171–1173.

Rohner, R. P. (1976). Sex differences in aggression: Phylogenetic and enculturation perspectives. *Ethos*, *4*, 57–72.

Rubin, J., & Provenzano, L. Z. (1974). The eye of the beholder: Parents' views on sex of newborns. *American Journal of Orthopsychiatry*, *44*, 512–519.

Scaramella, T., & Brown, W. (1978). Serum testosterone and aggressiveness in hockey players. *Psychosomatic Medicine*, *40*, 262–265.

Sears, R., Maccoby, E., & Levin, H. (1957). *Patterns of child rearing.* Stanford, CA: Stanford University Press.

Segall, M. (1983). Aggression in global perspective. In A. P. Goldstein & M. Segall (Eds.), *Aggression in global perspective.* New York: Pergamon Press.

Tieger, T. (1980). On the biological bases of sex differences in aggression. *Child Development*, *51*, 943–963.

White, J. (1983). Sex and gender issues in aggression research. In R. Geen & E. Donnerstein (Eds.), *Aggression: Theoretical and empirical reviews.* New York: Academic Press.

Whiting, B., & Edwards, C. (1973). A cross-cultural analysis of sex differences in the behavior of children aged three through eleven. *Journal of Social Psychology*, *91*, 171–188.

Wrong, D. (1961). The oversocialized conception of man in modern sociology. *American Sociological Review*, *26*, 183–193.

Yalom, I., Green, R., & Fisk, N. (1973). Prenatal exposure to female hormones. *Archives of General Psychiatry*, *28*, 554–561.

Young, W., Goy, R., & Phoenix, C. (1964). Hormones and sexual behavior. *Science*, *143*, 212–218.

*Acknowledgment.* This research was supported by a grant from the H. F. Guggenheim Foundation and by the University of California. Correspondence concerning this article should be sent to Dane Archer, Professor of Sociology, Stevenson College, UC Santa Cruz, Santa Cruz, CA 95064, 408-459-2555 or at one of the following: (FAX) 408-459-3334 or (Internet) archer@cats.ucsc.edu.

# 6

# Violence by and Against Women:
# A Comparative and Cross-National Analysis

## Candace Kruttschnitt

We have not yet seen a thorough cross-national synthesis of information on female involvement in violent crime across levels of analysis. To date, most cross-national analyses of female crime focus on offending and, by comparison to the work on males, have a very narrow theoretical scope. By contrast, this chapter attempts a more comprehensive understanding of women's involvement in violent crime, using offending and victimization data at both the individual- and aggregate-levels. First, there is an examination of individual-level data to determine what factors are associated with women's risks of offending and victimization within specific societies. Second, aggregate-level data is examined to assess how women's risks of violent offending and victimization are distributed across societies and what societal factors are associated with high rates of female violence.[1]

There are, however, numerous problems inherent in this undertaking. Estimating the relative percentage of violent female offenders and victims among different nations is impossible given both the limitations of large-scale cross-national surveys of crime and the lack of systematic research on women and crime in most nations. The major sources of cross-national data on violent female offending (International Criminal Police Organization, United Nations, Comparative Crime File Data) and victimization (World Health Organization, International Crime Survey) do provide information on the distribution of female involvement in violent crime. Nevertheless, as explicated by Gartner (1993), these surveys are hampered by issues of the reliability and validity of their measures of interpersonal violence which have yet to be systematically estimated or corrected. These large-scale cross-national datasets are best utilized for aggregate descriptive or analytic analyses of female involvement in violent crime.

At the national-level, systematic research on women offenders can be found in only a few developed nations (United States, Canada, selected European nations, and Australia). More generally, extant analyses of female violence vary tremendously in the years they encompass, the geographic regions they cover, the offenses they include, and the data sources they draw upon. For example, analyses include some countries that compile statistical data only on sentenced women or women in correctional facilities whereas others analyze only court records or arrest data. Even when the data sources are similar, the methods used to calculate crime rates vary across studies. Analyses of violent female victimizations are similarly limited and, increasingly, dominated by descriptive studies of domestic violence. Taken together, these data deficiencies constrain both our understanding of the behavioral trends in violent female offending and victimization and our ability to evaluate explanations for any observed trends.

Other limitations of available data and existing research shape the conclusions of this review. First, female involvement in acts of serious interpersonal violence (homicide, assault, robbery, rape) is the primary focus of this article. Analyses are excluded that confound property and violent crimes (e.g., combining burglary and robbery into one offense category) or report information only on the total female crime rate. Second, because the range of individual correlates of violence researched in the United States is not matched by other nations, the international data is used to guide what to include from the available U. S. publications. Third, authors do not consistently examine both the percentage of women involved in violent crime relative to other crimes (a within-sex analysis) and the proportional involvement of women in violent crime (a between-sex analysis). Although data limitations preclude a systematic examination of both methods of assessing violent female crime, every effort is made to clarify which method of measuring female crime is used. Finally, although there is an emphasis on studies based on large and representative samples, from which strong conclusions can be derived, cross-cultural and ethnographic data is also used when such data bear directly on the issues of concern.[2]

This review is divided into five sections. The first two consider individual-level data, reviewing the correlates of violent female offending and victimization. To explain the patterns observed in the individual-level data, the third section focuses on the contextual environment of violent female encounters. Section four turns to the aggregate-level data to assess the societal determinants of gender variations in violent offending and victimization.[3] Finally, section five summarizes the findings from this review as well as the potential weaknesses of the extant research and theory. In so doing, directions for future research are layed out.

## WOMEN AT RISK FOR VIOLENT OFFENDING

Every study of female crime, regardless of the data source or nation studied, notes that women represent a small proportion of the violent offender population (see e.g., Adler, 1981; Curtis, 1974; Ferracuti & Newman, 1974; Heindensohn, 1991; Heiland, Shelley, & Katoh, 1992). Most studies also find little evidence of change in this pattern. Data from the United States, the Federal Republic of Germany, and the Netherlands all suggest either stability over time in violence by young females or declines in their relative proportion of offending (Bruinsma, Dessaur, & Van Hezewijk, 1981; Kaiser, 1985; Karstedt, 1992; Kruttschnitt, in press). One possible exception to this pattern of stability is reported for England/Wales (Gibbens, 1981).

Unfortunately, perhaps because women only represent a small proportion of violent offenders, little scholarly work identifies characteristics or situations that increase women's risks for violent offending. The only characteristics of the offender on which meaningful statistics are available cross-nationally are age, race, and offender-victim relationship.

## Age

Although age is thought to be one of the major risk markers for violent offend-ing (Farrington, 1986), there is little evidence that particular ages place women at high risk for violent crime. Instead, the age-crime curve for women appears to vary across offenses, historical periods, and nations. In the United States, recent arrest rates for robbery and assault are highest from the mid-teens to the late-twenties, irrespective of gender. For murder, however, female involvement peaks later, in the 20s, and continues at a relatively stable, albeit low, rate through the 30s; the comparable male rate drops off in the 30s (Kruttschnitt, in press). Similar gender differences in the age distribution of homicide offending are reported for Canada during 1974-1983 (Daly & Wilson, 1988, p. 169). Some scholars believe that this relatively flat age distribution for female homicide is due to the greater tendency for women, as compared to men, to engage in intrafamilial homicides (Daly & Wilson, 1988; Wolfgang, 1958; see also Maxfield, 1989). However, it is unclear whether this finding can be general-ized to other times and places. For example, homicide data from Australia for 1933-1981 indicate that women's peak ages of offending have declined over time (Wallace, 1986).[4] Unfortunately, age-relevant data from other countries are either drawn from conviction statistics (Bhanot & Misra, 1981; Rasko, 1981) or are dichotomized at an arbitrary age (Kent, 1981).

## Race

Virtually all of the research pertaining to the interaction of gender, race, and violent crime is done in the United States and focuses on murder. Uniformly, these studies find that black women are more frequently involved in acts of lethal violence than white women and that the homicide rates of black females exceed even those of white males (Riedel, 1988). Arrest rates for assault and self-reports of violent juvenile offending appear to follow a similar pattern (Laub & McDermott, 1985; Steffensmeier & Allen, 1988).

Outside of the United States much less is known about gender, race, and violent offending. What is known, however, suggests that the high rates of ho-micide among black females in the United States have little to do with their race per se. First, black women living in other countries do not appear to have unusually high rates, or different patterns, of violent offending relative to those found among white women, as confirmed in studies of black women living in both predominantly black countries, like Nigeria, and predominantly white coun-tries, like Canada (Oloruntimehin, 1981; 1992; Wilson & Daly, 1992).[5] Sec-ond, marital status conditions the relationships among gender, race, and levels of lethal violence. The sex ratio of killing for blacks (homicides perpetrated by women per 100 perpetrated by men) is unusually high only for spousal homi-cides, a pattern which generally is not found among other minorities or whites in the United States or blacks in other nations (Mushanga, 1978; Wilson & Daly, 1992). Although far from complete, these findings indicate that cultural factors that may be unique to African-American women and their partners may explain their unusually high rates of lethal violence in the United States.

### The Targets of Female Violence

Researchers in countries other than the United States are far more concerned with the targets of female violence than the demographic correlates of female violence. Irrespective of time and place, they find that the bulk of lethal violence by females is directed toward family members, especially spouses.[6]

Examination was made of the relative proportions of female involvement in all homicides and spousal homicides using published data from two U. S. cities, Canada, England/Wales, Scotland, and Australia (Wallace, 1986; Wilson & Daly, 1992, Table 3). Table 6.1 reports the comparisons.

In each of these nations, the female share of homicide offenders is low, roughly 10%. Yet, for spousal homicides, women's involvement is far more substantial (ranging from 18% to 54%; see also Curtis, 1974; National Council for Crime Prevention, 1990; Rasko, 1981). With the exception of England/Wales, women are at least twice as likely to perpetrate a spousal homicide as any other type of homicide. Other analyses of the same Canadian and Australian data indicate that, while women are more likely to kill their spouses than their children, children represent the largest proportion of other homicides in which women are involved (Daly & Wilson 1988, p. 83; Wallace 1986). In fact, in some countries, children are reported to be the primary targets of women's homicides (Curtis, 1974; Katoh, 1992).

Interestingly, there are also indications that as women's legal relationships to intimates shift so also do their levels of lethal violence. For example, in the Netherlands, a decline in both the absolute number and the proportional involvement of women in offenses against life and person are attributed to increases in divorce and abortion (Bruinsma et al., 1981). In India, the lack of availability of divorce is thought to explain the murder rate among women (Hartjen, 1986).

## WOMEN AT RISK FOR VIOLENT VICTIMIZATION

There is more research on women as victims than as offenders. However, much of this research is anecdotal or otherwise limited in scope and methodology (see e.g., Dobash, Dobash, Wilson, & Daly, 1992; Heise, in press; Hoffman, Demo, & Edwards, 1993; Landau, 1989; Seventh United Nations Congress on the Prevention of Crime and the Treatment of Offenders, 1985). Few systematic national studies of crime victimization exist outside of the United States.

The 1989 International Crime Survey was designed, albeit with limited success, to address these concerns (van Dijk, Mayhew, & Killias, 1991). Men's and women's relative risks of robbery and assault victimization, and women's risks of serious sexual assaults, were examined in 14 developed nations.[7] Although, generally, women reported fewer incidents of violent victimization than men, gender differences were least apparent for robbery in the United States and for assault with force in the United States, Finland, Switzerland, Belgium, and Scotland (van Dijk et al., 1991, p. 66). Reported rates of serious sexual assaults (rape, attempted rape, and indecent assaults) were highest in the United

**Table 6.1 Percentage of Homicides Perpetrated by Women Contrasting Spousal to Other Homicides (adapted from Wilson and Daly 1992: Table 3 and Wallace 1986: Tables 7. 4 and 7. 6)**

| Data Set | Spousal Homicide | | | Other Homicides | |
|---|---|---|---|---|---|
| | % Women | % of all Homicides | (*n*) | % Women | Total |
| Chicago 1965-1985 | 50. 5 | 13. 3 | (1,706) | 9. 7 | (12,835) |
| Detroit 1972 | 54. 4 | 18. 2 | (79) | 11. 3 | (434) |
| Canada 1974-1983 | 23. 4 | 24. 2 | (1,060) | 10. 4 | (4,383) |
| England & Wales 1977-1986 | 18. 5 | 27. 8 | (1,204) | 12. 8 | (4,333) |
| Scotland 1979-1987 | 28. 8 | 20. 0 | (139) | 7. 2 | (694) |
| New South Wales 1968-1981 | 26. 7 | 30. 1 | (296) | 11. 5 | (982) |

States, Canada, Australia, and West Germany. This evidence of national variation in both serious sexual assaults, and other assaults, may however reveal more about women's willingness to report victimizations by nonstrangers to survey interviewers than their actual risks of being assaulted in these countries (see also Clark & Lewis, 1977; Chappell, 1989).

## Age

Younger women appear to be at greater risk of non-lethal violent victimizations than older women. National Crime Surveys in both the United States and Canada reveal that females 15-24 years of age report more robbery and assault victimizations than women of other ages (Kruttschnitt, in press; Sacco & Johnson 1990).[8] Age-relevant data on rape victims are not available from the Canadian survey because too few incidents were reported. Nevertheless, the comparable American survey, and police files of rape cases in Toronto, Canada; Melbourne, Australia; and six jurisdictions in England, covering various years between l968-1988, also indicate that women in their mid-to-late teens are at the greatest risk for violent victimization (Bush, 1977; Clark & Lewis, 1977; Kruttschnitt, in press; Wright, 1980).

As is true for offending, age appears to be less strongly related to victimizations that involve lethal violence. Data from three nations—Australia, Canada, and the United States—encompassing various time periods, suggest that women's risks of being killed are distributed relatively evenly over the life course (Daly & Wilson, 1988; Gartner & McCarthy, 1991; Riedel, 1988; Wallace, 1986). Specifically, rates of "femicide" begin to rise in the mid-to-late teens, peak in the 20s and gradually decline thereafter, but this age curve is less sharp for women than for men.[9]

## The Perpetrators in Female Victimizations

Just as women are more likely to offend against intimates than against strangers, so also are they more likely to be attacked by intimates than by strangers.

National Crime Victimization Survey (NCVS) data from the United States indicate that women's rates of being seriously assaulted by a relative are twice
that of men's (Reiss & Roth, 1993, pp. 232-233). Women's vulnerability to
victimization by relatives, however, may be even more pronounced than these
official data indicate. For example, findings from self-report surveys conducted
in the U. S. reveal that the number of females assaulted by their male partners
may be four times as high as the number reported by the NCVS (Young, 1992).
Data collected in various cities in Sweden also suggest that the under-repre-
sentation of women as official victims of violence is related to women's greater
likelihood of being assaulted by a family member (WilkstrÜm, 1985, p. 111).[10]
Additionally, because official data on sexual assaults exclude marital rape—
which some researchers (Young, 1992) believe is the most common form of
sexual assault—it seems likely that cross-national studies of rape have underestimated the frequency with which women are attacked by known, and especially intimate, offenders.[11]

   Data on homicide, which can be viewed as a special class of assault, are
more complete and accurate than data on other violent crimes (Loftin, Kindley,
Norris, & Wiersema, 1987; Maxfield, 1989, p. 80). Reports from a number of
countries indicate that lethal violence against women is most frequently perpetrated by family members. U.S. Supplemental Homicide Report data show that
whereas over one-half of all femicides are perpetrated by a family member
(with spouses representing the largest percentage of offenders) only about one-
fifth of male victims are killed by a family member (Reiss & Roth, 1993).
Comparable patterns occur in Australia, suggesting only a slightly larger percentage of family femicides in Australia as opposed to the U.S. (Wallace, 1986).
Further, evidence from Canada suggests that the domestic context of femicides
may be time invariant. Specifically, despite the changes occurring in women's
lives over roughly the last 70 years, the proportion of women killed by intimate
partners remained relatively constant (Gartner & McCarthy, 1991).

## THE CONTEXT OF VIOLENT FEMALE OFFENDING
## AND VICTIMIZATION

These individual-level data indicate that, in most times and places, women involved in nonlethal violent encounters are young and, irrespective of the type
of violence, are more likely than men to be intimately related to their attackers
and their victims. Nevertheless, the age distributions for assault and rape are
based on official data which undercount the actual incidence of female victimization due to the underreporting of crimes involving spouses and intimate partners. If women are more likely to be assaulted by intimate partners or family
members than official data indicate, their risks of encountering such victimizations are probably distributed more evenly over the life course than official
data indicate. Evidence for such an interaction between age and the victim-
offender relationship can be found in analyses of homicide data in both the
United States and Canada. These data show that lethal violence involving ac-
quaintances/strangers exhibits the traditional age curve for violent crime, which
peaks in the late teens, whereas lethal violence involving spouses and intimate
partners has a much flatter age curve (Gartner & McCarthy, 1991; Maxfield,

1989). The nature of women's involvement in violent encounters, then, may be dependent on their relationships to their victims and offenders.

## Female Violence in Encounters with Nonintimates

One perspective particularly relevant to violence among nonintimates is routine activity/lifestyle theory. This theory argues that the convergence of potential victims and offenders in the absence of suitable guardians will lead to a greater risk of crime, independent of individual motivations (Cohen & Felson, 1979; Hindelang, Gottfredson, and Garofalo, 1978). This approach identifies activities and situations—those outside of the household, away from family members who are potential guardians, and occurring at night—that are risk markers for violence.

It is difficult to determine whether this perspective provides an adequate explanation for women's involvement in violent encounters with strangers due to the lack of relevant research. However, preliminary evidence from homicide studies in the United States and Canada suggests that it may. Single women and young women appear to be over-represented as victims and offenders in nondomestic/nonintimate homicides (Gartner & McCarthy, 1991; Mann, 1988). These demographic characteristics are thought to be proxy measures of lifestyle since young single people pursue more social activities outside of the home. Employment status is a more direct measure of out-of-home activity. Being employed is thought to increase women's risks of victimization and offending throughout the world by increasing their exposure to high-risk individuals and situations (Curtis, 1974).[12] However, evidence suggests that, at least with regard to homicide victimizations, this relationship may be more complex. Analyses of femicides in Canada over the past 70 years show that, irrespective of the victim-offender relationship, employment increased women's risks of victimization only when it was less normative for women to work outside of the home (Gartner & McCarthy, 1991, p. 308). In the case of robbery and assault, however, the extent of Canadian women's nighttime activities still appear to have a direct effect on their risk of victimization (Sacco & Johnson, 1990).[13]

## Female Violence in Encounters with Intimates

Much of what is known about women's involvement in violent encounters with intimates comes from descriptive studies of domestic violence (see, e.g., Fergusson, Horwood, Kershaw, & Shannon, 1986; Freed & Freed, 1989; Heise, in press; Kumagai & Straus, 1983; Landau, 1989; Mushanga, 1978; Radford, 1992; Rodd, 1980; Scutt, 1983). These studies indicate that women in many, if not most, countries are at greater risk of encountering violence in their own homes than on the streets. At the same time, however, we know that women's risks of being attacked by, and attacking, intimates are not distributed equally among different nations, as revealed in spousal homicide data (Table 1) and ethnographic cross-cultural studies of family violence (Levinson, 1989; Wilson & Daly, 1993).

What explains such cross-national variation in the rates of female involvement in violence with intimates? In the case of offending, recent attempts to answer this question focus on hypotheses which address the comparable number of women and men who kill their spouses in the United States. These include, for example, the prevalence of gun use, the convergence of the sexes in their use of violence in other domains, the proportion of legally registered marriages, and ethnic group differences (Dobash et al., 1992; Wilson & Daly, 1992). Unfortunately, neither the individual nor the aggregate effects of these variables appear to explain the differences between the United States and other nations in the sex-ratio of spousal killings. Consequently, Wilson & Daly (1992, pp. 208-209; 1993) suggest an alternative set of hypotheses which are consistent with their evolutionary psychological perspective: women's lethality will approach men's when women are forced to defend their valued resources (e.g., their children from a former union/marriage) or when they are socially empowered to do so (e.g., matrilocal residential patterns).

Guided by patriarchy, resource, and exchange theories, the concepts of competition over valued resources and power differentials also appear as explanatory variables in individual studies of domestic violence conducted in the United States, the United Kingdom, Canada, and Thailand (Brinkerhoff & Lupri, 1988; Dobash & Dobash, 1979; Hoffman, Demo, & Edwards, 1993; Yllo & Straus, 1990). Nevertheless, due to differences in research designs and methodologies, these studies have not yet produced a cohesive body of research which convincingly advances these explanatory concepts or otherwise explains variations in wife abuse between or across nations.

## SOCIETAL LEVEL DETERMINANTS OF VIOLENT FEMALE OFFENDING AND VICTIMIZATION

Aggregate-level cross-national research on women and crime looks very different from individual studies of female offending and victimization. Whereas the latter focuses on the relational and domestic nature of female violence within particular nations, the former examines whether developmental, distributional, and demographic variables can explain female crime rates (particularly murder and theft) across nations.

### Offending

Aggregate-level cross-national research on female offending has been concerned primarily with testing the emancipation hypotheses as formulated by Adler (1975) and Simon (1975).[14] Both Adler and Simon hypothesized that, as a result of the Women's Movement, changes in gender roles and increasing opportunities for women outside of the home have produced changes in female offending. Adler draws more attention to the effects of the Women's Movement on violent female offending, whereas Simon stresses changes in employment opportunities for women and associated increases in women's involvement in white-collar and occupational crimes.

Nine quantitative cross-national studies of female offending, all of which either explicitly or implicitly test the emancipation hypothesis are summarized in Table 6.2. All of these studies use International Criminal Police Organization (INTERPOL) data, covering various years between 1950 and 1980, and most measure female crime as the proportion of total arrests for murder and theft which involve women. Only the findings for murder are reported here.

Overall, the findings add little to our understanding of the variation across nations in female violence. Of the 55 associations reported in this table, less than one-half are substantial or statistically significant. Among the significant associations, however, the data support the argument that economic development and social equality increase the female murder rate. Nevertheless, serious questions remain about whether emancipation increases women's motivation to engage in violent offenses.

First, female arrests for murder did not change appreciably over this thirty-year period, despite the associations mentioned above. In fact, evidence indicates a slight decline in the female share of arrests for homicide (Simon & Baxter, 1989). Second, female arrest rates for murder do not vary systematically with a nation's level of development or degree of modernization (see e.g., Simon, 1975; Steffensmeier, Allan, & Streifel, 1989). Third, the observed associations between national-level variables and female arrest rates for homicide tell us virtually nothing about what is occurring on the individual-level. Although some researchers are clearly aware of the ecological fallacy (Bowker, 1981; Marshall, 1982), most continue to draw implications about individuals' behaviors from aggregate observations.

The specific implications of these aggregate-level relationships are unknown and lend themselves to any number of interpretations. For example, in societies where women constitute a greater proportion of the paid labor force, we do not know whether working women or their unemployed counterparts are at greater risk of engaging in lethal violence. Both possibilities could be explained by an economic inequality perspective—in the case of the former, relative deprivation, and, in the case of the latter, absolute deprivation (Blau & Blau, 1982; Steffensmeier et al., 1989). The association between a nation's gross national product and the female arrest rates for murder also lends itself to different interpretations. All women in these countries may be at higher risk of committing murder due to weakened informal and formal social controls (Sampson, 1986; Steffensmeier et al., 1989). Or, alternatively, this association may be explained by differences in the professionalization of social control agencies in nations with low and high gross national products which, in turn, affect the rate of reporting and apprehending female murderers (Oloruntimehin, 1992; Steffensmeier et al., 1989).

## Victimization

The overview presented here of cross-national data on female homicides suggests that the predominant theoretical model—emancipation—has not been very successful in explaining women's violence. Aggregate-level research on homicide victimization draws attention to a wider range of explanations for sex-specific homicide rates and the gender gap in these rates. Coupled with cross-cultural data on domestic violence, this body of research provides some intriguing ideas about the social contexts in which females are at greatest risk of being violently victimized.

First, there is some evidence that attempts to derive gender-specific explanations for cross-national variations in the level of female violence may be misguided. Analysis of World Health Organization data on 18 developed nations, encompassing three decades, reveals substantial covariation between males'

**Table 6.2. Summary Data From Cross-National Studies of Female Offending**

| Study | Crime Data Source (Year) | Sample Size | Type of Analysis | Independent Variables | Relationship IV to DV | Dependent Variable |
|---|---|---|---|---|---|---|
| Simon (1975) | Interpol (1963-1968, 1970) | 25 | Bivariate correlations | 1. Total crime rates<br>2. Total arrest rates | ns<br>ns | Female arrest rates for murder |
| Bowker (1978) | Interpol (1950-1972) | 30 | Cross-tabulation[a] | 1. Social/educ. sexual equality<br>2. Economic sexual equality<br>3. Economic development | −<br>+<br>− | Proportionate female murder rate |
| Bowker (1981 | Interpol (1974)) | 92 | Bivariate correlations | 1. Female labor force participation rate<br>2. Femaleness in economic activity<br>3. Segregation of economic activity<br>4. Proportionate female illiteracy<br>5. Median female education, ages 15-24<br>6. Median female education, ages 35-64<br>7. Proportion of females who are single<br>8. Proportion of females who are divorced<br>9. Fertility rate<br>10. No. of national orgs. for gender equality<br>11. Year suffrage<br>12. No. of int'l women's non-gov't. orgs.<br>13. Urbanization<br>14. Per capita gross national product<br>15. Per capita protein consumption | ns<br>ns<br>ns<br>ns<br>ns<br>ns<br>ns<br>ns<br>ns<br>ns<br>−*[b]<br>ns<br>ns<br>+*<br>+* | Proportionate female murder rate |
| Hartnagel (1982) | Interpol (1971) | 40 | Bivariate correlations; Regression | 1. Marriage rate<br>2. Fertility rate<br>3. Year suffrage<br>4. Female labor force participation rate<br>5. Proportion of economic active females<br>6. Occupational segregation<br>7. Femaleness of illiteracy<br>8. Femaleness of higher education<br>9. Per capita gross national product<br>10. Urbanity | ns<br>ns<br>ns<br>ns<br>ns<br>ns<br>ns<br>ns<br>ns<br>ns | Proportionate female murder rate |

| Study (Year) | Data source (Years) | N | Method | Independent variable | Sign | Dependent variable |
|---|---|---|---|---|---|---|
| Marshall (1982) | Interpol (1963-1970) | 14 | Bivariate correlations[c] | 1. Female labor force participation rate | + | Proportionate female murder rate[d] |
| | | | | 2. Index of femaleness economic activity | + | |
| | | | | 3. Femaleness of admin. & managerial work | + | |
| | | | | 4. Femaleness of clerical work | | |
| | | | | 5. Occupational segregation | | |
| | | | | 6. Industrial segregation | − | |
| Messner (1985) | Interpol (1970-1974) | 29 | Regression | 1. Gini coeff. of family income | ns | Female arrest rate |
| | | | | 2. % Never married females | +* | |
| | | | | 3. % Never married males | ns | |
| | | | | 4. GNP/capita | ns | |
| | | | | 5. Population | ns | |
| Widom & Stewart (1986) | Interpol (1971-1972) | 43 | Bivariate correlations[e] | 1. Female-male life expectancy, 1 yr. | level of murder: − ; distribution of murder[f]: −* | level of murder / distribution of murder[f] |
| | | | | 2. Female-male infant mortality rate, 7-27 days | level of murder: −* | |
| | | | | 3. No. of years women had full vote | distribution of murder: + | |
| | | | | 4. % illegitimate births | level of murder: +* | |
| | | | | 5. Child/woman ratio | level of murder: +* | |
| Simon & Baxter (1989) | Interpol (1962-65, 1969-72, 1977-80) | 31 | Bivariate correlations[g] | 1. % female secondary education students | + | % of females arrested for homicide |
| | | | | 2. % of women in national labor force | | |
| | | | | 3. Per capita private consumption of GNP | + | |
| | | | | 4. % of labor force in industry | + | |
| Steffensmeier et al. (1989) | Interpol (1970-76) | 69 | Regression; Decomposition of effects of development on FP/A | 1. Kilowatt hours of energy per capita | ns | Female % arrests, homicide |
| | | | | 2. University students % female | ns | |
| | | | | 3. Occupational segregation | ns | |
| | | | | 4. Radios per capita | (h) | |
| | | | | 5. Years of interpol data | +* | |

(a) Bowker reports no significance tests; the signs refer to the direction of the relationships reported for gamma's ranging from .52 to .68.

(b) * p ≤ .05

(c) Marshall reports no significance tests because of the non-random nature of the sample. Signs are indicated for coefficients that ranged from .24 to .53

(d) The proportionate female robbery and burglary rate is also examined but these two offenses are treated as one crime category

(e) Widom and Stewart include 33 independent variables in their analysis; only those having a significant association with murder are shown here

(f) Level of female murder = percent of females arrested for murder/female population; distriburtion of female murder arrests = percentage of females arrested for murder/ total arrests

(g) No tests of statistical significance were reported; the signs refer to the strongest reported correlations for homicide: .51 to .56, all occurring in the last time period (1977-80)

(h) The most substantial indirect effect of development on the FP/A for homicide (.34) is through this indicator of opportunity for female based consumer crime.

and females' victimization rates and, not surprisingly, few gender differences the in predictors of these rates (Gartner, 1990). For both males and females, economic deprivation, weak social integration, and exposure to official violence increase the risk of homicide victimization. Only female labor force participation places women—but not men—at a significantly greater risk of homicide.

Second, these same data also show considerable cross-national variation in women's risks of victimization relative to men's risks. While women are less likely than men to be killed in virtually every country, deviations from the expected gender gap in homicide vary substantially by context and historical period (Gartner, Baker, & Pampel, 1990). To understand these variations, Gartner et al. (1990) use gender-linked situational and motivational models, focusing on women's participation in non-traditional domestic and economic roles. They found that women's risks of being killed are higher, and the gender gap is less pronounced, when women have a relatively greater involvement in non-traditional social roles (as represented by delayed marriage, divorce, single parenthood, and labor force participation). Nevertheless, this risk of victimization associated with non-traditional roles is conditioned by women's status. Specifically, the social and economic gains women obtain from participation in higher education appear to reduce women's vulnerability to violent victimization (Gartner et al., 1990, p. 608).[15] Similar to the aggregate-level offending data, these findings raise a number of questions about which women are most vulnerable within the context of non-traditional gender roles and which are most likely to be protected by women's fuller participation in higher education.

Cross-cultural and ethnographic studies provide one avenue for bridging the gap between the aggregate and the individual causal processes producing violence against women. Although these studies are limited to depictions of domestic violence in small-scale and peasant societies, and, as such, are restricted in their generalizability, their portrayals of the contexts in which spousal violence is most likely to occur are notably consistent with those from industrialized nations. These studies suggest that the protection women obtain from fuller participation in higher education may be due to the support networks they establish in this setting. Specifically, when wives are members of exclusively female economic groups, or when they have strong and close bonds to family members or work groups, they are unlikely to be beaten by their husbands (Baumgartner, in press; Levinson, 1989). The cross-cultural research also supports the motivational perspective which argues that perceived challenges to male dominance place women at particularly high risk from their spouses (Gartner et al., 1990, p. 597). Wife beating is most frequent where the male dominates all aspects of family life, including restricting the female's access to divorce (Levinson, 1989; see also, Sanday, 1981). Women who attempt to escape traditional domestic and economic roles (but have not yet completed the transition) may, therefore, be at greatest risk of being beaten and killed by their spouses (see also, Allen & Straus, 1980; Daly & Wilson, 1988; 1993; Wallace, 1986).

## CONCLUSIONS

This chapter reviewed current cross-national research on individual- and aggregate-level risk factors in women's violence. A cross-national perspective offers a number of unique contributions to understanding and preventing women's violence. For example, individual characteristics generally assumed to be important correlates of female violence (e.g., age, race) may be specific to particular offenses, nations, and perhaps even historical periods. Cross-national analyses can also reveal the validity of existing theoretical frameworks and the extent to which other pertinent observations suggest the need for new theoretical interpretations.

Of particular interest in this review of the cross-national data is the importance of domestic violence for understanding women's risk of both violent offending and victimization. In the United States, it has been known for some time that women's involvement in murder is confined primarily to their domestic relationships (Wolfgang, 1958). Data from other nations suggest that, while this may be a global pattern, considerable variation exists in women's risk of killing, and being killed by, intimates. To explain this variation we need to examine how individual, community, and structural factors interact to influence these violent experiences. Little work of this type exists. At present we can only infer how structural sources of gender stratification and gender relations may affect women's risks of intimate violence, while remaining cognizant of the limitations inherent in working with different levels of analysis (see, e.g., Lieberson, 1985).

The development of multilevel and contextual research in this area will be possible only if current theoretical and methodological limitations are addressed. Most of the individual-level research is atheoretical, despite the range of perspectives available for explaining intimate violence by and against women. For example, these include, but are not limited to, motivation, socialization, social learning, and cultural theories (see e.g., Fagan & Browne, in press). Most of the aggregate-level research focuses on testing the emancipation perspective (Adler, 1975; Simon, 1975) which has little relevance to the violence women direct against family members. However, even when the relevant theoretical perspectives are applied (see e.g., Gartner et al., 1990), the appropriate aggregate and individual measures are lacking.

Generally, since official measures of crime are not well-suited to estimating the incidence of violence among nonstrangers (Young, 1992), our understanding of women's involvement in violent crime will remain incomplete. Although we can be more confident about homicide data (Archer & Gartner, 1984; Gurr, 1989), we do not know if variations in women's proportional involvement in assault and rape are due to actual cross-national variations or instead merely to variations in their willingness to report nonstranger victimizations. We also have no knowledge of cross-national variations in women's participation in instrumental violence. Is this because the data are not systematically recorded or is this because women are generally not involved in these types of offenses?

Clearly, the gaps in our knowledge about women's violent offending and victimization are enormous. They result not only from under-reporting violence between intimates but also from a lack of systematic recording of violent female offending and victimization rates over time. Most of the research reviewed here covers a relatively short time span, and is based variously on arrests, convictions, and incarcerations. Accordingly, for most countries, we do not know whether the data accurately reflect either current or historical trends in women's violence (cf. e.g., Allen, 1990; Gartner & McCarthy, 1991; Wallace, 1986).

The major implication of this review is that theoretical and methodological development on violent female offending and victimization is imperative. Further, this work should proceed in tandem. Incorporating the work on offending with the work on victimization will enhance both our knowledge about women's roles in violent encounters and the explanatory power of existing theory derived from separate disciplines.

## NOTES

1. Sampson and Lauritsen (in press) completed the first synthesis of the causes and consequences of criminal violence in the United States using multiple levels of analysis. Consistent with their analysis, the individual level of explanation inquires as to the characteristics of individuals that explain behavior. An aggregate-level explanation corresponds closely to their definition of macrosocial or community-level explanations which ask what it is about societal structures or cultures that produce differential rates of crime.

2. One final issue deserves further clarification. Although this review examines multiple levels of analysis, the data cannot in their present form be used to make causal inferences between levels. This is not to say, for example, that the information contained in aggregate-level data are determined solely by macrosocial processes, but instead that the types of contextual analyses that would permit us to make such a determination are not yet available on a cross-national level (see e.g., Miethe & McDowall, 1993). Thus, while these cross-national studies do not permit us to bridge the individual-aggregate gap, both types of data are used to inform the other and, ultimately, to suggest directions for future research.

3. The term *gender* refers to the sociological, psychological, and cultural patterns that are used to evaluate and shape male and female behavior. By contrast, the term sex is used to refer to genetic sex or the chromosomal makeup of the individual. Because gender is imposed on sex by acculturation and socialization, it is not surprising to find that these two concepts are still used interchangeably. Nevertheless, this distinction can be quite significant for cross-national and cross-cultural studies of violence. For example, a reference to sex differences in violent crime rates implies a biological basis for the disparate rates which should be observed universally. By contrast, a reference to gender differences assumes variability in violent crime rates either across or within societies based on situational, social, or cultural factors. This distinction has been most carefully addressed in the empirical research on sex and gender differences in aggression (see e.g., Macaulay, 1985; Maccoby & Jacklin, 1974; Tieger, 1980; White, 1983).

4. Interestingly, data on convictions and cautions for indictable offenses in England and Wales covering roughly the same time period (1939-1983) also shows a convergence in the relationship between age of peak offending and gender. The peak age of offending declined significantly for females and increased slightly for males (Farrington, 1986, p. 191-193).

5. Strictly speaking, race is a biological characteristic. Its significance in the United States is derived from its correspondence to specific social statuses and locations (Black, 1976; 1993). To the extent that ethnicity, or tribal or clan membership, is similarly associated with specific social statuses or locations, it should also be important for understanding variations in women's rates of violent offending in other societies (see e.g., Black, 1984; Hagan, 1985).

6. Women's involvement in instrumental acts of violence, such as robbery, might show different patterns. For example, data from the United States indicate that of all violent crimes, robbery is least likely to involve a victim who is known to the offender (Reiss & Roth, 1993, p. 79).

7. Problems specific to the International Crime Survey, which should be considered when reviewing these results, are reviewed in another paper in this volume (see Gartner, 1993).

8. In reviewing the results of victim crime surveys, it is important to remember that these surveys rely on the victim's judgement and memory about whether a crime has occurred and analyses suggest that memory fade may vary with the relational distance between the victim and offender (Law Enforcement Assistance Administration, 1972, Table 5).

9. Gartner and McCarthy (1991), among others, use the nonlegal term "femicide" to refer to the killing of women.

10. The Canadian victimization survey did not include information on the victim-offender relationship (Sacco & Johnson, 1990).

11. NCVS rape data show that 61% of the forcible rapes that are reported in the U. S. involve offenders who were known to the victim (Reiss & Roth, 1993, p. 79). Although comparable figures have been reported for England, Malaysia and selected cities in South America (Heise, in press; Wright, 1980), data from Canada, Australia and the International Crime Survey indicate higher rates of stranger victimization (Bush, 1977; Clark & Lewis, 1977; van Dijk et al., 1991). These differences are explained, at least partially, by methodological variations in surveys across nations (cf. e.g., Allen, 1990; Bush, 1977; Clark & Lewis, 1977).

12. Data from the International Crime Survey indicate that, generally, in countries where women's employment rate is high, the gender disparity in victimization is low (van Dijk et al., 1991). It is unclear, however, whether this relationship would hold with offense type and victim-offender relationship held constant.

13. Similar examinations have not been conducted in the United States because the National Crime Victimization Survey does not include direct measures of routine activities.

14. Although Adler and Simon can be credited with the recent popularization of the emancipation/liberation perspective, this perspective has a long history in criminology (see, Bishop, 1931; Bonger, 1916; Lombroso & Ferrero, 1895; Pollak, 1950; Thomas, 1923).

15. Interestingly, these findings may also explain why South and Messner (1986) found that societal-level population sex-ratio's do not significantly influence female homicide victimization rates. The lack of an association may be due to the way in which the effects of a high ratio of males to females in the population operate in different social contexts. For example, in societies where women adopt primarily traditional social roles, a high sex-ratio should reduce women's rates of being killed but, in societies where women adopt less traditional roles, the same high sex-ratio may serve to increase male attempts to dominate women and women's risks of victimization (see also Daly & Wilson, 1992; Sanday, 1981).

## REFERENCES

Adler, F. (1975). *Sisters in crime.* New York: McGraw-Hill.

Adler, F. (1981). *The incidence of female criminality in the contemporary world.* New York: New York University Press.

Allen, C. M. & Straus, M. A. (1980). Resources, power, and husband-wife violence. In M. A. Straus, & G. T. Hotaling (Eds.), *The social causes of husband-wife violence* (pp. 188-209). Minneapolis: University of Minnesota Press.

Allen, J. A. (1990). *Sex and secrets. Crimes involving Australian women since 1880.* Oxford: Oxford University Press.

Archer, D., & Gartner, R. (1984). *Violence and crime in cross-national perspective.* New Haven: Yale University Press.

Baumgartner, M. P. (in press). Violent networks: The origins and management of domestic conflict. In R. B. Felson, & J. Tedeschi (Eds.), *Violence and aggression: The social interactionist approach.* Washington: American Psychological Association.

Bhanot, M. L., & Misra, S. (1981). Criminality amongst women in India: A study on female offenders and female convicts. In F. Adler (Ed.), *The incidence of female criminality in the contemporary world* (pp. 228-258). New York: New York University Press.

Bishop, C. (1931). *Women and crime.* London: Chalto & Windus.

Black, D. (1976). *The behavior of law.* New York: Academic Press.

Black, D. (1984). Crime as social control. In D. Black (Ed.), *Toward a general theory of social control, Vol. 2: Selected Problems* (pp. 1-27). Orlando: Academic Press.

Black, D. (1993). *The social structure of right and wrong.* San Diego: Academic Press.

Blau, J. R., & Blau P. M. (1982). Metropolitan structure and violent crime. *American Sociological Review, 47,* 114-128.

Bonger, W. (1916). *Criminality and economic conditions* (1967 reprint ed.) New York: Agathon.

Bowker, L. H. (1978). *Women, crime and the criminal justice system.* Lexington: D. C. Heath.

Bowker, L. H. (1981). The institutional determinants of international female crime. International Journal of *Comparative and Applied Criminal Justice, 5:,* 11-28.

Brinkerhoff, M. B., & Lupri, E. (1988). Interspousal violence. *Canadian Journal of Sociology, 13,* 407-431.

Bruinsma, G. J. N., Dessaur, C. I., & Van Hezewijk, R. W. J. V. (1981). Female criminality in the Netherlands. In F. Adler (Ed.), *The incidence of female criminality in the contemporary world* (pp. 14-63). New York: New York University Press.

Bush, J. P. (1977). *Rape in Australia.* Melbourne: Sun Books.

Chappell, D. (1989). Sexual criminal violence. In N. A. Weiner, & M. E. Wolfgang (Eds.), *Pathways to criminal violence* (pp. 68-108). Newbury Park: Sage.

Clark, L. M. G., & Lewis, D. J. (1977). *Rape: The price of coercive sexuality.* Toronto: Women's Press.

Cohen, L., & Felson, M. (1979). Social change and crime rate trends: A routine activity approach. *American Sociological Review, 44,* 588-607.

Curtis, L. A. (1974). *Criminal violence. National patterns and behavior.* Lexington: Lexington Books.

Daly, M., & Wilson, M. (1988). *Homicide.* New York: Aldine De Gruyter.

Dobash, R. E., & Dobash, R. P. (1979). *Violence against wives: A case against the patriarchy.* New York: Free Press.

Dobash, R. P., Dobash, R. E., Wilson, M., & Daly, M. (1992). The myth of sexual symmetry in marital violence. *Social Problems, 39,* 71-91.

Fagan, J., & Browne, A. (in press). Marital violence: Physical aggression between women and men in intimate relationships. In A. J. Reiss, Jr., & J. Roth (Eds.), *Understanding and preventing violence: Vol. 3. Social and psychological perspectives on violence.* Washington, DC: National Institute of Mental Health.

Farrington, D. P. (1986). Age and crime. In M. Tonry, & N. Morris (Eds.), *Crime and justice, Vol. 7* (pp. 189-250). Chicago: University of Chicago Press.

Fergusson, D. M., Horwood, L. J., Kershaw, K. L., & Shannon, F. T. (1986). Factors associated with reports of wife assault in New Zealand. *Journal of Marriage and the Family, 48,* 407-412.

Ferracuti, F., & Newan, G. (1974). Assaultive offenses. In D. Glaser (Ed.), *Handbook of Criminology* (pp. 175-207). Chicago: Rand McNally.

Freed, R. S., & Freed, S. A. (1989). Beliefs and practices resulting in female deaths and fewer females than males in India. *Population and Environment, 10,* 144-161.

Gartner, R. (1990). The victims of homicide: A temporal and cross-national comparison. *American Sociological Review, 55,* 92-106.

Gartner, R., Baker, K., & Pampel, F. C. (1990). Gender stratification and the gender gap in homicide victimization. *Social Problems, 37,* 593-612.

Gartner, R., & McCarthy, B. (1991). The social distribution of femicide in urban Canada, 1921-1988. *Law and Society Review, 25,* 287-313.

Gartner, R. (1993). Methodological Issues in Cross-Cultural Large-Survey Research on Violence. *Violence & Victims, 8,* 199-216.

Gibbens, T. C. N. (1981). Female crime in England and Wales. In F. Adler (Ed.), *The incidence of female criminality in the contemporary world* (pp. 102-121). New York: New York University Press.

Gurr, T. R. (1989). Historical trends in violent crime: Europe and the United States. In T. R. Gurr (Ed.), *Violence in America, Vol. 1* (pp. 21-54). Beverly Hills: Sage.

Hagan, J. (1985). Toward a structural theory of crime, race, and gender: The Canadian case. *Crime and Delinquency, 31,* 129-146.

Hartnagel, T. F. (1982). Modernization, female social roles, and female crime: A cross-national investigation. *The Sociological Quarterly, 23,* 477-490.

Hartjen, C. A. (1986). Crime and development: Some observations on women and children in India. *International Annals of Criminology, 24,* 39-57.

Heidensohn, F. (1991). Women and crime in Europe. In F. Heidensohn, & M. Farrell (eds.), *Crime in Europe* (pp. 55-71). London: Routledge.

Heiland, H., Shelley, L. I., & Katoh, H. (Eds.). (1992). *Crime and control in comparative perspectives.* Berlin: Walter de Gruyter.

Heise, L. (in press). Violence against women: The missing agenda. In M. Koblinsky, J. Timyan, & G. Gay (Eds.), *Women's health: A global perspective.* Westview Press.

Hindelang, M. J., Gottfredson, M. R., & Garofalo, J. (1978). *Victims of personal crime: An empirical foundation for a theory of personal victimization.* Cambridge: Ballinger.

Hoffman, K. L., Demo, D. H., & Edwards, J. N. (1993). *Wife abuse: A test of resource, structural, and social psychological theories in a non-western society.* Unpublished manuscript, Virginia Polytechnical Institute and State University, Department of Sociology, Blacksburg, VA.

Kaiser, G. (1985). Trends and related factors of juvenile delinquency in Europe. In P. R. David (Ed.), *Crime and criminal policy* (Publication 25, pp. 395-412). Milan: United Nations Social Defense Research Institute.

Karstedt, S. (1992, November). *Emancipation and antisocial behavior: New and old myths.* Paper presented at the annual meeting of the American Society of Criminology, New Orleans, LA.

Katoh, H. (1992). The development of delinquency and criminal justice in Japan. In H. Heiland, L. I. Shelley, & H. Katoh (Eds.), *Crime and control in comparative perspectives* (pp. 69-81). Berlin: Walter de Gruyter.

Kent, J. N. (1981). Argentine statistics on female criminality. In F. Adler (Ed.), *The incidence of female criminality in the contemporary world* (pp. 188-214). New York: New York University Press.

Kruttschnitt, C. (in press). Gender and interpersonal violence. In A. J. Reiss Jr., & J. Roth (Eds.), *Understanding and preventing violence: Vol. 3. Social and psychological perspectives on violence*. Washington, DC: National Institute of Mental Health.

Kumagai, F., & Straus, M. A. (1983). Conflict resolution tactics in Japan, India, and USA. *Journal of Comparative Family Studies, 14*, 377-392.

Landau, S. F. (1989). Family violence and violence in society. In E. C. Viano (Ed.), *Crime and its victims: International research and public policy issues. Proceedings of the fourth international institute on victimology* (pp. 25-33). New York: Hemisphere.

Laub, J. H., & McDermott, M. J. (1985). An analysis of serious crime by young black women. *Criminology, 23*, 81-99.

Law Enforcement Assistance Administration (1972). *San Jose methods test of crime victims* (Statistics Technical Report No. 1). Washington, DC: U. S. Government Printing Office.

Levinson, D. (1989). *Family violence in cross-cultural perspective*. Newbury Park: Sage.

Lieberson, S. (1985). *Making it count: The improvement of social research and theory*. Berkeley: University of California Press.

Loftin, C., Kindley, K., Norris, S., & Wiersema, B. (1987). An attribute approach to relationships between offenders and victims in homicide. *Journal of Criminal Law and Criminology, 78*, 259-271.

Lombroso, C., & Ferrero W. (1915). *The female offender* (Originally published in 1895). New York: D. Appleton & Co.Macaulay, J. (1985). Adding gender to aggression research: Incremental or revolutionary change? In, V. E. O'Leary, R. K. Unger, & B. S. Wallston (Eds.), *Women, gender and social psychology* (pp. 191-224). Hillsdale, N. J: Lawrence Erlbaum.

Maccoby, E. E., & Jacklin, C. N. (1974). *The psychology of sex differences*. Stanford: Stanford University Press.

Mann, C. R. (1988). Getting even? Women who kill in domestic encounters. *Justice Quarterly, 5*, 33-51.

Marshall, I. H. (1982). Women, work and crime: An international test of the emancipation hypothesis. *International Journal of Comparative and Applied Criminal Justice, 6*, 25-37.

Maxfield, M. G. (1989). Circumstances in supplementary homicide reports: Variety and validity. *Criminology, 27*, 671-695.

Messner, S. F. (1985). Sex differences in arrest rates for homicide: An application of the general theory of structural strain. *Comparative Social Research, 8*, 187-201.

Miethe, T. D., & McDowall, D. (1993). Contextual effects in models of criminal victimization. *Social Forces, 71*, 741-759.

Mushanga, T. (1978). Wife victimization in East and Central Africa. *Victimology, 2*, 479-485.

National Council for Crime Prevention (1990). *Crime trends in Sweden, 1988*. Stockholm: Allmanna Forlaget.

Oloruntimehin, O. (1981). A preliminary study of female criminality in Nigeria. In F. Adler (Ed.), *The incidence of female criminality in the contemporary world* (pp. 158-175). New York: New York University Press.

Oloruntimehin, O. (1992). Crime control in Nigeria. In H. Heiland, L. I. Shelley, & H. Katoh (Eds.), *Crime and control in comparative perspectives* (pp. 164-188). Berlin: Walter de Gruyter.

Pollak, O. (1950). *The criminality of women.* Philadelphia: University of Pennsylvania Press.

Radford, J. (1992). Woman slaughter: A license to kill? The killing of Jane Asher. In J. Radford, & D. E. H. Russell (Eds.), *Femicide. The politics of woman killing* (pp. 253-266). New York: Twayne Publishers.

Rasko, G. (1981). Crimes against life committed by women in Hungary. In F. Adler (Ed.), *The incidence of female criminality in the contemporary world* (pp. 145-157). New York: New York University Press.

Reiss, A. J. Jr., & Roth, J. (Eds.), (1993). *Understanding and preventing violence.* Washington D. C.: National Academy Press.

Riedel, M. (1988, November). *Black women and homicide: Rates, patterns, and perspective.* Paper presented at the annual meeting of the American Society of Criminology, Chicago, IL.

Rodd, T. (1980). Marital murder. In J. Scutt (Ed.), *Violence in the family: A collection of conference papers* (pp. 95-105). Canberra: Australian Institute of Criminology.

Sacco, V. F., & Johnson, H. (1990). *Patterns of criminal victimization in Canada.* Statistics Canada. General Social Survey Analysis Series.

Sampson, R. J. (1986). Neighborhood, family structure and the risk of personal victimization. In J. M. Byrne, & R. J. Sampson (Eds.), *The social ecology of crime* (pp. 25-46). New York: Springer-Verlag.

Sampson, R. J., & Lauritsen, J. L. (in press). Violent victimization and offending: Individual, situational, and community-level risk factors. In A. J. Reiss Jr., & J. Roth (Eds.), *Understanding and preventing violence: Vol. 3. Social and psychological perspectives on violence.* Washington, D. C. : National Institute of Mental Health.

Sanday, P. R. (1981). The socio-cultural context of rape: A cross-cultural study. *Journal of Social issues, 37,* 5-27.

Scutt, J. (1983). *Even in the best of homes: Violence in the family.* Ringwood, Vic: Penguin.

Seventh United Nations Congress on the Prevention of Crime and the Treatment of Offenders (1985). *Victims of crime. The situation of women and victims of crime.* Milan: United Nations.

Simon, R. J. (1975). *Women and crime.* Lexington: D. C. Heath.

Simon, R. J., & Baxter, S. (1989). Gender and violent crime. In N. A. Weiner & M. E. Wolfgang (Eds.), *Violent crime, violent criminals* (pp. 171-197). Newbury Park: Sage.

South, S. J., & Messner, S. F. (1986). The sex ratio and women's involvement in crime: A cross-national analysis. *Sociological Quarterly, 28,* 171-188.

Steffensmeier, D. J., & Allan, E. (1988). Sex disparities in arrests by residence, race, and age: An assessment of the gender convergence/crime hypothesis. *Justice Quarterly, 5,* 53-80.

Steffensmeier, D., Allan, E., & Streifel, C. (1989). Development and female crime: A cross-national test of alternative explanations. *Social Forces, 68,* 262-283.

Thomas, W. I. (1923). *The unadjusted girl.* New York: Harper & Row.

Tieger, T. (1980). On the biological basis of sex differences in aggression. *Child Development, 51,* 943-963.

Van Dijk, J. J. M., Mayhew, P., & Killias, M. (1991). *Experiences of crime across the world.* Deventer: Kluwer Law & Taxation Publishers.

Wallace, A. (1986). *Homicide: The social reality.* New South Wales: Bureau of Crime Statistics and Research, Attorney General's Dept.

White, J. W. (1983). Sex and gender issues in aggression research. In R. G. Green, & E. I. Donnerstein (Eds.), *Aggression: Theoretical and empirical reviews, Vol. 2, issues in research* (pp. 1-26). New York: Academic.

Widom, C. S., & Stewart, A. J. (1986). Female criminality and the status of women. *International Annals of Criminology, 24,* 137-162.

Wikström, P. H. (1985). *Everyday violence in contemporary Sweden: Situational and ecological aspects.* (Report no. 15). Stockholm: National Council for Crime Prevention, Research Division.

Wilson, M., & Daly, M. (1992). Who kills whom in spousal killings? On the exceptional sex ratio of spousal homicides in the United States. *Criminology, 30,* 189-215.

Wilson, M., & Daly, M. (1993). An Evolutionary Psychological Perspective on Male Sexual Proprietariness and Violence Against Wives. *Violence & Victims, 8,* 271-294.

Wright, R. (1980). Rape and physical violence. In D. J. West (Ed.), *Sexual offenders in the criminal justice system: Proceedings of the 12th Cropwood Conference* (pp. 100-113). Cambridge: Cambridge University, Institute of Criminology.

Wolfgang, M. (1958). *Patterns in criminal homicide.* New York: Wiley.

Yllo, D., & Straus, M. A. (1990). Patriarchy and violence against wives: The impact of structural and normative factors. In M. A. Straus, & R. J. Gelles (Eds.), *Physical violence in American Families: Risk factors and adaptations to violence in 8,145 families* (pp. 383-399). New Brunswick: Transaction

Young, V. D. (1992). Fear of victimization and victimization rates among women: A paradox? *Justice Quarterly, 9,* 419-441.

# 7

# An Evolutionary Psychological Perspective on Male Sexual Proprietariness and Violence Against Wives

Margo Wilson
Martin Daly

A particularly nasty husband might hit his wife with the sharp edge of a machete or axe or shoot a barbed arrow into some nonvital area, such as the buttocks or the leg. Another brutal punishment is to hold the glowing end of a piece of fire-wood against the wife's body, producing painful and serious burns. Normally, however, the husband's reprimands are consistent with the perceived serious-ness of the wife's shortcomings, his more drastic measures being reserved for infidelity or suspicion of infidelity. It is not uncommon for a man to seriously injure a sexually errant wife, and some husbands have shot and killed unfaithful wives.

I was told about one young man in Monou-teri who shot and killed his wife in a rage of sexual jealousy, and during one of my stays in the villages a man shot his wife in the stomach with a barbed arrow ... Another man chopped his wife on the arm with a machete; some tendons to her fingers were severed ... A club fight involving a case of infidelity took place in one of the villages just before the end of my first field trip. The male paramour was killed, and the enraged husband cut off both of his wife's ears ...

– Yanomamö (Venezuela); from Chagnon (1992, p.147)

"N/ahka, a middle aged woman, was attacked by her husband. His assault re-sulted in injuries to her face, head and lips. Her husband accused her of sleeping with another man ... N/ahka and her husband had been married for many years but had no children together. Her only child was a girl of about fourteen years whose father was a Herero, and to whom N/ahka had not been married. The father had never contributed to his daughter's support, and for many years the child had been reared by N/ahka's parents who lived in a different village. When N/ahka's parents heard about the beating, they made plans to lodge a formal complaint ... against their son-in-law. Other people, not close relatives of N/ahka or her husband, claimed that the couple had a long history of discord, al-legedly because the wife liked to sleep with Bantu men.

- !Kung San (Botswana); from Draper (1992, p. 54)

The prevalence, forms, severity, circumstances, and legitimacy of violence against wives are cross-culturally variable. Indeed, the variability is such that many writers feel that the only valid propositions about violence against wives are necessarily culturally specific. These violent narratives, however, strike chords that transcend cultural variability. We do not find the people in these ethnographic accounts unintelligibly alien, nor, we propose, would normal adults anywhere. One implication is that both violence against wives and cross-cultural variations therein can usefully be discussed in terms of panhuman phenomena and concepts. One such approach, attempted here, is to discuss these phenomena in terms of a putatively panhuman evolved psychology and to propose hypotheses about cross-cultural variation in this light.

Cross-cultural diversity in social phenomena is, of course, anthropology's domain, and some prominent anthropologists (e.g. Geertz, 1984; Leach, 1982) have rejected the quest for truths of cross-cultural applicability. But others (e.g., Brown, 1991; Tooby & Cosmides, 1992) have criticized such cultural particularism as both unwarranted by the ethnographic record and antiscientific. Our sympathies reside with the latter school, which in no way denies the diversity of cultural manifestations but treats them as things to be explained rather than as irreducibles.

Why did N/ahka's husband assault her? To deter future infidelity? Because her relatives were not at hand to deter him? To disfigure her and make her unattractive to other men? Because San society legitimizes violence against women? Because he was socialized to be violent by a violent father? Because of neural impacts of testicular hormones? Because he lost his temper? It should be clear that these "answers" are not alternatives. In principal, all could be true, or all false, and if evidence were to persuade us to accept or reject any one of them, we would be none the wiser about the validity of any of the others.

All behavioral phenomena can and must be explained at multiple levels. "Causes" include extrinsic eliciting circumstances, relevant states and events in the brain, and a personal developmental history. There is also an evolutionary history, which is just as directly causal to a person's actions as any present stimulus or past experience, since the mental mechanisms processing present or past experiences were created by the process of evolution by selection.

In this chapter, we argue that the violent rages of husbands, as illustrated in our opening quotations, are diversely manifested cross-culturally, but reflect an evolved, sexually proprietary, masculine psychology that is panhuman. We also advance several hypotheses about cross-cultural variations in violence against wives in light of this proposal.

## AN EVOLUTIONARY APPROACH TO THE SOCIAL SCIENCES

An impediment to the identification of panhuman underpinnings of phenomena like violence against wives is that basic universals of human existence may be so taken for granted as to be invisible. In this regard it is helpful to situate human sociality within a comparative biological perspective. Biology is the study of living things, and its unifying conceptual framework is Darwin's theory of evolution by selection.

Living creatures are hugely complex systems. How can their adaptive organization have come into being? Darwin discovered the answer, "natural selection": Adaptive complexity emerges over generations because random variation is ceaselessly generated in populations of reproducing organisms and is then winnowed by nonrandom differential survival and reproduction, resulting in the more successful forms proliferating while their alternatives perish.[1]

Darwinian selection is more than a simple matter of differential survival. It is successful traits that "survive" over generations, not individuals, and this sort of long-term survival depends not merely on the longevity of those with a given trait, but on the abundance of their progeny. Imagine, for example, an aggressively coercive, mutant variety of male in a population of risk-averse pacifists, and imagine that these mutants tend to fertilize more females than the pacifists, but die younger. In such a case, the mutation will spread through the population over generations and male lifespan will decline. The general point is that adaptive traits have been "designed" by selection to contribute to a single outcome: outreproducing other members of one's species ("fitness")[2], in environments whose relevant aspects are not crucially different from those in which the history of selection has occurred. Every living creature has been shaped by such a history of Darwinian selection, and so has every complex functioning constituent part of every living creature. The "adaptationist" enterprise of elucidating the evolved functional designs of organisms and their constituent parts is the cornerstone of biological discovery (Mayr, 1983).

Psychologists are wary of "purposive" concepts, but Darwin made seemingly "teleological" reasoning scientific, by showing that the consequences of biological phenomena constitute an essential part of their explanation: what they achieve is in a specific, concrete sense why they exist (Daly & Wilson, 1993). Natural selection provided a materialistic explanation for the previously incomprehensible fact that living things have purposiveness instantiated in their structures. Unfortunately, psychologists have not always understood this implication of Darwinism, imagining that its concept of adaptive function is isomorphic with an account of goals and drives: evolutionists are regularly misunderstood to be invoking fitness as a goal like a full belly or self-esteem. In fact, when fitness consequences are invoked to explain behavior, they are invoked not as objectives or motivators, but to explain why particular objectives and motivators have evolved to play particular roles in the causal control of behavior. Selection designs organisms to cope with specific adaptive problems which have been sufficiently persistent across generations to have favored particular solutions. These evolved solutions necessarily entail contingent responsiveness to environmental features that were statistical predictors of the average fitness consequences of alternative courses of action in the past. Adaptation is not prospective; the apparent purpose in organismic design depends upon the persistence of essential features of past environments.

Another impediment to evolutionary sophistication in social science is the popular but false dichotomy of "social" versus "biological" explanations. Subscribers to this dichotomy equate "biology" with its mechanistic subdisciplines (genetics, endocrinology, etc.) and think of biological influences as intrinsic and irremediable, to be contrasted with extrinsic, remediable social influences. Moreover, since "biological" effects are irremediable, those who propose their existence (the "nature" crowd) are unmasked as pessimists and reactionaries, while advocates of "alternative" social influences (the "nurture" crowd) are optimists and progressives. This ideology, predicated on ignorance of evolutionary biology, pervades the social sciences, where it may be accepted by "nature" advocates as thoroughly and thoughtlessly as by their "nurture" foes. One presumption of this world-view is that biology is mute about anything manifesting developmentally, experientially, or circumstantially contingent variation; indeed, the very demonstration of such contingency is seen as an exercise in the alternative, anti-biological mode of explanation. The irony is that developmentally, experientially and circumstantially contingent variation is precisely what evolutionary biological theories of social phenomena are about. What sorts of contingent social responsiveness would we expect selection to have favored, in what circumstances, and why? These are the issues that occupy theorists of social evolution.

## PANHUMAN ATTRIBUTES IN COMPARATIVE BIOLOGICAL PERSPECTIVE

The first thing to note about *Homo sapiens* in comparative biological perspective is that people reproduce sexually. The evolutionary consequences of this mundane fact are immense. Many creatures reproduce without sex, producing offspring genetically identical to mother and thus assuring that whatever resource allocation is optimal for maternal fitness is optimal for offspring fitness, too. In sexual reproducers like ourselves, by contrast, "parent-offspring conflict" (Trivers, 1974) is endemic: the allocation of resources which would maximize maternal fitness is not identical to that which would maximize offspring fitness, a fact with innumerable consequences for maternal and infantile physiology and psychology (Haig, 1993).

Besides engendering parent-offspring conflict, sexual reproduction introduces a new social relationship: that between mates. This relationship entails both a fundamental commonality of purpose and a fundamental arena of potential conflict. First, since preferences have been shaped by selection and since the well-being and eventual reproduction of offspring contribute to the fitness of both parents, the resource allocations and other exigencies that appeal to one parent are likely to have appeal for the other, too. However, the fact that both parties gain expected fitness from either's investments in their joint offspring also opens the door to the evolution of "parasitic" exploitation of one sex's reproductive efforts by the other sex, and to escalated "evolutionary arms races" between the sexes (Davies, 1992).

The second thing to note about *Homo sapiens* in comparative biological perspective is that people are *dioecious*: Individuals come in two varieties, female and male, and successful reproduction requires one of each. Not all sexually reproducing creatures are dioecious, but in those that are, selection has acted partly in a sexually differentiated manner and partly not, producing some adaptations that are sexually differentiated and others that are species-typical.

The female is, by definition, the sex that produces the larger gamete: eggs are bigger than sperm. Thus, internal fertilization (the union of parental gametes inside one parent's body, which has evolved independently many times) almost invariably occurs within the female. Further evolutionary consequences include the elaboration of diverse copulatory devices (Eberhard, 1985) and all of the psychophysiological paraphernalia dubbed "sexuality" (Symons, 1979).

Moreover, wherever additional modes of internal nurturance such as mammalian pregnancy have evolved, these too are sexually differentiated. Sexual asymmetry in internal gestation and lactation, characteristic of mammals, opens the door to the evolution of "parasitic" exploitation of the female's reproductive efforts by the male.

Indeed, insofar as reproductive efforts can be partitioned into the pursuit of matings vs parental investment (Trivers, 1972; Low, 1978), male mammals generally specialize in the former and females in the latter. One consequence is that male fitness tends to be limited by the number of matings, female fitness by nutrient availability. Because the minimal time and energy cost of producing a viable offspring is much lower for a male than for a female, the ceiling on potential reproduction is higher. Hence variance in reproductive success is usually higher for males ("effective polygyny"; Daly & Wilson, 1983), engendering more intense same-sex competition and the selective favoring of more expensive, dangerous, competitive traits, both morphological (e.g., weapons like antlers) and psychological (e.g., risk acceptance). Moreover, insofar as males are specialized for aggressive competition and male fitness is largely determined by the frequency and exclusivity of mating access, it is hardly surprising that males commonly attempt to exert aggressive control of females, too. Also noteworthy is that the greater size and aggressivity of males tend to be associated with greater vulnerability to threats of starvation, disease, and even predation, as the demands of same-sex competitive prowess compromise male design efficiency for other aspects of the species' ecological niche (Gaulin & Sailer, 1985).

This generic characterization must be tempered, however, by recognition of cross-species diversity. The extent to which male mammals have higher fitness variance than females, grow larger, die younger, etc., varies greatly even among closely related species, and these sex differences are correlated with one another. Most notably, when the sexes share parenting (as in foxes, various monkeys, beavers, etc.), these sex differences are reduced or abolished. Shared parenting is rare in mammals, however, presumably at least partly because male mammals lack reliable cues of paternity, with the result that fathers are vulnerable to "cuckoldry" (unwitting investment in young sired by rivals) and paternal investment is therefore evolutionarily unstable.

The third thing to note about *Homo sapiens* in comparative perspective, then—and the first in which we differ from closely related species—is that people form mateships of some stability, with biparental investment in young. Our nearest relatives, chimpanzees and gorillas, cleave much closer to the mammalian stereotype above, with males very much larger than females and parental investment predominantly or solely maternal.

Ours is hardly an exemplary monogamous species, however. Sex differences in body size, maturation schedules, intrasexual combat, and senescence are vestiges of effective polygyny, and human sex differences in these domains, although smaller than in extremely polygynous mammals, exceed those of monogamous species. A likely implication is that biparental pair-formation is an ancient hominid adaptation, but that competitively ascendant men continued to be polygamous. That is exactly what the ethnographic record of marriage practices suggests. Also, in the majority of known human societies (including all who subsist by foraging, as everyone did until the relatively recent invention of agriculture), most marriage is at least serially monogamous, but some men of high status are polygamous (Murdock, 1967; Betzig, 1986).

## MARITAL ALLIANCE IS A PANHUMAN INSTITUTION

In all societies, women and men enter individualized marital alliances, with publicly recognized entitlements and obligations. Marital status everywhere entails the legitimation of sexual access (often but not always exclusive) and the possibility of reproduction and biparental care. (Marriages fail, but, unlike most mammalian sexual alliances, marriage is not embarked upon with the expectation or intent of dissolution when conception or some other landmark has been attained.) Details of obligation and entitlement, stability, number of simultaneous marital partners, rules of marital eligibility, sex roles, and so forth, all vary in time and place, and yet marriage is everywhere a socially recognized sexual and reproductive alliance between a woman and a man, institutionalizing the partners' mutual entitlements and obligations.

In the contemporary West, we tend to view the mating game as a marketplace of individuals, but in the sort of kin-based society in which the human social psyche evolved, people take a strong manipulative interest in the marital transactions of others. Marriage in such societies is most often patrilocal, and the bride is incorporated into her husband's kinship group (Murdock, 1967; cross-cultural variability in these and related phenomena is discussed below). Indeed, many anthropologists view marriage in nonstate societies as a contract between kin groups, with women and their reproductive capabilities treated as exchangeable goods; even where kin groups exert less influence, as in modern nation states, a proprietary construction of the marriage's significance remains ubiquitous (Wilson & Daly, 1992).

## THE EVOLVED PSYCHOLOGY OF SEXUAL PROPRIETARINESS AND VIOLENCE

### Sexual Proprietariness is a Psychological Adaptation of the Human Male

In proposing that men take a proprietary view of women's sexuality and reproductive capacity, we mean that men are motivated to lay claim to particular women as songbirds lay claim to territories, as lions lay claim to a kill, or as people of both sexes lay claim to valuables. Proprietariness has the further implication, possibly peculiar to the human case, of a sense of entitlement. Trespass provokes not only hostility but grievance, which has a more broadly social function: hostile feelings motivate action against rivals, but grievance motivates appeals to other interested persons to recognize the trespass as a wrong against the property holder and hence as a justification for individual retaliation or for more collective sanctions. The violent rage of a husband is a private response to a perceived threat, but acknowledgement by others that a husband was wronged adds another layer of social complexity. Indeed, entitlement and grievance are elements of human social psychology that would be pointless without the social complexity entailed by coalitions, reputations and politics. (Possible positive feedback effects of others' recognition of husbands' proprietary entitlements warrant study.)

Because claims of proprietary entitlement are responses to rivalry over limited resources, they necessarily exist in an arena of actual or potential conflicts of interest. These conflicts increase in number and complexity when the "property" is another person, since the owner must be concerned not only with rivals but with the property's own antagonistic interests, and with the property's relatives or other allies. Women's variably effective resistance to men's coercion and violence thus reflects, in part, the relative power of the two parties as affected by each's material and social resources (e.g., Thornhill & Thornhill, 1983; Smuts, 1992).

Sexual competition and cuckoldry risk are potent selection pressures affecting the evolution of psychological mechanisms and processes. We suggest that men's attitudes, emotions, and actions indicative of sexual proprietariness and the commoditization of women are contingent products of sexually differentiated evolved mental mechanisms in the contexts of particular historical and cultural circumstances. The social complexity of our species—with its alliances based on both kinship and reciprocity, its moral systems and consequential personal reputations, and its cultural and ecological diversity—provides an arena within which male sexual proprietariness is diversely manifested (Dickemann, 1979;1981). Nevertheless, a ubiquitous core mindset can be discerned from numerous phenomena which are culturally diverse in detail but monotonously alike in the abstract: socially recognized marriage, the valuation of female fidelity, the equation of the "protection" of women with protection from sexual contact, the conception of adultery as a property violation, and the special potency of wifely infidelity as a provocation to violence (Wilson & Daly, 1992a).

## Sexual Proprietariness and the Double Standard in Adultery Laws

All indigenous legal codes address the issue of men's entitlements to sexual access to women, and all define an offense of adultery: unauthorized sex with a married woman, the man's marital status being immaterial (Daly, Wilson, & Weghorst, 1982). Adultery is generally conceived of as a property violation, and often quite explicitly so; the victim is the husband, who may be entitled to damages, to violent revenge, or to divorce with refund of brideprice.

Adultery compensations are as prominent in Anglo-American legal history as in tribal bridewealth societies. Relevant tort actions remedying illicit sexual poaching include "adultery," "loss of consortium," "criminal conversation," "alienation of affection," "enticement," "seduction," and "abduction," actions. Plaintiffs were husbands, fathers, or fiancés, and the conditions for a successful action show that the issue was lost sexual exclusivity, not lost labor: the woman's prior chastity was crucial, since a man who steals an already unchaste woman has stolen nothing. Also clearly indicative of men's proprietary construction of the women involved in these cases was the irrelevance of their consent, which did not mitigate the wrong against the husband, father or fiancé (Wilson & Daly, 1992a). Besides these entitlements to compensation for infringements of their proprietary rights, Anglo-American husbands have enjoyed other owners' privileges, too. Until recently, husbands were legally entitled to confine wives against their will and to use force to enjoy their conjugal rights (Dobash & Dobash, 1979; Edwards, 1985). Persons who gave sanctuary to a fleeing wife, including even her relatives, were legally obliged to give her up or be liable for the tort of "harboring," and Englishmen remained entitled to restrain wives intent on leaving them until a 1973 ruling made such acts kidnappings (Atkins & Hoggett, 1984).

Besides being treated as a tort, adultery has sometimes been criminalized as well (i.e., treated as an offense against the state as well as the husband). Adultery was a capital crime in 17th-century England, for example (Quaife, 1979). Cross-cultural and historical correlates of the criminalization of adultery have not, to the best of our knowledge, been explored. We would expect harsh criminal sanctions to be especially characteristic of highly stratified, polygynous societies in which powerful men use state power to enforce and legitimize their monopoly over their wives and concubines. (See Thornhill, 1991, for tests of an analogous argument about cross-cultural variability in definitions of "incest" and in the severity of sanctions against it.)

Several authors (Ford & Beach, 1952; Leacock, 1980; Stephens, 1963; Whyte, 1978) have claimed that certain exotic societies lack double standards of sexual morality or male resentment of adultery or both. These claims have then been widely cited as proof that sexual jealousy and proprietariness are cultural artifacts and not masculine psychological adaptations. But the claims are without foundation. Eleven societies (Baiga, Dieri, Gilbertese, Gilyak, Hidatsa, Lesu, Marquesas, Masai, Naskapi-Montagnais, Toda, and Yapese) have been listed as cases in point, and yet the relevant ethnographies explicitly describe men's violent reactions to adultery in all eleven (Daly, Wilson, & Weghorst, 1982). Three factors appear to have contributed to this confusion. One is that Ford and Beach (1952) and Stephens (1963) merely listed societies lacking collective criminal sanctions against adulterers, but have been misread as demonstrating that violent and other private responses to adultery were absent. Secondly, Whyte (1978) miscoded the double standard as "absent" if adulterous women and men were punished equally although adultery was itself defined asymmetrically (i.e., with respect only to the woman's marital status) in all cases. Finally, the issue has been muddied by what Bloch (1977) and Brown (1991) decry as "anthropological malpractice": the exaggeration of cultural difference to titillate and astonish. The idea that there are cultures in which sex is freely undertaken without interference or resentment is a persistently popular but groundless myth.

## The Psychological Link Between Male Sexual Jealousy and Violence

"Fearful or wary of being supplanted; apprehensive of loss of position or affection" is a dictionary definition of "jealous" (Morris, 1976). Jealousy is best characterized as a complex psychological state or mode of operation, activated by a perceived threat that a third party might usurp one's place in a valued relationship, which generates a diversity of circumstantially contingent responses ranging from vigilance to violence, aimed at countering such threats (Wilson & Daly, 1992a). Jealousy is sexual if the valued relationship is sexual.

The state of sexual jealousy is one component of the sexually proprietary mindset: a relatively dynamic state of attentional allocation and readiness to act, normally aroused by imminent cues of rivalrous threat. (Although jealous arousal can be chronic in some individuals, the inappropriate persistence of the jealous state is likely to be deemed pathological; see below.) In addition to jealous arousal, sexual proprietariness encompasses motives and actions that may be effective in the prevention of a threat of trespass or usurpation, as well as responses thereto.

As noted earlier, sexual rivalry is ubiquitous in male mammals because their fitness has been limited by access to female reproductive efforts. But where males, too, invest parentally, cuckoldry risk adds a further dimension: Bad enough to lose a fertilization to a rival, but a much greater selective penalty befell the cuckold who invested in the rival's child as his own. If there is a corresponding threat to woman's fitness, it is not that she would be analogously cuckolded, but rather that her mate would channel resources to other women. It follows that men's and women's proprietary feelings toward mates are likely to have evolved to be qualitatively different, men being more intensely concerned with sexual infidelity per se and women more intensely concerned with the allocation of their mates' resources and attentions. This is precisely what psychological studies of sex differences in jealousy show (Buss, Larsen, Westen, & Semmelroth, 1992; Daly, Wilson, & Weghorst, 1982; Teismann & Mosher, 1978).

Of special interest in the present context are jealousy's psychological links to anger and violent action, links which also appear to be sexually differentiated (Wilson & Daly, 1992a). The most direct testimony to this linkage is to be found in homicides. Daly & Wilson (1988a) reviewed studies of the motives and circumstances in uxoricides (wife-killings) from a variety of societies, and found that the majority of cases in every well-described sample were precipitated by suspected or actual female infidelity and/or by the woman's decision to leave the marriage. "Jealousy" furthermore led the list of police attributions of substantive issues in spousal homicides, and the jealous party was generally the man, regardless of which partner ended up dead. For subsequent corroborative evidence, see Allen (1990), Campbell (1992), Crawford and Gartner (1992), Mahoney (1991), Polk and Ranson (1991), and Wilson & Daly (1992b,c).

A minority of wife-killers are found "unfit to stand trial" or "not guilty by reason of insanity," and these are often diagnosed as psychiatric cases of "morbid jealousy" (e.g., Mowat, 1966) on the basis of obsessive concern with suspected infidelity and a tendency to invoke bizarre "evidence" in support. However, most jealous wife-killers are not considered insane. Quite the contrary: Anglo-American common law specifically deems killing upon the discovery of a wife's adultery to be the act of a "reasonable man" and deserving of reduced penalty (Wilson & Daly 1992 a,b). Other legal traditions—European, Oriental, Native American, African, Melanesian—all concur (Daly, Wilson, & Weghorst, 1982). Not only is jealousy deemed "normal," but so even is lethal reaction, at least if perpetrated by a man and in the heat of passion.

Moreover, violent sexual jealousy is deemed normal or at least unsurprising both in societies in which the cuckold's violence is seen as a reprehensible loss of control (e.g. Dell, 1984) and in those where it is seen as a praiseworthy redemption of honor (e.g. Safilios-Rothschild, 1969; Besse, 1989). The cross-cultural familiarity of jealous rages supports the view that the psychological links between sexual proprietariness and violent inclinations are not arbitrary aspects of particular cultures, but are evolved aspects of human male psychology.

## A Wife's Desertion Is an Impetus to Male Violence

The distinction between a woman's adultery and her wanting to end the relationship altogether illustrates two related but distinct adaptive problems underlying male sexual proprietariness. Although only the former places the man at risk of misdirected paternal investment in another man's offspring, most homicide researchers have lumped them as "jealousy" cases, apparently because of the similar aggressively proprietary attitude of the killers, who seem to react to adultery and desertion as more or less the same thing. From the perspective of natural selection, they are in a sense similar: the important commonality is that the man loses control of female reproductive capacity and hence loses ground in the reproductive competition between men.

Women attempting to leave men are frequent homicide victims (Allen, 1990; Barnard, Vera, Vera & Newman, 1982; Crawford & Gartner, 1992; Mahoney, 1991; Wallace, 1986; Wilson & Daly, 1993), and killers' vows that "If I can't have her, nobody can" are recurring features of such cases (e.g. Campbell, 1992). Despite reduced access or "opportunity," wives often incur greater risk of homicide by their husbands when separated from them than when coresiding (Figure 7.1). Coresidency status does not appear to have a similar bearing on the risk to husbands. Moreover, the excess risk incurred by separating wives is much worse than Figure 7.1 conveys, since the homicide rates were computed with population-at-large denominators of all separated women regardless of the duration of separation whereas the homicides occurred mainly within the first couple of months (Wilson & Daly, 1993). Manifestations of the woman's intention of terminating the relationship may also increase the risk of uxoricide while the couple still coreside (Crawford & Gartner, 1992; Wallace, 1986; Wilson & Daly, 1993). Reasons for concluding that separation is itself a risk factor rather than a mere correlate of some more relevant factor are discussed by Wilson & Daly (1993).

When a wife is pursued and killed by a husband she has left, the killer's motive is obviously not merely to be rid of her. Yet if keeping her is his aim, killing is even more clearly counterproductive. Thus, although such killings are often deliberate and even carefully planned, they are anything but rationally instrumental. We propose that such homicides are best interpreted as the dysfunctionally extreme manifestations of violent inclinations whose lesser expressions are effective in coercion, for although uxoricide may seldom serve the interests of the killer, it is far from clear that the same can be said of sublethal wife abuse. This interpretation is reinforced by evidence that the motives and risk factors relevant to uxoricide have similar relevance for sublethal wife-beating (Wilson & Daly, 1992; Wilson, Daly, & Wright, 1993). A credible threat of violent death can very effectively control people, and the risks to estranged wives suggest that such threats by husbands are often sincere. Moreover, unlike threats or assaults directed at strangers, the coercive use of violence by husbands has often had a legitimacy that enhances the coercive power of the threats.

## Violence Is a Male Resource

There is a broad sex difference in human violence, whether in fisticuffs, warfare, or the slaughter of game (Murdock, 1967). Men possess evolved morphological, physiological, and psychological means for effective use of violence

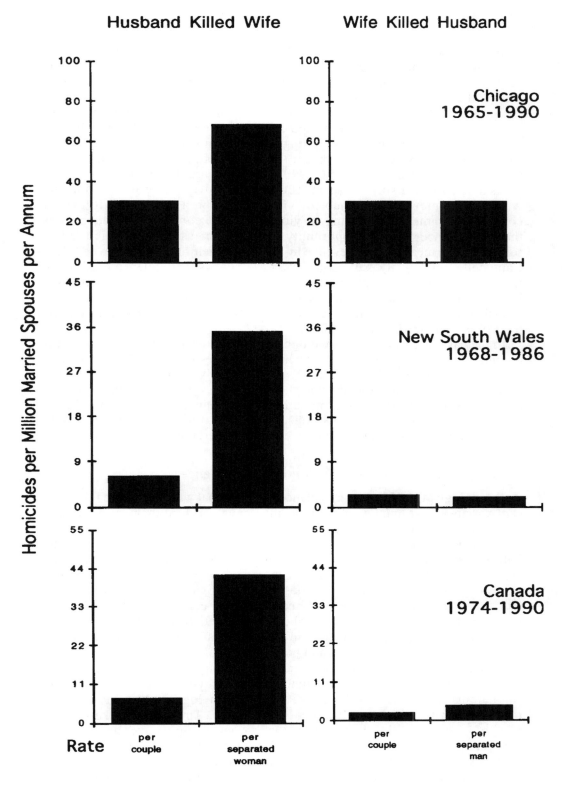

**Figure 7.1.** Homicides per million registered-marriage spouses per annum, according to whether the couple were coresiding or separated at the time of the homicide.

(Daly & Wilson, 1988a; 1990; 1993; Wilson & Daly, 1985). In modern nations where the state monopolizes legitimate use of violence, we easily forget the value of a credible threat of violence, but in non-state societies, such a threat was (and is) essential for deterring violations of one's interests and a crucial component of the reputation needed to acquire and maintain status and power (Chagnon, 1992). If men have indeed evolved violent capabilities to compete with other men, it is hardly surprising that they should sometimes use those capabilities in conflicts with women; the objects of male violence are mostly male rivals (e.g., Daly & Wilson, 1990), but wives are the victims too.

As noted above, uxoricide seems counterproductive. The utility of sublethal wife-beating may also be doubted. Violence can be a costly way to extract compliance: rather than making its victims wish to comply, violence inspires them to defiance when the opportunity arises. Severe assaults can elicit severe self-defensive measures and revenge by victims or their relatives (Browne, 1989; Campbell, 1992b; Daly & Wilson, 1988a). It follows that violence is often the recourse of desperate people lacking access to the positive incentives that might inspire more "voluntary" compliance. Moreover, a seemingly inexpensive and effective initial use of violence can embroil one in escalating hostilities, closing off any possibility of negotiation.

In the case of wife-beating, one implication would seem to be that a man is especially likely to resort thereto when he perceives his control of his wife to be tenuous and he lacks material or other incentives to retain her. Another implication is that the violence, once begun, is likely to escalate, because each beating, even if effective in intimidating the woman and reducing her likelihood of imminent departure, also raises her general level of incentive to quit the relationship, inspiring the man to escalated coercion.

## Coercive Control of Women Without Overt Violence

Anthropological and historical evidence suggests that wherever there is significant variance in resources, high status men have parlayed their resources and power into polygynous monopolization of women (wives and/or concubines) and have been concerned to "protect" their women from potential rivals (Betzig, 1986). Relatively recently in human history, with the inequities engendered by agricultural surpluses and the rise of complex, role-differentiated societies, extreme polygyny and extreme sequestering of women became possible. The most despotic harem holders confined women in cells guarded by eunuchs, maintained records of their menstrual cycles, farmed them out to the harems of underlings when they got too old, and even killed and replaced them *en masse* in the event of security failures and possible cuckoldry.

Harem acquisition is a novelty on an evolutionary timescale, and is neither an evolved adaptation in its own right nor a consequential selection pressure. But harems provide evidence about evolved psychology in the same way that refined sugar does: they testify to evolved appetites. The widespread establishment of harems falsifies the theory that men want multiple wives because they are economic assets. Proponents of this view have insisted that wives are sought as means to wealth, power, and status rather than as perquisites thereof, but harem occupants are typically maintained at great expense and prevented from being productive. This oddly recurring institution also demonstrates that men who collect women are not simply pursuing sexual variety, for in every independent invention of the harem phenomenon, exclusivity of sexual access appears to have been one of the despot's main preoccupations (Betzig, 1986).

Only the richest and most powerful men could collect harems, but millions of men have guarded and constrained "their" women by practices that seem to depart from those of despots only in degree. Veiling, chaperoning, purdah, and incarceration of women are common social institutions of patrilineal-patrilocal societies, and the significance of these practices is evident when one notes that it is only women of reproductive age who are confined. Prepubertal children and postmenopausal women enjoy considerable freedom. Coercive control is also achieved by genital mutilations designed to destroy the sexual interest of women and even their penetrability until surgically reopened (Hicks, 1986; Hosken, 1979); less violent solutions are chastity belts of countless variety. Claustration and chastity belts might be interpreted simply as solutions to male-male competition, but practices like clitoridectomy and infibulation show that the women are being "guarded" not only from "predatory" males but from their own inclinations.

Moreover, claustration practices are status-graded (Dickemann, 1979, 1981). The higher her social status, the more restricted the woman, a seemingly paradoxical correlation until one considers that high-status men have both a relatively great concern about the paternity of their heirs and the wherewithal to confine women even if it requires foregoing their productive labor. (Chinese foot-binding was a status-graded practice that simultaneously made an ostentation of the male owner's capacity to dispense with the woman's labor and rendered her incapable of flight.) Economic inequities persist in modern state societies, but the variance in men's access to women has been greatly tempered in comparison to despotic harem societies. Most notable in this regard is the rapid spread of legislated monogamy. Why this happened in spite of the persisting polygynous inclinations of powerful men has been considered by Betzig (1986; 1991) and MacDonald (1990). We would expect that the prevalence and intensity of coercive control of women is lessened when the variance in men's access to women is reduced.

## SOURCES OF VARIABILITY IN THE VIOLENT MANIFESTATIONS OF MEN'S SEXUAL PROPRIETARINESS

Social phenomena vary systematically both within and between societies. An evolutionary psychological perspective can shed light on both sorts of variability in violence against wives, by suggesting which social cues are likely to activate sexually proprietary psychological mechanisms. Wherever the relevant cues are salient, recurring and prevalent, manifestations of male sexual proprietariness are expected to be diverse, culturally elaborated, and frequent. The psychological link between jealousy and anger suggests that cues of imminent threat of loss of sexual exclusivity may be manifested in violent action. Moreover, the prevalence and intensity of such violence is expected to reflect local sanctions. The target of a jealous man's rage may be the woman, the rival, or both, and again, the target(s) selected may be expected to reflect sanctions, as well as the social status of each party, and the circumstances of the alleged trespass.

## Hypotheses about Patterned Variations
## in Male Sexual Proprietariness and Violence

If male sexual proprietariness represents complex evolved psychological adaptation, designed by selection to promote male fitness in ancestral environments, and if, like any adaptation, it is costly (since mate-guarding takes time away from other potentially useful activities, while violence and even threats entail risk of injury from retaliatory or defensive violence), then sexually proprietary attentions and actions should have evolved to be allocated in response to cues of expected utility. Many male birds, for example, guard their mates closely during their fertile phase, but cease once the last egg is laid.

In human beings, we hypothesize that such variable cuing of sexual proprietariness affects behavioral variability both within and between societies. Some phenomena, such as age-related changes in fertility, are cross-culturally general and likely to account for within-society variability in more or less similar ways. Others, such as the risk imposed by desperate, disenfranchised male rivals, vary across societies and may therefore be expected to account for some of the between-society variance in proprietary manifestations. We have organized the following hypotheses suggested by our evolutionary psychological perspective on violence against wives according to five thematic issues.

### 1. Intensity of Intrasexual Competition.

The degree of coercive constraint of wives, including violence, is predicted to reflect cues of the local, contemporaneous intensity of male sexual competition and poaching. Relevant cues may include encounter rates with potential male rivals; whether they are encountered alone or in all-male groups as opposed to being accompanied by women (that is, cues of bachelor pressure); cues of the status, attractiveness, and resources (hence, mate value) of rivals relative to oneself, and of other social groups or categories (lineages, castes, etc.) relative to one's own social group or category; and cues of local marital (in)stability.

Local cues of life trajectory and life expectancy are also predicted to be relevant. Evolved psychologies use cues of future prospects and expected lifespan in assessing whether to accept present risks (Daly & Wilson, 1990; Wilson & Daly, 1985); one's rivals are likely to be relatively undeterred by the dangers associated with adulterous overtures, for example, when their own life prospects are poor. Being part of a relatively large age cohort should also be expected to intensify male-male competition, especially where same-age women are unavailable; thus, cohort size effects on intrasexual rivalry and hence on the coercive constraint of women may be especially evident where age disparities at marriage are large.

Parameters like relative cohort size, expected lifespan, local marital stability, local prevalence of adultery, and so forth, clearly cannot be "cued" simply by stimuli present at the time of behavioral decisions, but must instead be apprehended cumulatively over large parts of the lifespan. This implies that people develop mental models which cannot be quickly modified or discarded, and that the "inertial" aspects of such development help explain why emigrants, for example, may not easily assimilate new cultures (see Tooby & Cosmides, 1992).

When individual men monopolize multiple women, whether as wives or concubines, others are consigned to bachelorhood, and male-male competition is exacerbated (Betzig, 1986; 1991). On this basis, we may expect marital coercion and violence to be more extreme in polygynous than in monogamous populations. Levinson (1989) indeed found a significant correlation across non-state societies between his wife-beating codes and a dimension ranging from polyandrous through monogamous to polygynous marriage. We hypothesize that the real relationship will prove to be stronger than his results indicated, since he rank-ordered polygyny in a manner unrelated to the crucial consideration of the variance in men's access to women, and since marital polygyny is an imperfect indicator of the breeding system and hence of the intensity of intrasexual competition.

## 2. Factors Affecting the Woman's Attractiveness to Rivals.

*(a) Risk of conception.* Men's jealousy should prove to be variably aroused at least partly in relation to variable attributes of women. A man is vulnerable to cuckoldry as a result of wifely infidelity, for example, only when his wife is fertile; while he may be concerned to protect a pregnant wife from various sorts of harms, he need not protect her from insemination by rivals.

In a rare investigation of human mate-guarding, Flinn (1988) found that men indeed appear to be sensitive to correlates of cuckoldry risk. Flinn recorded the identity, whereabouts, and activities of everyone he saw during standardized walks through a Caribbean village, in which heterosexual relationships were unstable and often nonexclusive, and in which men directed paternal investments selectively to their own offspring rather than to their stepchildren or to the woman's children sired by other men. He found that men spent more time with partners who reported having menstrual cycles than with those who were pregnant or postmenopausal; that men displayed more agonism both to their wives and to other men when their wives were cycling than in other reproductive conditions; that there was more agonistic interaction between sexual partners whose relationship was nonexclusive than between monogamous pairs; and that hostile male-male interactions were especially characteristic of men who were simultaneously sexually involved with a nonmonogamous woman. We expect that these patterns will prove to be widespread.

*(b) Reproductive Value.* The statistically expected future reproduction of an individual, given her age, condition and circumstances, is her "reproductive value" (RV: Fisher, 1958). Evolutionary biologists find this quantity a useful predictor of intraspecific variations in reproductive behavior and physiology. In animals that exhibit mate fidelity across successive reproductive episodes, RV is a measure of the fitness value and hence the attractiveness of potential mates.

The RV of women is maximal soon after puberty, and begins to decline steeply in the 30's. As one would then expect, youth is a major determinant of women's sexual (Kenrick & Keefe 1992) and marital (e.g. Borgerhoff Mulder, 1988; Buss & Barnes 1986; Glick & Lin 1987) attractiveness. These age-related "opportunity" and "motivational" considerations, as well as other factors including childlessness, suggest that young wives may be more likely than older wives to terminate an unsatisfactory marriage, more likely to be approached by sexual rivals of the husband, and more likely to form new sexual relationships. Hence, we hypothesize that men will be especially jealous, proprietary and coercive toward younger wives.

Uxoricide risk is indeed maximal for the youngest wives in the modern west (Daly & Wilson, 1988a; b; Mercy & Saltzman, 1989; Wilson, Daly, & Wright, 1993); this seems paradoxical given that men allegedly "value" young wives maximally, unless one views uxoricides as the dysfunctional extremes of "normal" coercive violence. The direct relevance of wife's youth to husband's violence has not been established, however, since many other variables are confounded with her age, including parity and childlessness, duration of the union, and the man's own age. Since young men are the most violent age-sex class generally (e g. Daly & Wilson, 1990; Wilson & Daly, 1985), an obvious hypothesis is that male age is actually the relevant factor. This seems not to be the case, however, or at least not the whole story, since young wives married to older husbands actually incur greater risk than those married to young husbands (Wilson & Daly, unpublished data).

It is sometimes suggested that male jealousy cannot be an evolved adaptation because men remain jealous of postmenopausal or otherwise infertile women. This argument ignores the fact that adaptations can only have evolved to track ancestrally informative cues of fertility, and not fertility itself. In a modern society with contraception and diverse cosmetic manipulations, postmenopausal women are likely to exhibit fewer cues of age-related declining RV than still-fertile women in foraging societies.

### 3. Situational Cues of Possible Infidelity.

In addition to attributes of the woman that affect rivals' interest in her, husbands have access to situational information concerning risks of infidelity. A man whose wife has been under continuous surveillance, either by himself or by trusted allies such as close kin, can be relatively confident; conversely, unmonitored absences may be deemed cause for concern (e.g. Fricke, Axinn, & Thornton, 1993). Baker and Bellis (1989) report a particularly interesting psychophysiological response to lapses of personal surveillance: the number of sperm transferred in stable couples' copulations tracks the proportion of the time since their last copulation that they spent apart, paralleling findings of modulated "sperm competition" tactics in other pair-forming animals. We hypothesize that, all else equal, men will also be more sexually demanding, threatening and coercive when circumstances dictate that their wives are relatively unmonitored.

Where control of women by husbands and husbands' kin is constrained, as for example in matrilineal-matrilocal societies in which men make prolonged foraging excursions, men sometimes play little paternal role and direct their "parental" efforts to known relatives, especially their sisters' children. Evolution-minded anthropologists have interpreted such "avuncular" investment and inheritance as a facultative response to uncertain paternity (e.g. Flinn, 1981; Flinn & Low, 1986). Critics of this argument have sometimes noted that the rate of misattributed paternity would have to be implausibly high for sisters' sons to have a higher expected relatedness to a man than his wife's children, but the issue is not simply which heir an adaptive male psychology "should" prefer. Any degree of paternity uncertainty makes daughter's children surer grandchildren than son's children, for example, and so men may be pressured by their own parents to invest avuncularly; the question, then, is how uncertain paternity interacts with other factors to affect the resolution of conflicts (see

Hartung, 1985). In the absence of risk of misdirected paternal investment, men in avuncular societies may be expected to be relatively less concerned about wifely fidelity, but male sexual proprietariness may still be aroused by cues of the intensity of male intrasexual competition.

Even if we accept as a given that wifely infidelity is an exceptionally potent elicitor of anger, there remains a question about the anger's target. We have argued above that violent inclinations toward the wife are functionally coercive, implying that the sexually proprietary male psyche treats knowledge or suspicion of an episode of adultery as predictive of repeat episodes, unless the woman's unfaithful inclinations are deterred. But what if the man is presented with evidence that unfaithful inclination on the part of his wife was not at issue? If infidelity seems clearly to have been coerced, as in rape with injury, violent anger ought mainly to be directed at the usurper, although signs of weak resistance might elicit hostility directed at the woman, too (see Thornhill & Thornhill, 1983; 1992). Moreover, it is noteworthy that even unequivocally blameless rape victims are often devalued as "damaged goods" by husbands and relatives with proprietary interests in them (Wilson & Daly, 1992a).

## 4. Female Choice.

(a) *Coerced marriage.* As we noted earlier, people take a strong manipulative interest in others' marriages. In many societies, marriage is arranged, with the very real possibility that the bride and/or groom are dissatisfied with the choice. In mediaeval England, for example, children could be "espoused" as early as 7 years of age, with the Christian church sanctifying the commitment; a recalcitrant bride who eloped with the man of her choice before her espoused marriage was consummated could cause severe repercussions for her father who had promised her to another man, and a father was likely to launch proceedings against his daughter's "abductor" in such circumstances. Legislation reinforced fathers' interests by stripping eloping daughters of all claims against their families' property. It would not be surprising to discover that wives in unsatisfactory arranged marriages incurred risk of violence by jealous husbands.

One vivid example of the violence that women will risk to escape from their husbands comes from Chagnon's (1992) study of the Yanomamö. Men in this society sometimes raid other villages, killing the men and capturing the women. Violence and threats of violence are effective in deterring these "wives" from escaping. But a woman may take the risk, and "on her own, flees from her village to live in another village and find a new husband there. If the woman's own [husband's] village is stronger than the one she flees to, the men will pursue her and forcibly take her back—and mete out a very severe punishment to her for having run away. They might even kill her. Most of the women who have fled have done so to escape particularly savage and cruel treatment, and they try to flee to a more powerful village" (Chagnon, 1992, p. 149).

(b) *A reputation for violence as a desirable trait in a man.* Given the costs to women of enduring a husband's violence, it may initially seem counterintuitive that violence might be useful and hence attractive in a man. But it is often clearly useful in a kinsman: women commonly rely on brothers and other male kin to protect them from abusive husbands (Campbell, 1992b; Smuts, 1992). Yanomamö women, for example "dread the possibility of being married to men in distant villages, because they know that their brothers will not be able to protect them" (Chagnon, 1992, p. 149). Moreover, in communities where women are at risk of being abducted by other men, as among the Yanomamö, or even where sexual harassment and assault by strangers and acquaintances are chronic, a husband with a reputation for vengeful violent action can be a valued social resource. However, violent men as husbands or brothers may be risky propositions for women. We would anticipate that wherever local rates of sexual assault are chronically high or where material and social rewards are gained by the effective use of violence, a reputation for controlled use of violence may be perceived as a valuable trait in a husband. In the absence of marital conflict such a choice may run little risk for the woman.

## 5. Costs to Husbands of Using Violence.

*(a) Social sanctions.* Evolved psychologies are sensitive to costs, so we hypothesize that violence against wives will be more prevalent where it is more legitimate. However genuine rage may be, angry men are seldom impervious to social controls. Quantitative data bearing on this issue are regrettably sparse, but the ethnographic record at least impressionistically supports the generalization that societies vary greatly in their incidences of severe wife assault, and that even vengeful husbands are sensitive to the probable costs of violence.

Several authors have argued that wife battering is rarer or less severe in societies where wives retain close contact with genealogical kin, who deter husbands from serious abuse (e.g., Campbell, 1992b; Chagnon, 1992; Draper, 1992; Smuts, 1992). Variation in access to male kin is apparently related to variable vulnerability of wives within societies, too, even relatively matrilocal societies (H. Kaplan & K. Hill, pers. comm., 1990). Oddly, however, Levinson (1989) found no support for the hypothesis that access to kin protects wives from abuse in non-state societies: prevalence of wife-beating was apparently unrelated to postmarital residence practices in a cross-cultural tabulation. One problem with this null result is that wife-beating codes based on ethnographic materials are noisy; however, Levinson's codes were significantly related to variables like widow remarriage proscriptions and the presence or absence of all-female work groups. A more important problem is that Levinson's test of relationship was a rank-order correlation even though postmarital residence practices were coded on a five-point scale whose ordering did not correspond to lesser/greater access to genealogical kin. We hypothesize that better cross-cultural methods will overturn Levinson's null result.

*(b) Wives' Resistance.* Wives sometimes kill husbands, perhaps mainly in self-defensive resistance to male coercive control (Wilson & Daly, 1992c). In some societies, wives vastly outnumber husbands as victims, while body counts are more nearly equal in others (Table 7.1). The contrast between the United States and other English-speaking industrialized nations is especially striking, and Wilson & Daly (1992c) showed that this contrast cannot be attributed to greater gun use in the United States. Neither is it due to a general diminution of sex differences in the use of lethal violence regardless of victim-killer relationship; variability in the sex ratio of killing (SROK) is specific to the marital relationship. Moreover, despite large differences in the spousal SROK between the United States and other nations, several factors affecting this ratio had similar

**Table 7.1. Number of Spousal Homicides and the Spousal Sex Ratio of Killing (SROK = Homicides Perpetrated by Women per 100 Perpetrated by Men) in Various Homicide Samples**

| Data Set | Killer | | |
|---|---|---|---|
| | Man | Woman | SROK |
| United States 1976-1985 | 10,529 | 7,888 | 75 |
| Chicago, Ill. 1965-1989 | 844 | 862 | 102 |
| Detroit, Mich. 1972 | 36 | 43 | 119 |
| Detroit, Mich. 1982-1983 | 28 | 56 | 200 |
| Houston, Tex. 1969 | 19 | 26 | 137 |
| Miami, Fla. 1980 | 23 | 20 | 87 |
| Philadelphia, Pa. 1948-1952 | 53 | 47 | 89 |
| New South Wales 1968-1986 | 303 | 95 | 31 |
| Canada 1974-1983 | 812 | 248 | 31 |
| Denmark 1933-1961 | 96 | 16 | 17 |
| England/Wales 1977-1986 | 981 | 223 | 23 |
| Scotland 1979-1987 | 99 | 40 | 40 |
| Africa, Mid-20th Century | | | |
| Tiv, Luo, Soga, Gisu, | | | |
| Nyoro, Luyia | 70 | 4 | 6 |
| India | | | |
| Bison-Horn Maria 1930-1940s | 20 | 0 | 0 |
| Munda, Oraon, Bhil 1960s | 14 | 0 | 0 |

NOTE: Most published studies of homicides do not classify cases in a manner permitting inclusion in this table; often, the set of cases has been selected on some potentially biasing criterion, such as arrest or conviction, and even where all cases known to the police have been tabulated, spousal cases have seldom been distinguished from others. (See Wilson & Daly 1992c for sources.)

impacts across the board: the victimization of wives was greater relative to that of husbands (the SROK was lower) in registered than in de facto marriages, in separated couples than in those still coresiding, in markedly age-discrepant couples where the wife was older, and in cases where a gun was used.

One thing that is clearly common to these western nations with their variable SROKs (and variable rates of spouse-killing) is the relevance of male sexual proprietariness, as discussed earlier. The high SROK in the United States does not imply that wives' and husbands' actions or motives are more alike in that country. Rather, in the United States as elsewhere, men often pursue and kill estranged wives while women hardly ever behave similarly; men, but not women, kill spouses as part of planned murder-suicides; men perpetrate familicidal massacres, killing spouse and children together, while women do not; men, but not women, kill after prolongedly subjecting spouses to coercive abuse; men kill in response to revelations of wifely infidelity, while women almost never react similarly; and women, unlike men, kill mainly in circumstances with strong elements of self-defense or defense of children (references in Wilson & Daly, 1992c).

So whence the variability in SROK? One hypothesis is that wives' lethality approaches husbands' specifically when women feel the need to defend children of former unions against their current mates. By the same reasoning by which a man may be expected to possess evolved defenses against cuckoldry, we may expect him to exhibit less than full paternal commitment to stepchildren; his wife's investments in his predecessors' children (and demands that he, too, invest) can thus be a potent source of marital conflict (Daly & Wilson, 1988c). Stepchildren themselves incur greatly elevated risks of both fatal and nonfatal abuse (Wilson, Daly, & Weghorst 1980; Daly & Wilson 1985; 1988b), and their presence is a major risk factor for violence against wives, too (Daly, Singh, & Wilson, 1993). We would therefore expect that wherever stepfather families are prevalent, women would be readier to use dangerous defensive tactics, and the SROK values would be higher. We hypothesize that the incidence of steprelationship will prove relevant to relatively high SROK values in, for example, American cities and in *de facto* as compared to registered marriages.

Another hypothesis is that the spousal SROK value rises when wives feel socially empowered to retaliate against male coercion. The Indian and African peoples in Table 7.1, among whom women scarcely ever killed their husbands, were strongly patrilineal societies with brideprice and patrilocal residence. In such societies, an abused wife, cut off from her kin, may feel she has no recourse other than suicide or flight; violence against the husband is futile and almost unthinkable (e.g. Counts, 1990)[3]. Conversely, an abused wife surrounded by supportive relatives has more assertive options available, and she may be especially tempted to react violently in the absence of the services of protective legal or political institutions.

## CONCLUDING COMMENTS

Many other factors influence the utility and the costs of sexually proprietary violence, and are therefore likely to affect its prevalence insofar as men are facultatively responsive to appropriate cues. Reputational effects, for example, can run either way: wife-beating is a shameful act of cowardice in some societies and an obligation for salvaging honor in others. The proposition that angry resentment of infidelity is an evolved characteristic of the male mind in no way implies that men should be impervious to these social pressures. Rather, an evolutionary psychological perspective helps clarify why such initially puzzling variability in norms about wife-beating exist. Wife-beaters are considered bullies, for example, where alternative means of controlling female sexuality make such violence superfluous.

Some prominent anthropologists have insisted that cultural variations are without utilitarian significance (e.g. Sahlins, 1976). Indeed, arbitrariness with respect to function ("dog" versus "chien") is sometimes deemed definitional of a cultural distinction. But societal differences in social practices and institutions are clearly not always arbitrary, and perhaps hardly ever. We know that they are not arbitrary because of powerful statistical associations among marriage practices, modes of kinship reckoning, subsistence ecology, inheritance, incest rules, childhood socialization practices, and so forth, associations which have been increasingly successfully elucidated and predicted by evolution-minded anthropologists (e.g., Flinn, 1981; Flinn & Low, 1986; Gaulin & Schlegel, 1980; Low, 1989; Thornhill, 1991).

We have argued that the particular cues and circumstances which inspire men to use violence against their partners reflect a domain-specific masculine psychology which evolved in a social milieu in which assaults and threats of violence functioned to deter wives from pursuing alternative reproductive opportunities, which would have represented consequential threats to husbands' fitness. Although the motives in the majority of uxoricides and sublethal wife-beating across cultures and across centuries indeed reflect male sexual proprietariness, it is important to note that the actual rates at which women are slain or beaten by husbands are enormously variable. Women in the United States today face a statistical risk of being slain by their husbands that is about five to ten times greater than that faced by their European counterparts, and in the most violent American cities, risk is five times higher again. It may be the case that men have proprietary inclinations toward their wives everywhere, but they do not feel equally entitled to act upon them everywhere.

## NOTES

1. Biologists note that there are additional sources of evolutionary change, including mutation, migration, and fortuitous differential mortality. But only selection generates functional complexity.

2. This process is defined in evolutionary biology more technically and precisely as promoting the relative replicative success of one's genes, in competition with alternative forms of the same gene (alleles). The term "fitness" (which was coined by the sociologist Herbert Spencer) has produced a lot of misunderstanding, for it has been used by evolutionists in several slightly different senses, none of which corresponds to its vernacular meaning of physical condition (Dawkins, 1982).

3. These considerations suggest the following cross-cultural hypothesis: the suicide rate of married women will be higher, relative to that of other demographic groups, in patrilocal societies than in neolocal, and higher in neolocal societies than where wives have continuing contact with their relatives.

## REFERENCES

Allen, J. A. (1990). *Sex and secrets. Crimes involving Australian women since 1880.* Melbourne: Oxford University Press.

Atkins S., & Hoggett B. (1984). *Women and the law.* Oxford: Blackwell.

Baker, R. R., & Bellis, M. A. (1989). Number of sperm in human ejaculates varies in accord with sperm competition theory. *Animal Behaviour, 37,* 867-869.

Barnard, George W., Vera, H., Vera, M. I., & Newman, G. (1982). Till death do us part: A study of spouse murder. *Bulletin of the American Association of Psychiatry and Law, 10,* 271-280.

Besse, S. K. (1989). Crimes of passion: The campaign against wife killing in Brazil, 1910-1940. *Journal of Social History, 22,* 653-666.

Betzig, L. (1986). *Despotism and differential reproduction: A darwinian view of history.* Hawthorne, NY: Aldine de Gruyter.

Betzig, L. (1991). History. In M. Maxwell, (Ed.), *The sociobiological imagination.* Albany, NY: SUNY Press.

Bloch, M. (1977). The past and the present in the present. *Man, 12,* 278-292.

Borgerhoff Mulder, M. (1988). Kipsigis bridewealth payments. In L. Betzig, M. Borgerhoff Mulder., & P. Turke, (Eds.), *Human reproductive behaviour*. Cambridge: Cambridge University Press.

Brown, D. (1991). *Human universals*. New York: McGraw-Hill.

Browne, A. (1985). Assault and homicide at home: When battered women kill. In M. J. Saks & L. Saxe (Eds.), *Advances in applied social psychology*, (vol. 3). Hillsdale NJ: Erlbaum.

Browne, A. (1987). *When battered women kill*. New York: Free Press.

Buss, D. M., & Barnes, M. F. (1986). Preferences in human mate selection. *Journal of Personality & Social Psychology*, *50*, 559-570.

Buss, D., Larsen, R. J., Westen, D., & Semmelroth, J. (1992). Sex differences in jealousy: Evolution, physiology, and psychology. *Psychological Science*, *3*, 251-255.

Campbell, J. C. (1992a). If I can't have you, no one can: Issues of power and control of homicide of female partners. In J. Radford & D. E. H. Russell, (Eds.), *Femicide: The politics of woman killing*. New York: Twayne.

Campbell, J. C. (1992b). Wife-battering: Cultural contexts versus Western social sciences. In D. A. Ayers, J. K. Brown, & J. C. Campbell, (Eds.), *Sanctions and sanctuary: Cultural perspectives on the beating of wives*. Boulder, CO: Westview Press.

Chagnon, N. A. (1992) *Yanomamö. The last days of Eden*. San Diego, CA: Harcourt Brace Jovanovich.

Counts, D. C. (1990). Beaten wife, suicidal woman: Domestic violence in Kaliai, West New Britain. *Pacific Studies*, *13*, 151-169.

Crawford, M. & Gartner, R. (1992). *Woman killing: Intimate femicide in Ontario 1974-1990*. Toronto: Women We Honour Action Committee.

Daly, M., Singh, L., & Wilson, M. (1993). Children fathered by previous partners: A risk factor for violence against women. *Canadian Journal of Public Health*, *84*, 209-210.

Daly, M., & Wilson, M. (1983) *Sex, evolution, and behavior* (2nd edition). Belmont, CA: Wadsworth.

Daly, M., & Wilson, M. (1985) Child abuse and other risks of not living with both parents. *Ethology & Sociobiology*, *6*, 197-210.

Daly, M., & Wilson, M.(1988a) *Homicide*. Hawthorne NY: Aldine de Gruyter.

Daly, M., & Wilson, M. (1988b) Evolutionary social psychology and family homicide. *Science*, *242*, 519-524.

Daly, M., & Wilson, M. (1988c). The Darwinian psychology of discriminative parental solicitude. *Nebraska Symposium in Motivation*, *35*, 91-144

Daly, M., & Wilson, M. (1990). Killing the competition: Female/female and male/male homicide. *Human Nature*, *1*, 81-107.

Daly, M., & Wilson, M. (1993) The evolutionary psychology of male violence. In J. Archer (Ed.), *Male violence*. London: Routledge Kegan Paul.

Daly, M., Wilson, M., & Weghorst, S. J. (1982). Male sexual jealousy. *Ethology and Sociobiology*, *3*, 11-27.

Davies, N. B. (1992). *Dunnock behaviour and social evolution*. Oxford: Oxford University Press.

Dawkins, R. (1982). *The extended phenotype*. Oxford: W. H. Freeman.

Dell, S. (1984). *Murder into manslaughter: The diminished responsibility defence in practice*. Oxford: Oxford University Press.

Dickemann, M. (1979). The ecology of mating systems in hypergynous dowry societies. *Social Science Information*, *18*, 163-195.

Dickemann, M. (1981). Paternal confidence and dowry competition: a biocultural analysis of purdah. In R. D. Alexander & D. W. Tinkle (Eds.), *Natural selection and social behavior*. New York: Chiron Press.

Dobash, R. E., & Dobash, R. P. (1979) *Violence against wives*. New York: Free Press.

Draper, P. (1992) Room to maneuver: !Kung women cope with men. In D. A. Counts, J. K. Brown, & J. C. Campbell (Eds.), *Sanctions and sanctuary. Cultural perspectives on the beating of wives*. Boulder, CO: Westview Press.

Eberhard, W. G. (1985). *Sexual selection and animal genitalia*. Cambridge, MA: Harvard University Press.

Edwards, S. (1985). Male violence against women: Excusatory and explanatory ideologies in law and society. In S. Edwards (Ed.), *Gender, sex and the law*. London: Croom Helm.

Fisher, R. A. (1958). *The genetical theory of natural selection*. (2nd revised edition, originally published 1930.) New York: Dover Press.

Flinn, M. V. (1981). Uterine vs. agnatic kinship variability and associated cousin marriage preferences. In R. D. Alexander and D. W. Tinkle, (Eds.), *Natural selection and social behavior*. New York: Chiron Press.

Flinn, M. V. (1988). Mate guarding in a Caribbean village. *Ethology & Sociobiology*, *9*, 1-28.

Flinn, M., & Low, B. (1986). Resource distribution, social competition, and mating patterns in human societies. In D. I. Rubenstein & R. W. Wrangham, (Eds.), *Ecological aspects of social evolution*. Princeton, NJ: Princeton University Press.

Ford, C. S., & Beach, F. A. (1952) *Patterns of sexual behavior*. New York: Harper and Row.

Fricke, T., Axinn, W. G., & Thornton, A. (1993). Marriage, social inequality, and women's contact with their natal families in alliance societies: Two Tamang examples. *American Anthropologist*, *95*, 395-419.

Gaulin, S. J. C., & Sailer, L. D. (1985) Are females the ecological sex? *American Anthropologist*, *87*, 111-119.

Gaulin, S. J. C., & Schlegel, A. (1980). Paternal confidence and paternal investment: A cross-cultural test of a sociobiological hypothesis. *Ethology & Sociobiology*, *1*, 301-309.

Geertz, C. (1984). Anti-anti-relativism. *American Anthropologist*, *86*, 263-278.

Glick, P., & Lin, S.L. (1987). Remarriage after divorce: Recent changes and demographic variations. *Sociological Perspectives*, *30*, 162-179.

Haig, D. (1993). Genetic conflicts in human pregnancy. *Quarterly Review of Biology*, *68*, 495-531.

Hartung, J. (1985). Matrilineal inheritance: New theory and analysis. *Behavioral & Brain Sciences*, *8*, 661-688.

Hicks, E. K. (1986). *Infibulation: Status through mutilation*. Alblasserdam, The Netherlands: Offsetdrukkerij Kanters B. V.

Hosken, F. P. (1979). *The Hosken report. Genital and sexual mutilation of females*. 2d revised edition. Lexington, MA: Women's International Network News.

Kenrick, D., & Keefe, R. C. (1992). Age preferences in mates reflect sex differences in reproductive strategies. *Behavioral & Brain Sciences*, *15*, 75-133.

Leacock, E. (1980). Social behavior, biology, and the double standard. In G. W. Barlow & J. Silverberg, (Eds.), *Sociobiology: Beyond nature/nurture?* Boulder, CO: Westview Press.

Leach, E. (1982). *Social anthropology*. Oxford: Oxford University Press.

Levinson, D. (1989). *Family violence in cross-cultural perspective*. Newbury Park, CA: Sage.

Low, B. S. (1978). Environmental uncertainty and the parental strategies of marsupials and placentals. *American Naturalist, 112*, 197-213.

Low, B. S. (1989). Sex, power, and resources: Ecological and social correlates of sex differences. *International Journal of Contemporary Sociology, 27*, 45-71.

MacDonald, K. (1990). Mechanisms of sexual egalitarianism. *Ethology & Sociobiology, 11*, 1-27.

Mahoney, M. R. (1991). Legal images of battered women: Redefining the issue of separation. *Michigan Law Review, 90*, 1-94.

Mayr, E. (1983). How to carry out the adaptationist program? *American Naturalist, 121*, 324-334.

Mercy, J. A., & Saltzman, L. E. (1989). Fatal violence among spouses in the United States, 1976-85. *American Journal of Public Health, 79*, 595-599.

Morris, W. (1969). *The American heritage dictionary of the English language*. Boston: Houghton Mifflin.

Mowat, R. R. (1966). *Morbid jealousy and murder*. London: Tavistock.

Murdock, G. P. (1967). *Ethnographic atlas*. Pittsburgh: University of Pittsburgh Press.

Polk, K., & Ranson, D. (1991). The role of gender in intimate violence. *Australia and New Zealand Journal of Criminology, 24*, 15-24.

Quaife, G. R. (1979). *Wanton wenches and wayward wives*. London: Croom Helm.

Safilios-Rothschild, C. (1969). 'Honor' crimes in contemporary Greece. *British Journal of Sociology, 20*, 205-218.

Sahlins, M. D. (1976). *The use and abuse of biology*. Ann Arbor, MI: University of Michigan Press.

Smuts, B. (1992). Male aggression against women: An evolutionary perspective. *Human Nature, 3*, 1-44.

Stephens, W. N. (1963). *The Family in cross-cultural perspective*. New York: Holt, Rinehart, and Winston.

Symons, D. (1979). *The evolution of human sexuality*. New York: Oxford University Press.

Teismann, M. W., & Mosher, D. L. (1978). Jealous conflict in dating couples. *Psychological Reports , 42*, 1211-1216.

Thornhill, N. W. (1991). An evolutionary analysis of rules regulating human inbreeding and marriage. *Behavioral and Brain Sciences, 14*, 247-293.

Thornhill, R., & Thornhill, N. W. (1983). Human rape: An evolutionary analysis. *Ethology & Sociobiology, 4*, 137-183.

Thornhill, R., & Thornhill, N. W. (1992).The evolutionary psychology of men's coercive sexuality. *Behavioral and Brain Sciences, 15*, 363-421.

Tooby, J., & Cosmides, L. (1992). The psychological foundations of culture. In J. H. Barkow, L. Cosmides, & J. Tooby, (Eds.), *The adapted mind: Evolutionary psychology and the generation of culture*. New York: Oxford University Press.

Trivers, R. L. (1972).Parental investment and sexual selection. In B. Campbell (Ed.), *Sexual selection and the descent of man, 1871-1971*. Chicago: Aldine.

Trivers, R. L. (1974). Parent-offspring conflict. *American Zoologist, 14*, 249-264.

Wallace, A. (1986). *Homicide: The social reality*. Sydney: New South Wales Bureau of Crime Statistics and Research.

Whyte, M. K. (1978). *The status of woman in preindustrial societies*. Princeton, NJ: Princeton University Press.

Wilson, M., & Daly, M. (1985). Competitiveness, risk-taking and violence: The young male syndrome. *Ethology & Sociobiology*, *6*, 59-73.

Wilson, M., & Daly, M. (1992a). The man who mistook his wife for a chattel. In J. H. Barkow, L. Cosmides, & J. Tooby (Eds.), *The adapted mind: Evolutionary psychology and the generation of culture*. New York: Oxford University Press.

Wilson, M., & Daly, M. (1992b). Til death us do part. In J. Radford & D. E. H. Russell (Eds.), *Femicide*. New York: Twayne.

Wilson, M., & Daly, M. (1992c). Who kills whom in spouse killings? On the exceptional sex ratio of spousal homicides in the United States. *Criminology*, *30*, 189-215.

Wilson, M., & Daly, M. (1993). Spousal homicide risk and estrangement. *Violence & Victims*, *8*, 3-16.

Wilson, M., Daly, M., & Weghorst, S. (1980). Household composition and the risk of child abuse and neglect. *Journal of Biosocial Science*, *12*, 333-340.

Wilson, M., Daly, M., & Wright, C. (1993). Uxoricide in Canada: Demographic risk patterns. *Canadian Journal of Criminology*, *35*, 263-291.

*Acknowledgments*. We wish to acknowledge the support of the Arts Research Board of McMaster University, the Harry Frank Guggenheim Foundation, the Rockefeller Foundation, the Natural Sciences & Engineering Research Council of Canada, and the Social Sciences & Humanities Research Council of Canada. We thank Joanna Scheib and Jennifer Davis-Walton for critical comments.

# 8

# Homicide and U.S. Regional Culture

Richard E. Nisbett
Gregory Polly
Sylvia Lang

White southern culture has long been considered to be more violent than northern culture—by foreigners, by northerners, and by southerners themselves. *The Encyclopedia of Southern Culture* (Wilson & Ferris, 1989) devotes 39 pages to the topic of violence. None of the historians and cultural observers contributing to the section expresses doubt that the South deserves its reputation for violence, including a greater proclivity toward homicide as a means of resolving conflicts.

There have been many theories, not necessarily contradictory, to account for southern violence. One candidate is the weather. The South is hotter than the North, and there is evidence that homicide and other violent crimes are more common on hot days than on cool ones (Anderson, 1989). A second candidate is poverty. The South is poorer than the rest of the country, and poverty in all regions of the country is associated with violence. A third candidate is the tradition of slavery. Whites might have extended their violent treatment of slaves to other whites. Alternatively, the fact that work was unnecessary for whites may have encouraged violent behavior. In Tocqueville's (1835/1969) view, slavery meant that the white population was idle, and this idleness gave rise to an interest in arms and violence.

Many other writers (e.g., Crèvecoeur, 1782/1981; McWhiney, 1988) have noted that the hunting and herding life, which was far more common in the South than in the North, also leaves plenty of free time and in addition pits one man against his fellows in competition for limited resources. They have proposed that it was these aspects of economic life rather than, or in addition to, slavery that encouraged the violent pastimes.

Herding may have been important in another sense. In contrast to the sober Puritan, Quaker, and Dutch farmer-artisans who settled New England and the mid-Atlantic states, the dominant economic and cultural influence on the South came from the herding peoples of the fringes of Britain (McWhiney, 1988). These so-called Scotch-Irish, like many peoples whose livelihood is based on herding, faced the risk of loss of wealth by theft. It was very easy for one man to take another's animal or his entire herd. To prevent such a thing from happening, herding peoples often develop a "culture of honor," responding to threats to property or reputation for strength and toughness with savage violence (Lowie,

1954; Peristiany, 1965). Even an insult or unfavorable comment may be construed as a threat to the individual's reputation for manhood and strength and so must be dealt with violently. The conditions of the U.S. South were, if anything, more favorable for the herding practices of the Scotch-Irish than Britain had been; and until the invention of the cotton gin, herding was a highly important economic activity even in the Deep South. Moreover, the low population density, together with the weakness of legal institutions in the South, would have favored self-defense and a belligerent stance as the chief viable means of protection. Thus, like herding peoples elsewhere in the world, the original southerners participated in a culture in which violence might have been a frequent form of response to threats concerning property or reputation (Cash, 1941; Fischer, 1989; Wyatt-Brown, 1986).


## THE CULTURE OF HONOR

Testing such a broad hypothesis as the present one—that cultural differences in norms concerning violence exist between regions of the country—requires a wide variety of methods with converging results. The hypothesis is simultaneously a hypothesis about individuals and a hypothesis about society. Evidence of different kinds, at both levels, is needed to support the cultural view. At the individual level, attitudinal and behavioral data concerning preference for violence are relevant to the hypothesis, especially data indicating specific preference for violence related to the concerns of the culture of honor. At the societal level, regional differences in rates of occurrence of violent acts and regional differences in laws and social policies accepting or endorsing violence are relevant to the hypothesis, especially data indicating a particular preference for types of violence that would be predicted to characterize members of a culture of honor.

Nisbett and Cohen and their colleagues have recently begun to test the notion that white southerners still participate to a degree in a culture of honor. Cohen and Nisbett (1994) have found in surveys that although southerners do not endorse violence in the abstract any more than do northerners (for example, they are no more likely to agree with the statement "Violence deserves violence" or the statement "Many people only learn through violence"), they are more likely to endorse violence for purposes of protection ("A man has the right to kill a person to defend his house") and in response to an affront (for example, when "an acquaintance looks over Fred's girlfriend and starts to talk to her in a suggestive way"). It is important to note that, though poverty predicts attitudes toward violence, the constellation of attitudes associated with poverty is different from that associated with region, sometimes actually the opposite of regional differences.

Cohen, Nisbett, Bowdle, and Schwarz (1994) have conducted a series of experiments examining the response of northern and southern college students to insults in the laboratory. In these experiments, a confederate pushes his shoulder against the subject and calls him an "asshole." Southerners express more anger and less amusement in response to this insult, as rated by observers, and are more likely to mention violence when asked to complete a subsequently presented scenario containing an affront than are insulted northerners. Physiological measures show that the cortisol and testosterone levels of southerners show greater increases in response to an insult than do those of northerners, indicating higher stress levels and greater preparedness for aggression. Insulted southerners engage in more aggression, being unwilling to move out of the way for someone to pass; and they engage in more dominance-related behavior, giving firmer handshakes and acting in a tougher manner. (Noninsulted southerners are trivially less aggressive than noninsulted northerners.) Finally, the insulted southerner, but not the insulted northerner, believes that a person who has witnessed the insult regards him as unmanly and weak.

At the societal level, several investigators (Baron & Strauss, 1988; Cohen et al., 1994; Reed, 1981) have observed that southern states are more likely to have laws and social policies that promote or accept violence in some way—including allowing capital punishment for crime, corporal punishment in schools, and the killing of an intruder or a person fleeing with property, as well as having higher rates of production of military men and football players. Thus, there is evidence both at the individual level and at the societal level that a version of the culture of honor still exists in the South. In the next section, we examine the implications of this hypothesis for the rates and types of homicides to be expected in the South versus the North.

## IMPLICATIONS OF THE CULTURE OF HONOR FOR HOMICIDE RATES

Most homicides take place between acquaintances (Reed, 1981; Simpson, 1985; Smith & Parker, 1980), and a very high fraction of homicides are argument-related (Daly & Wilson, 1988; Lundsgaarde, 1977; Wolfgang & Ferracuti, 1967). If there is still a southern culture of honor, it seems reasonable to predict several things about regional differences in homicide.

1. Homicide rates should be higher for whites in the South than in the North.
2. Homicide rates should be particularly elevated for whites in smaller cities, which are in general closer to rural areas, rather than in larger cities, which are less tied to agricultural concerns and reflect more cosmopolitan influences.
3. Homicide rates for blacks should be relatively unrelated to region. The great black migrations to northern cities are a recent phenomenon (Bailey, 1989), and there is no reason to assume that anything like the long-standing cultural differences for whites in different regions characterize blacks in different regions.
4. Homicide rates for argument- and conflict-related homicides should be more elevated in the South than rates for homicides not involving arguments, such as those conducted in the course of another felony (e.g., robbery). This is because arguments are likely to involve behavior that is interpreted as insulting and therefore requires a violent response. On the other hand, nothing about the culture-of-honor hypothesis leads to the expectation that either felonies in general, or homicide in the context of felonies, should be higher in the South.

In order to test these hypotheses, homicide data were compiled from the *Supplementary Homicide Reports* (U.S. Department of Justice, 1984) for 1976–

1983. These reports break the homicide data down by race and by circumstances (arguments, felonies, etc.). The homicide rates for non-Hispanic whites and for blacks in cities of different sizes, in different regions, were examined.

## PREVIOUS STUDIES OF REGIONAL DIFFERENCES IN HOMICIDE

There already exists a literature comparing homicide rates of North and South, but this is not relevant to present concerns because it does not distinguish between white and black homicide rates (with two exceptions—Harer & Steffensmeier [1992] and Messner & Golden [1992]) and because all studies examine only large population units. Some studies examine entire states (Baron & Straus, 1988; Gastil, 1971; Huff-Corzine, Corzine, & Moore, 1986; Loftin & Hill, 1974; Parker & Smith, 1979; Smith & Parker, 1980). But, of course, states differ in many ways that are associated with homicide rate, including percentage living in large metropolitan areas (Archer & Gartner, 1984; Friday, 1983; Harries, 1974, 1980; Nettler, 1984; Wolfgang & Ferracuti, 1967), average population density (Galle, Gove, & McPherson, 1972; McPherson, 1972; Schmitt, 1966; Winsborough, 1970), and the nature of the economy and ecology, including factors that are plausibly related to gun ownership such as percentage of the population involved in agrarian activities. Other studies examine cities or Standard Metropolitan Statistical Areas (SMSAs) (Blau & Blau, 1982; Gastil, 1971; Loftin & Parker, 1985; McCarthy, Galle, & Zimmern, 1975; Messner, 1982, 1983; Parker, 1989; Simpson, 1985; Williams, 1984). But when cities or SMSAs are studied, it is only the largest units that are examined, and these are studied in the same aggregated analysis; that is, rates for cities of all sizes are included in the dependent variable, as are rates for both blacks and whites. In the first-order correlational analyses, South–North as a dummy variable or southernness defined as the degree to which the state was initially settled by southerners, is usually found to be slightly to moderately associated with homicide rates. But when homicide rate is regressed on a package of variables including city size, percentage nonwhite, and percentage living in poverty, the Southernness variable ceases to be significant or is at least substantially diminished in power. In explaining this pattern, investigators characteristically note that the South has more blacks and more people living in poverty and declare that these variables, rather than cultural ones, account for the regional differences.

However, to examine homicide rates of all races as the dependent variable and then attempt to pull out the effects of race by including percentage nonwhite as an independent variable risks obscuring real regional differences. Such differences can be obliterated when one includes factors in the regression analyses such as race that are correlated more highly with the dependent variable (in this case, homicide rate) than is the variable of primary interest (in this case, regional differences), as was pointed out many years ago by Klein (1962). This point has been noted specifically in relation to studies of the association between region and delinquency by Gordon (1968). (These issues have been brought to the fore again by Land, McCall, & Cohen, 1990.) Thus, if one wishes to know whether there are differences in homicide rates for either race, it is essential to examine each race separately.

As a comparison with other investigations, we examined the variables that are standard in the literature just described, comparing the results of regression analyses using highly aggregated data with results using disaggregated data. The variables were poverty; population density; income inequality, or GINI (Baron & Straus, 1988; Blau & Blau, 1982); and percentage of the population who are males between the ages of 15 and 29 (Greenberg, 1983; Hindelang, 1981; Hirschi & Gottfredson, 1983).

The anticipation was that we would duplicate the pattern of modest zero-order correlations between southernness and homicide rates and weak regression coefficients for race-aggregated, larger city data, while showing strong relationships for white homicide rates for smaller cities, using the same control variables.

## METHODS

### Homicide Variables

Homicide rates reported are based on the detailed U.S. Department of Justice data on homicide and nonnegligent manslaughter presented in the supplementary homicide records in *Uniform Crime Reports* (Fox & Pierce, 1987). We report two different types of rates for the time period 1976–1983: (1) the rate for males of murder and nonnegligent homicide offenders and (2) the rate for both sexes for victims of murder and nonnegligent homicide. The two variables have different and probably largely independent sources of error. The offender rate is subject to errors of misidentification; the victim rate includes homicide cases where the perpetrator was a person of a race different from that of the victim. We report homicide rates for cities of 10,000–50,000, 50,000–200,000, and more than 200,000, based on the 1980 census (1980 rather than 1990 census data were used because the detailed data are available for the 1976–1983 period). The data for all 70 central cities larger than 200,000 are reported. The other cities were randomly sampled from those for each state to select four of each size (unless there were four or fewer in a given category, in which case all cities of the size were included in the sample). This resulted in a sample of 188 small cities and 141 medium-size cities.

### Demographic Variables

*Poverty Index.* Some investigators use as their index of poverty the percentage earning less than a given amount per year. Others employ an index composed of a variety of factors indicative of poverty. These factors are invariably highly intercorrelated, but a composite of several factors obviously offers higher reliability than any single measure. The poverty index we employed was composed of five different variables, all of which have been used by other investigators, drawn from the U.S. Census for 1980. The variables, which were transformed to standard scores and weighted equally, were the following: (1) percentage of persons in the city below the poverty line, (2) percentage of households on public assistance, (3) percentage of persons over 25 years old with less than 5 years of education, (4) percentage of children living in one-parent homes, and (5) adult unemployment rate. Unfortunately, for reasons of confidentiality, the census does not break down these data into racial and ethnic categories for all smaller cities. Thus, we analyzed the data both for all cities in the sample and for just those cities that are 90% or more white and non-Hispanic. Cities consisting of 90 percent or more non-Hispanic whites only exist at the smaller two city sizes, so it was possible to perform regression analyses only for these.

*GINI Index.* The index of economic inequality was based on Adams's (1991) technique, which can be used to assess this variable for communities of relatively small size as well as cities of larger size.

*Density.* Density, or number of people per square mile in 1980, was obtained from the *County and City Data Book* (U.S. Bureau of the Census, 1983).

*Percentage of Males Age 15-29 in the White Non-Hispanic Population in 1980.* This variable was obtained from the National Planning Data Corporation, Ithaca, NY, using the U.S. census.

*Southernness Index.* Gastil's (1971) index of southernness, based on the degree to which the state was initially settled by southerners, was used as the indicator of southernness of the cities studied. States of the Confederate South (except Florida) receive a value of 30 in the index; states such as Oklahoma, with populations that initially were overwhelmingly from the South, receive a 25; those such as Colorado, with populations about half from the South at the time of settlement, receive a 20; and so on, down to those such as the New England states with very little southern population at any time, which receive a 5. Gastil's index has been criticized on several grounds, mainly because it rests on early immigration data rather than more contemporary data on the percentage in the state of southern birth. But the Gastil index and percentage of the current population born in the South are correlated beyond the .90 level (Huff-Corzine et al., 1986), so there seems to be no reason not to employ the more frequently used Gastil index.


## RESULTS

### Replicating Prior Results

It will be recalled that investigators who examine homicides in large population units, by members of all races, find small to moderate correlations between southernness and homicide rate, which then disappear or are greatly diminished when regressions are performed controlling for a package of other variables, including percentage blacks and percentage living in poverty. When we examine our data at these highly aggregated levels, using our independent variable definitions, we find the same pattern as found in the literature in general. Table 8.1 presents zero-order correlations among all variables for cities of 50,000 or more. It may be seen that southernness is correlated with both male offender rates and victim rates at moderate levels but that the percentage of the city population living in poverty and the percentage of the city population that is black are both better predictors of homicide rates than southernness. This reflects precisely the sort of situation in which the effect of southernness is likely to be underestimated by regression analyses.

It may be seen in Table 8.2 that southernness is only a very weak predictor of homicide rates net of the more powerful variables. The standardized coeffi-

**Table 8.1. Bivariate Correlations between Homicide Rates and Predictor Variables for Cities of 50,000 or More**

| | 1 | 2 | 3 | 4 | 5 | 6 | 7 | 8 | 9 |
|---|---|---|---|---|---|---|---|---|---|
| 1 Male offender | | | | | | | | | |
| 2 Victim | .97*** | | | | | | | | |
| 3 GINI | .44*** | .40*** | | | | | | | |
| 4 Density | .31*** | .31*** | .06 | | | | | | |
| 5 Poverty index | .73*** | .72*** | .55*** | .47*** | | | | | |
| 6 % Males 15–29 | –.11 | –.12 | .17 | –.15* | –.02 | | | | |
| 7 Southernness index | .40*** | .35*** | .29*** | –.28*** | .16** | .14* | | | |
| 8 Population | .35*** | .35*** | .13 | .50*** | .26*** | –.06 | –.03 | | |
| 9 % Black | .79*** | .78*** | .38*** | .29*** | .74*** | –.05 | .40*** | .19** | |

*N* of cities = 211.
* *p* < .05.
** *p* < .01.
*** *p* < .001.

**Table 8.2.  Regression Coefficients for Homicide Rates in Cities of 50,000 or More**

| Variable | Standardized Coefficient | Unstandardized Coefficient | Standard Error | *t* value |
|---|---|---|---|---|
| | | Male Offender Rate | | |
| GINI index | .044 | .195 | .208 | .937 |
| Density | −.044 | .000 | .000 | −.867 |
| Poverty index | .312 | 1.100 | .242 | 4.535*** |
| % Males 15−29 | −.109 | −.473 | .163 | −2.908** |
| Southernness index | .160 | .252 | .072 | 3.497*** |
| Population | .203 | .000 | .000 | 4.817*** |
| % Black | .449 | .355 | .048 | 7.336*** |
| | | | | Adjusted $R^2$ = .74 |
| | | Victim Rates | | |
| GINI index | −.009 | −.030 | .159 | −.187 |
| Density | −.062 | .000 | .000 | −1.129 |
| Poverty index | .352 | .889 | .184 | 4.819*** |
| % Males 15−29 | −.105 | −.329 | .124 | −2.652** |
| Southernness index | .128 | .145 | .055 | 2.628** |
| Population | .206 | .000 | .000 | 4.594*** |
| % Black | .439 | .249 | .037 | 6.742*** |
| | | | | Adjusted $R^2$ = .70 |

** $p \leq .01$.
*** $p \leq .001$.

cient for southernness is only .16 for male offender rates and approximately .13 for victim rates. The other variables also duplicate the most frequent patterns of other studies—that is, important contributions made by the poverty index, size of the city population, and percentage of blacks in the population and weak contributions made by the GINI index of inequality and by the population density variable when other variables are controlled for. Thus, our procedures reflect the general findings in the literature when highly aggregated data are analyzed.

## Differential Prediction for Whites and Blacks

Table 8.3 shows correlation coefficients and regression coefficients relating southernness to homicide rates in each of three city sizes for whites and blacks. Table 8.3 makes clear why the procedure of examining simultaneously the data for both races and all city sizes gives such a misleading picture. There is no relationship between region and homicide rates for blacks at all, except for offender rates for the smallest cities. Thus, it is not merely potentially misleading to fail to disaggregate the two races; Table 8.3 shows that it is empirically a mistake if one wishes to know the relationship between region and homicide rates for either race separately. Table 8.2 indicates only a very weak relationship between southernness and homicide when other variables are controlled, whereas Table 8.3 shows that, for whites there actually is a relationship for

**Table 8.3. Correlations and Regression Coefficients Relating Southernness and Homicide Rates for Whites and Blacks as a Function of City Size (Regression Coefficients in Parentheses)**

| City Size | Whites | | Blacks | |
|---|---|---|---|---|
| | Male Offender Rate | Victim Rate | Male Offender Rate | Victim Rate |
| 10–50,000 | .37*** | .42*** | .35*** | .14 |
| | (.20)** | (.23)** | (.21)* | (.11) |
| 50–200,000 | .40*** | .39*** | .10 | .06 |
| | (.32)*** | (.31)*** | (.14) | (−.02) |
| > 200,000 | .10 | .06 | −.03 | .02 |
| | (.29)* | (.28)† | (.05) | (.14) |

  † $p < .10$.
  * $p < .05$.
 ** $p < .01$.
*** $p < .001$.

whites that has been obscured. A similar point can be made for city size. Table 8.1 indicates moderate zero-order correlations between population size and homicide rates when medium and large cities are examined together, whereas Table 8.3 shows that this is misleading. There is a moderate zero-order association for medium-size cities (and for small cities) but essentially no zero-order relationship among the very largest cities.

There are two puzzles in Table 8.3. The first is, why are the null zero-order correlations between southernness and white homicide rates for large cities replaced by moderate coefficients from the regression analyses? We suspect this is the case because, unlike the situation in small and medium cities, poverty is less common for whites in the large cities of the South than for whites in the large cities of the North. Hence, controlling for poverty in the regression analyses has the effect of revealing an association between southernness and homicide net of poverty differences favoring the South. The second puzzle is, why is there a significant association between southernness and black homicide rates for small cities only, for male offender rates only? We have no good speculation about this.

## Examining Relationships for Cities that Are Overwhelmingly White

The analyses in Table 8.3 probably underestimate substantially the relationship between southernness and homicide for whites. It will be recalled that the poverty and GINI variables (and the population density variable) are defined over the whole population for the analyses in Tables 8.1–8.3. But of course, this procedure introduces a substantial source of systematic error into the data. Blacks and Hispanics are poorer than whites, and yet their data are used to estimate the values for whites as well (in our study as in the literature in general). The

**Table 8.4. Standardized Regression Coefficients for White Non-Hispanic Homicide Rates for Cities That Are 90% or More White and Non-Hispanic**

| | City Size | | | |
| --- | --- | --- | --- | --- |
| | 10,000–50,000 | | 50,000–200,000 | |
| Variable | Male Offender Rate | Victim Rate | Male Offender Rate | Victim Rate |
| --- | --- | --- | --- | --- |
| GINI Index | −.03 | .15 | .26* | .14 |
| Density | −.05 | −.08 | −.11 | −.14 |
| Poverty Index | .38*** | .25* | .42*** | .46*** |
| % Males 15–29 | −.10 | −.06 | −.22* | −.20* |
| Southernness index | .37*** | .43*** | .52** | .64** |
| $R^2$ | .29 | .33 | .49 | .57 |

*Note.* N of cities of size 10–50,000 = 101; N of cities size 50–200,000 = 60.
  \* $p < .05$.
 \*\* $p < .01$.
\*\*\* $p < .001$.

analyses in Table 8.4 avoid this problem to a degree by examining the white homicide data only for cities that are 90% or more white and non-Hispanic. (Data are presented only for small and medium-size cities; there are no large cities having populations that are 90 percent or more non-Hispanic whites.) Table 8.4 shows that the relationships between region and homicide rate for whites are slightly stronger than those presented in Table 8.3 when these more refined independent variables are entered into the regression analyses.

The results in Table 8.4 are thoroughly in agreement with the findings of other studies of the entire population of larger cities—for all variables *except* southernness. As in studies of large cities, we find poverty to be a very strong predictor of homicide; and we do not find income inequality (GINI), population density, or percentage of males 15–29 to be very important predictors. In contrast with other studies, however, we find southernness to be a very important variable, even in comparison with poverty. (We do not include a variable representing the percentage of blacks in the population in the analyses in Table 8.4 because the percentage of blacks in the population should be irrelevant, theoretically, to white homicide rates in a sample of cities in which the great majority of the citizens are white. However, when regression analyses are conducted including percentage of blacks as an independent variable, the results are virtually identical to the ones reported in Table 8.4.)

## Magnitude of Regional Differences in Homicide Rates

The magnitude of the differences in white homicide rates between North and South is revealed in Table 8.5 showing rates at each of the three different city sizes. For ease of presentation, we clustered homicide rate data for the 48 contiguous states into seven different regions: New England (CT, MA, ME, NH,

**Table 8.5. White Non-Hispanic Homicide Rates from 1976 to 1983 as a Function of Region and City Size (Ordered by Increasing Southernness of Origin of the Region's Inhabitants)**

| | City Size | | | | | | | | |
| | 10,000–50,000 | | | 50,000–200,000 | | | More than 200,000 | | |
| Region | Male Offender Rate | Victim Rate | N | Male Offender Rate | Victim Rate | N | Male Offender Rate | Victim Rate | N |
|---|---|---|---|---|---|---|---|---|---|
| New England | 2.72 | 1.88 | 23 | 4.58 | 2.76 | 15 | 13.88 | 10.69 | 1 |
| Middle Atlantic | 4.21 | 2.47 | 18 | 3.74 | 3.27 | 13 | 14.08 | 13.02 | 8 |
| Midwest | 3.08 | 2.26 | 52 | 5.07 | 3.95 | 40 | 14.25 | 10.92 | 15 |
| Pacific | 6.65 | 3.77 | 31 | 7.36 | 5.20 | 18 | 17.38 | 13.66 | 6 |
| Mountain | 6.60 | 4.80 | 12 | 6.28 | 4.36 | 10 | 13.35 | 11.81 | 12 |
| Southwest | 6.58 | 4.87 | 12 | 8.70 | 6.14 | 12 | 19.33 | 17.50 | 9 |
| South | 9.16 | 6.35 | 40 | 9.36 | 6.74 | 33 | 13.79 | 11.80 | 19 |
| Ratio of South to New England | 3.36 | 3.38 | | 2.04 | 2.44 | | .99 | 1.10 | |

**Table 8.6. White Non-Hispanic Homicide Rates from 1976 to 1983 for Cities That Are 90% or More White and Non-Hispanic (Ordered by Increasing Southernness of Origin of the Region's Inhabitants)**

| | City Size | | | | | |
|---|---|---|---|---|---|---|
| | 10,000–50,000 | | | 50,000–200,000 | | |
| Region | Male Offender Rate | Victim Rate | N | Male Offender Rate | Victim Rate | N |
| New England | 2.62 | 1.77 | 22 | 3.16 | 1.63 | 11 |
| Middle Atlantic | 1.90 | 1.02 | 10 | 3.35 | 2.49 | 7 |
| Midwest | 2.92 | 1.97 | 45 | 3.37 | 2.20 | 24 |
| Pacific | 4.62 | 2.64 | 8 | 6.10 | 4.26 | 5 |
| Mountain | 4.67 | 3.26 | 14 | 4.56 | 3.14 | 8 |
| Southwest | 5.13 | 4.69 | 4 | 4.47 | 2.84 | 2 |
| South | 8.23 | 4.85 | 9 | 6.63 | 4.49 | 4 |
| Ratio of South to New England | 3.14 | 2.74 | | 2.10 | 2.75 | |

RI, VT), the Mid-Atlantic region (NJ, NY, PA), the Midwest (IA, IL, IN, KS, MI, MN, MO, NB, ND, OH, SD, WI), the Pacific region (CA, OR, WA), the Mountain region (AZ, CO, ID, MT, NM, NV, UT, WY), the Southwest (AR, LA, OK, TX), and the South (AL, DE, FL, GA, KY, MD, MS, NC, SC, TN, WV, VA). The regions are listed in Table 8.5 in order of their degree of southernness as defined by Gastil's index, but the ordering of regions would be the same if we used the percentage of residents born in the South as our indicator of southernness.

It may be seen in Table 8.5 that there is no regional difference at all at the very largest city sizes (over 200,000), whereas there are differences between the South and New England of more than two to one for cities between 50,000 and 200,000 and between 10,000 and 50,000. There are comparable differences for the southern and southwestern states versus the eastern and midwestern states. Table 8.6 shows that the situation is the same for that portion of the sample composed only of cities for which the population consists of 90% or more non-Hispanic whites. Recall that for these cities the poverty data are relatively meaningful for the white population because they are based largely on whites.

## Conflict-Related versus Felony-Related Homicides

If it is the residue of the culture of honor that fuels high homicide rates in the South, then one would expect that it would be argument- and conflict-related homicide, not felony-related homicide, that would be more common in the South. Arguments are likely to result in affronts that might prompt violence. In contrast, homicides occurring in other contexts, such as a robbery or burglary, should probably differ little by region. The Fox and Pierce (1987) *Supplemen-*

**Table 8.7. White Male Homicide Rates for Felony-Related and Argument-Related Murders as a Function of Region of the U.S. and City Size**

| Murders | City Size Less Than 200,000 | City Size 200,000 or More |
|---|---|---|
| Felony-related | | |
| Non-South | .88 | 3.22 |
| South and Southwest | 1.16 | 2.25 |
| Argument-related | | |
| Non-South | 2.13 | 6.51 |
| South and Southwest | 4.77 | 7.66 |

*tary Homicide Reports* code homicides in such a way that one may classify them as argument- or conflict-related (for example, barroom quarrels, lover's triangles) versus felony-related. (Some homicide types cannot be placed unambiguously into one category or the other—for example, "drug-related" homicides.) We added together all the plausibly argument-related homicide categories and added together all the homicides occurring in the context of some other felony, and we compared the two sorts of homicides in cities of different sizes in the South and Southwest versus other regions of the country.

It may be seen in Table 8.7 that white male homicide rates in smaller cities in the South and Southwest are elevated only for argument-related murders. The interaction based on raw frequencies is significant at beyond the .001 level. For larger cities, there are more argument-related homicides proportionately in the South and Southwest and fewer felony-related homicides, so the same interaction obtains, again significant at beyond the .001 level.

## DISCUSSION

### Homicide Rates for Whites in South versus North

We have found that white homicide rates are higher in the South than in the North. For small and medium-size cities the differences in homicide rate as a function of southernness are dramatic. These differences survive regression analyses controlling for variables that have been studied by others who examine homicide rates. And the differences are particularly strong when the error in the covariates is reduced by examining cities with populations consisting of 90% or more whites. For large cities, there is no zero-order relationship between Southernness and homicide rates, but a relationship emerges when regression analyses are performed. This pattern likely occurs because, unlike the pattern in small and medium-size cities, large southern cities have fewer people living in poverty than do large northern ones. Since white rates of homicide are the same for large southern and northern cities despite the fact that there are fewer impoverished people in southern cities than in northern ones and because poverty in all regions is associated with high homicide rates, regression analyses show southern rates for whites to be higher than would be expected on the basis of the wealth of the cities. This prevents us from confirming the hypothesis that regional differences are more marked for smaller cities than for larger ones. One simply cannot answer the question until more precise data are available. It should be noted, however, that differences in the very most rural counties of the South have homicide rates more than four times higher than those of the North, despite the fact that income is virtually the same in northern and southern rural counties (Reaves & Nisbett, 1994).

Except for our findings about southernness, our results for whites concur with those of investigators using aggregated data. We find that poverty is associated with higher homicide rates at all city sizes, and we find population density, GINI, and percentage of population who are young males to be only very weakly related to homicide rates.

## Culture and Homicide

Despite the fact that relationships between southernness and homicide rates are large and clear for whites, they are virtually nonexistent for blacks. We believe this is because black culture is less different from region to region than is white culture. To the extent that homicide rates are influenced by culture, one would not expect large regional differences for blacks.

Our results support a cultural interpretation of homicide rates in another important respect as well. It is rates for argument- and conflict-related homicide, not felony-related homicide, that are particularly elevated in the South. This is precisely the pattern predicted by the culture-of-honor thesis.

There are also several respects in which our results speak against any purely non-cultural explanations of southern violence. Though poverty accounts for a substantial amount of the difference between regions, it can scarcely be the sole explanation. First, when our analyses are conducted, they show that regional effects are important independent of poverty. Second, the results of Cohen and Nisbett (1994) on attitudes toward violence in highly rural counties show that there are strong regional differences even though the counties do not differ in income levels. Moreover, income and education are not related to attitudes toward violence in the same way that region is. (It is also important to note that northern and southern counties do not differ in the fraction of homes where a gun is present.)

The temperature explanation of homicide differences cannot be the sole one. It should be noted first that the differences reported here are completely outside the range of differences associated with temperature. Temperature differences between North and South do not appear likely to account for more than a 25% difference in homicide rates. The differences we report here go as high as 3 to 1. Second, temperature differences could not account for the fact that differences in homicide rate between regions of the country rise dramatically as size of the locality decreases. (A third point against temperature is that the herding regions of Britain, which are in the North, have higher homicide rates today than the farming regions. Similarly, the herding regions in the north of

India are reputedly more violent than the farming regions in the South and the herding regions in the North of Mexico are reputedly more violent than the farming regions in the South.)

Finally, slavery seems less likely in view of the finding by Reaves and Nisbett (1994) that homicide rates today are higher in the herding, nonslavery parts of the South than in the nonherding parts. (In addition, the reputation of the South for violence much precedes the point at which there were substantially more slaves in the South than in the North.)

Of course, the present results cannot establish conclusively that it is southern culture, rather than something correlated with it, that affects white homicide rates. It remains possible that something else, noncultural, not yet examined, is correlated with southernness and that that noncultural variable is the causally important one.

But the present study, together with converging evidence from our program at both the societal and individual levels, serves to rescue the culture explanation of regional differences in homicide from the oblivion into which it has been consigned by the recent literature. The cultural hypothesis will remain a viable hypothesis until someone finds that there is indeed some noncultural factor, associated with southernness for whites but not for blacks, that accounts for the relationship.

## REFERENCES

Adams, T. K. (1991). *Calculation of GINI index for low-population areas of the U.S.* Ann Arbor: University of Michigan, Institute for Social Research Technical Report.

Anderson, C. A. (1989). Temperature and aggression: Ubiquitous effects of heat on occurrence of human violence. *Psychological Bulletin, 106,* 74–96.

Archer, D., & Gartner, R. (1984). *Violence and crime in cross-national perspective.* New Haven, CT: Yale University Press.

Bailey, R. (1989). Blacks in northern cities. In C. R. Wilson & W. Ferris (Eds.), *Encyclopedia of southern culture.* Chapel Hill: University of North Carolina Press.

Baron, L., &, Straus, M. A. (1988). Cultural and economic sources of homicide in the United States. *Sociological Quarterly, 29,* 371–390.

Blau, J. R., & Blau, P. M. (1982). The cost of inequality: Metropolitan structure and violent crime. *American Sociological Review, 47,* 114–129.

Cash, W. J. (1941). *The mind of the South.* New York: Knopf.

Cohen, D., & Nisbett, R. E. (1994). Self-protection and the culture of honor: Explaining southern violence. *Personality and Social Psychology Bulletin, 20,* 551–567.

Cohen, D., Nisbett, R. E., Bowdle, B., & Schwarz, N. (1994). *Regional culture and response to insults: An experimental ethnography.* Unpublished manuscript, University of Michigan.

Crèvecoeur, J. H. St. J. (1981). *Letters from an American farmer.* Hammondsworth, England: Penguin Books. (Original work published 1782)

Daly, M., & Wilson, M. (1988). *Homicide.* New York: Aldine de Gruyter.

Fischer, D. H. (1989). *Albion's seed: Four British folkways in America.* New York: Oxford University Press.

Fox, J. A., & Pierce, G. L. (1987). *Uniform crime reports: United States Supplementary homicide reports 1976–1983*. Boston: Northeastern University, Center for Applied Social Research.

Friday, P. C. (1983). Urban crime. In S. H. Kadish, (Ed.), *Encyclopedia of criminal justice*. New York: Free Press.

Galle, O., Gove, W., & McPherson, J. M. (1972). Population density and social pathology: What are the relationships for man? *Science, 176,* 23–30.

Gastil, R. D. (1971). Homicide and a regional culture of violence. *American Sociological Review, 36,* 416–427.

Gordon, R. A. (1986). Issues in multiple regression. *American Journal of Sociology, 78,* 592–616.

Greenberg, D. F. (1983). Age and crime. In S. H. Kadish (Ed.), *Encyclopedia of criminal justice*. New York: Free Press.

Harer, M. D., & Steffensmeier, D. (1992). The differing effects of economic inequality on Black and White rates of violence. *Social Forces, 70,* 1035–1054.

Harries, K. D. (1974). *The geography of crime and justice*. New York: McGraw-Hill.

Harries, K. D. (1980). *Crime and the environment*. Springfield, IL: Charles C. Thomas.

Hindelang, M. J. (1981). Variations in sex-race-age-specific incidence rates of offending. *American Sociological Review, 46,* 461–474.

Hirschi, T., & Gottfredson, M. (1983). Age and the explanation of crime. *American Journal of Sociology, 89,* 552–584.

Huff-Corzine, L., Corzine, J., & Moore, D. C. (1986). Southern exposure: Deciphering the South's influence on homicide rates. *Social Forces, 64,* 907–924.

Klein, L. R. (1962). *An introduction to econometrics*. Englewood Cliffs, NJ: Prentice-Hall.

Land, K. E., McCall, P. L., & Cohen, L. E. (1990). Structural covariates of homicide rates: Are there any invariances across time and social space? *American Journal of Sociology, 95,* 922–963.

Loftin, C., & Hill, R. H. (1974). Regional subculture and homicide: An examination of the Gastil-Hackney thesis. *American Sociological Review, 39,* 714–724.

Loftin, C., & Parker, R. N. (1985). An errors-in-variable model of the effect of poverty on urban homicide rates. *Criminology, 23,* 269–287.

Lowie, R. H. (1954). *Indians of the plain*. New York: McGraw-Hill.

Lundsgaarde, H. P. (1977). *Murder in Space City: A cultural analysis of Houston homicide patterns*. New York: Oxford University Press.

McCarthy, J. D., Galle, O. R., & Zimmern, W. (1975). Population density, social structure, and interpersonal violence. *American Behavioral Scientist, 18,* 771–791.

McPherson, J. M. (1972). *Lacunae in causal model research*. Unpublished doctoral dissertation, Vanderbilt University, Nashville, TN.

McWhiney, G. (1988). *Cracker culture: Celtic ways in the old South*. Tuscaloosa: University of Alabama Press.

Messner, S. F. (1982). Poverty, inequality, and the urban homicide rate. *Criminology, 20,* 103–114.

Messner, S. F. (1983). Regional and racial effects on the urban homicide rate: The subculture of violence revisited. *American Journal of Sociology, 88,* 997–1007.

Messner, S. F., & Gordon, R. M. (1992). Racial inequality and racially disaggregated homicide rates: An assessment of alternative theoretical explanations. *Criminology, 34,* 421–445.

Nettler, G. (1984). *Explaining crime* (3rd ed.). New York: McGraw-Hill.

Parker, R. N. (1989). Poverty, subculture of violence, and type of homicide. *Social Forces*, *67*, 983–1007.

Parker, R. N., & Smith, M. D. (1979). Deterrence, poverty, and type of homicide. *American Journal of Sociology*, *85*, 614–624.

Peristiany, J. G. (Ed.). (1965). *Honour and shame: The values of Mediterranean society*. London: Weidenfeld & Nicolson.

Reaves, A., & Nisbett, R. E. (1994). *Ecology, culture and homicide.* Unpublished manuscript, University of Michigan, Ann Arbor.

Reed, J. S. (1971). To live—and die—in Dixie: A contribution to the study of southern violence. *Political Science Quarterly*, *3*, 429–443.

Reed, J. S. (1981). Below the Smith and Wesson line: Reflections on southern violence. In M. Black & J. S. Reed (Eds.), *Perspectives on the American South: An annual review of society, politics, and culture.* New York: Cordon & Breach Science Publications.

Schmitt, R. C. (1966). Density, health, and social organization. *Journal of the American Institute of Planners*, *32*, 38–40.

Simpson, M. E. (1985). Violent crime, income inequality, and regional culture: Another look. *Sociological Focus*, *18*, 199–208.

Smith, M. D., & Parker, R. N. (1980). Type of homicide and variation in regional rates. *Social Forces*, *59*, 136–147.

Tocqueville, A. (1969). *Democracy in America* (J. P. Mayer, Ed.; G. Lawrence, Trans.). Garden City, NY: University of Chicago Press. (Original work published 1835)

U.S. Bureau of the Census. (1983). *County and city data book.* Washington, DC: U.S. Government Printing Office.

U.S. Department of Justice. (1984). *Uniform crime reports: U. S. supplementary homicide reports, 1976–1983.* Washington, DC: U.S. Government Printing Office.

Williams, K. R. (1984). Economic sources of homicide: Reestimating the effects of poverty and inequality. *American Sociological Review*, *49*, 283–289.

Wilson, C. R., & Ferris, W. (Eds.). (1989). *Southern culture.* Chapel Hill: University of North Carolina Press.

Winsborough, H. H. (1970). The social consequences of high population density. In T. Ford & C. DeJong (Eds.), *Social demography* (pp. 84–90). Englewood Cliffs, NJ: Prentice-Hall.

Wolfgang, M. E., & Ferracuti, F. (1967). *The subculture of violence.* London: Tavistock Publications.

Wyatt-Brown, B. (1986). *Honor and violence in the Old South.* New York: Oxford.

*Acknowledgments*: We are indebted to Terry Adams for making available his GINI data and to Christopher Achen, David Buss, Dov Cohen, Reynolds Farley, Susan Jenkins, Hazel Markus, Andrew Reaves, and Claude Steele for helpful advice and criticism. Some of the data reported in this chapter appeared in summary form in Nisbett (1993).

**9**

# A Social Interactionist Approach to Violence: Cross-Cultural Applications

**Richard B. Felson**
**James T. Tedeschi**

Interpersonal violence is more prevalent in some cultures than in others. While the rate of interpersonal violence varies across cultures, the goals may be the same everywhere. In this chapter we apply a "social interactionist theory" to cross-cultural data on aggression and violence. We propose that all violence is goal-oriented and that the incentives and at least some of the social dynamics leading to such behavior are similar in different cultures.

A social interactionist perspective, as proposed by Tedeschi and Felson (1994), is an attempt to provide a comprehensive theory of goal-oriented or instrumental aggression (see also Felson & Tedeschi, 1993). This approach attempts to integrate previously separate literatures on aggression and violence, social power and influence, social conflict and negotiations, retributive justice, and self-presentation. According to social interactionist theory, an individual engages in harmful actions in order to gain compliance, redress grievances, and promote or defend valued identities. This chapter applies the theory to the cross-cultural literature on aggression and violence with the goal of providing an integration of the evidence.

We first provide an overview of the social interactionist approach. The basic assumptions of the theory, its major concepts, and its relationship with other theories of aggression are briefly presented. Then we indicate how the theory interprets incidents of violence in different cultures. Our goal is to illustrate how the theory can be applied cross-culturally rather than to exhaustively review the available data. While our selection of cases is not systematic, in no case did we omit cases because they did not fit our scheme.

## THE SOCIAL INTERACTIONIST PERSPECTIVE

A social interactionist perspective rests on three major assumptions. First, harm-doing and the threat of harm are motivated to achieving interpersonal goals. The actor is viewed as a decision-maker who acts in terms of benefits, costs, and moral values. Second, the approach emphasizes situational factors in the development of coercive interactions. The relationship between the parties, the dynamics of the interchange between them, and the presence or absence of third parties are all relevant for explaining harm-doing. While the focus is on situational factors, it is recognized that individual differences are also important. Third, a social interactionist perspective requires an understanding of the phenomenology of actors, who often view their own harm-doing as legitimate and even moralistic. To understand why people engage in harm-doing it is necessary to examine their perceptions, judgments, expectations, and values.

A social interactionist approach is an alternative to the frustration-aggression hypothesis, which views aggression and violence as involuntary responses to frustration or aversive stimuli (e.g., Berkowitz, 1993). The latter viewpoint assumes some biological basis for the connection between frustration and aggression, but there is no evidence for a special system of aggressive behavior in humans.[1]

In our overview of the theory we first define coercive actions and relate them to concepts of aggression and violence. Then we describe the factors considered by the person in making decisions to perform coercive actions. Finally, we examine the processes leading to the use of coercion when individuals are attempting to force compliance, restore justice, and assert or defend identities.

## Coercive Actions

A coercive action is one where the intent is to either to impose a harm on another person or to force compliance. In a coercive action, harm or compliance is valued because it will lead to some distal (or more remote) outcome that is valued. For example, actors might value harm to the target because they believe it will result in justice or they might value compliance because they believe it will lead to tangible benefits.

There are three kinds of coercive actions: threats, bodily force, and punishment. The communication of an intent to do harm is a threat. Bodily force involves the attempt to physically constrain the target to force compliance. Punishment involves an act performed with the intention of causing harm to another person. Tedeschi and Felson (1994) distinguished between three types of punishment: physical punishments, deprivation of resources, and social punishments (e.g., insults). In this chapter "violence" refers to the use of physical punishments, threats of physical punishments, or bodily force.[2]

## Decision Making

The use of coercion is viewed as the result of a decision-making process. A coercion action, no matter how impulsive or spontaneous it appears, involves a string of decisions. The actor must decide not only whether to attack but how to carry it out. Even those theorists who posit a frustration-aggression mechanism implicitly include a decision-making process (e.g., Berkowitz, 1993). While for them the impulse to aggression is involuntary they acknowledge that decisions about costs may inhibit aggressive behavior. We differ from them in seeing both instigation and inhibition as a function of decision-making.

The basic elements involved in a decision include the expectations of success in achieving outcomes, the values of outcomes, and the expectations and negative values of costs. The greater the expected value and the lower the expected cost associated with a coercive action, the greater the likelihood of a coercive action. A weak form of rationality is relevant in many coercive interactions since these encounters often involve quick decisions, strong emotions, and alcohol intoxication. These factors may lead to a failure to consider costs or alternative behavior. In addition, individuals may enact some script they have learned, without giving their decision much thought. Scripts are programs for behavior stored in memory that when elicited may serve as guides to behavior (Abelson, 1976). When the behavior associated with a script has been used repeatedly and successfully in the past, one might call it habitual. However, the effect of scripts on behavior is not automatic; the individual retains the capacity to veto scripted or habitual action, depending on the evaluations of costs.

Our perspective is compatible with social learning theory, which also views harm-doing as instrumental behavior (Bandura, 1973). Social learning theory focuses on the learning of scripts, primarily through observation, instruction, and trial-and-error behavior, and the activation of the relevant behavior by the expectation of rewards (Huesmann, 1988). Social learning theory is useful primarily as a theory of socialization but it ignores the social context of aggressive behavior. It has little to say about the situational factors that lead to aggression or about what the incentives (or motives) for aggression are.[3]

### Incentives for Using Coercion

As indicated above, an act of coercion is intended to produce behavioral compliance or harm to the target. Compliance is valued primarily because it brings tangible benefits. Harm is valued because it produces justice, favorable identities, and compliance. We discuss compliance first as an incentive for coercion and then justice and identity as special motives.

*Compliance*.  One major reason for using coercion is to control the behavior of other people. Threats may be used to compel or deter specific behaviors, when the source expects compliance to mediate desired outcomes. Punishments are used to deter unwanted behavior and to encourage future compliance by the target. Compliance may mediate a wide range of values for a coercive actor, ranging from the material possessions desired by a robber to the rule conformity by children that is valued by parents.

There are many ways to achieve behavioral changes in others. Among such influence tactics are promises, persuasion, control of environmental contingencies, and so on (Cf., Tedeschi, Schlenker, & Bonoma, 1973). Sometimes, coercion is the influence tactic of last resort (Schank & Abelson, 1977; Bisanz & Rule, 1989). Nevertheless, in conflict situations noncoercive means become less effective because of self-interest and distrust, and coercion may become the means of first resort. Also, there are individual differences in social learning so that some people have a coercive influence style and tend to use it as a first choice in certain situations.

*Justice*.  Coercion may be used in the pursuit of retributive justice. The motive to restore justice is associated with grievances. Grievances are complaints based on the perception by grievants that they have been treated unfairly and that an offender is blameworthy. Grievances are common in social life since people frequently break rules or otherwise engage in behavior that is offensive to others. In addition, various attributional biases lead people to attribute blame to others for negative outcomes when none is warranted. Blaming people can help explain traumatic events that are otherwise difficult to understand. Blaming others can be a way of avoiding self-blame when joint effort produces negative outcomes. Also, people have a tendency to attribute the behavior of others to internal factors and to ignore situational factors (Heider, 1958). Finally, some people have a paranoid bias in making attributions, and are more likely to perceive hostile intentions in ambiguous circumstances (Dodge and Crick, 1990).

While there are a number of ways in which justice might be restored, such as by restitution or an apology, the grievant may seek to restore justice by punishing the offender. The grievant views the punishment as retribution, i.e., as a legitimate and justifiable response to the misdeeds of the other. The proximate goal is to harm the offender and the distal value is the restoration of justice. This type of coercion is "moralistic" in the sense that the actor feels justified in punishing the wrongdoer. The degree of punishment is a function of the severity of the offense, the reaction of the offender to the accusation, and other factors. The grievant may also use punishment to deter the target and others from repeating the offense. Because of this deterrent function, the use of coercion by grievants is sometimes described as a form of informal social control.[4]

***Identity***. Coercion may be used to establish or to protect identities. Coercion as an assertive form of self-presentation may be intended to establish an identity as a tough and courageous person. Such behavior is particularly common among young men. School-aged bullies, for example, prey on vulnerable targets in order to demonstrate their power (Besag, 1989). Coercion, in the form of criticism and gossip, may also be used to make another person seem inferior, so that the actor appears superior in comparison (Wills, 1981; Melburg & Tedeschi, 1989).

Defensive self-presentation occurs when a person is attacked by another person. Any attack casts the target into a negative identity by making the target appear weak and ineffectual. A counter-attack can nullify that image, and maintain one's honor. Retaliation is therefore a way of "saving face" when one has been attacked—a form of defensive self-presentation (Arkin, 1981). Since a counter-attack casts its target into a negative identity, it often motivates a counter-counter-attack, creating a "conflict spiral." Antagonists attempt to win these character contests rather than limit their punishments to fit the offense. Partly due to the involvement of social identities, small disputes sometimes escalate into incidents involving physical violence (Felson & Steadman, 1983; Luckenbill, 1977).

***Multiple Goals***. Any particular real world coercive episode may involve multiple goals for the interactants. The theory of coercive actions artificially untangles the processes for purposes of analysis and research, but applications to everyday events may often involve overlapping processes and goals. For example, dispute-related violence often begins with the expression of a grievance and then escalate when identities are attacked (Felson, 1984; Luckenbill, 1977). Concern for justice and deterrence may be central in the initial stages of the encounter whereas social identities become more salient as the incident escalates.

# CROSS-CULTURAL APPLICATIONS

Despite the tendency of some theorists to label cultures as "aggressive" or "nonaggressive," coercion is used in all societies. However, the form of coercion varies considerably across cultures. The Utku Eskimo is proscribed from using physical forms of coercion, while Yanamomo boys are encouraged to hit and kick others to get their way in social interactions (Briggs, 1970; Chagnon, 1977).[5] The Utku Eskimo however, do use other forms of coercion such as insults, gossip, withdrawal of affection, and shunning. Ostracism is the most severe form of punishment in Utku society.

In this section we provide examples from the literature of the processes we described above. Some of the coercive interactions described are common and some are unusual; hopefully our theory can account for both. By providing these examples, we give some idea of situational factors that instigate coercive actions and what the social context of that behavior is.

First, we discuss the use of coercion to force compliance, usually for economic or sexual purposes. Then we consider the use of coercion by grievants to restore justice and exact social control. We give examples from different cultures of the types of offenses that produce grievances and the way grievances are expressed. We pay particular attention to the role of third parties who sometimes intervene on behalf of the aggrieved party. Finally, we discuss the role of social identities in coercive interactions. We give examples of insults and other violations of politeness norms, and describe the effect of third parties who may witness these events.

## Coercion and Compliance

Violence is frequently used to force compliance and obtain some economic or sexual benefit. In large-scale societies, robbers use threats or bodily force to get money or material goods from their victims. Their anonymity often protects them from criminal prosecution, thereby lowering their expected costs. People who live in tribal societies have little opportunity to harm another member of the group and remain anonymous. In tribal societies, it is more common for members of one group to raid another group in order to achieve an economic benefit. Raids may be used to acquire food, cattle, or some other valued good.

Conflict over scarce resources is an important factor in producing coercive episodes. Felson (1983) found that the most important source of conflict between siblings in the United States was over the use and distribution of property in the home. For example, siblings frequently fought over what television show to watch. Among the Mbuti, men fight over hunting territories (Turnbull, 1965). The scarcity of females is a key feature of fighting and killing among the Yananomo men of Brazil (Chagnon, 1970). When several people want the same resource and cannot or are not willing to share it, the incentives for using coercion are likely to be high.

It is the rule rather than the exception for the Yanomamo to intimidate others to obtain food or resources. Chagnon (1970) writes "... it was not as difficult to become calloused to the incessant begging as it was to ignore ... the intimidation and aggression with which the demands were made. It was likewise difficult to adjust to the fact that the Yanomamo refused to accept "no" for an answer until or unless it seethed with passion and intimidation" (p. 8). Chagnon reported that he was initially confused over reciprocity patterns and when he offered anything to villagers they would return in droves to demand or beg for more. Asking or demanding with intimidation reflects the normative pattern of influence used.

The social organization of a society affects the types of conflicts that arise. In polygynous societies, co-wives tend to quarrel over sexual access to husbands, wealth distribution, and disciplining of children (Levinson, 1989). In tribal societies that are egalitarian, conflicts seldom occur about political control (Knauft, 1987). In societies where property is shared, conflicts seldom develop over property.

Coercion is sometimes used by males to force females to have sex with them. In 77% of a sample of tribal societies (N=65) males were described as either verbally or physically aggressive in their sexual advances (Broude & Greene, 1976). The use of coercive and non-coercive influence techniques by males may be based in part on sex differences in sexual selectivity.[6] The fact that females are more selective than males creates conflict between the sexes; as a result some males use coercion to produce sexual compliance.

When the people involved know each other, sexual coercion tends to be used as a last resort, after other influence techniques have failed (Kanin, 1983; 1985). The use of sexual coercion following failed attempts using other techniques was apparent in a study of the Mehinaku Indians of Brazil (Gregor, 1990). The males in this society show a much stronger proclivity than females to engage in sexual activity and they initiate most sexual interactions. The men attempt to encourage women to engage in sexual relations frequently by offering fish in exchange. They describe unwilling females as "stingy with their genitals, when the women refuse, their sexual overtures, the men may use some level of coercion—described vaguely as "pulling"— to force the women into the bush.

Among the Gusii of southwestern Kenya (Levine, 1959) males sometimes use sexual coercion when they lack the resources to obtain sexual experiences in other ways. When a Gusii man does not have the economic means, the attractiveness, or social skill to acquire a wife, he may abduct a woman from another clan for sexual purposes. According to Levine, inflation in the bridewealth price (the number of cattle transferred from the father of the groom to the father of the bride) resulted in an increase in the incidence of rape.

In some cultures, males use the threat of rape to deter certain offenses by females (see, e.g., Murphy, 1959). For example, among the Mehinaku Indians of Brazil (Gregor, 1990), the threat of group rape is used to prevent women from observing certain male ritual objects. The method is apparently successful as a form of social control: because of their intense fear of rape, the women never violated the rule, and a group rape had not occurred for at least forty years. Rape is condoned as a method of keeping females away from male ritual objects in a number of tropical forest societies in South America and in Highland New Guinea (for a review, see Sanday, 1981).

In these societies rape is a legitimate sanction specifically designed to deter particular forms of deviant behavior. The social control function is straightforward and unambiguous. In most societies, rape is not condoned by the group—in fact, it is a criminal act subject to severe punishment. In addition, most rapists do not specifically target deviant women in a conscious attempt to deter future violations.[7] We could conclude that in most societies, rape is not used as a form of social control (Tedeschi & Felson, 1994).

## Justice and the Grievance Process

Dispute-related violence usually begins with the expression of a grievance. The sequence of events in the development of a grievance begins with some negative event. The victim tries to discern whether the event was caused by another person, and whether the action was intentional or malevolent (Ferguson & Rule, 1981). Intentional actions that are perceived as malevolent are seen as particularly blameworthy.[8] The tendencies to make internal and external attributions, to perceive intentions, and to see a person as responsible for some of their actions but not others, are apparently human universals (Brown, 1991).

If blame is assigned a grievance is formed. A person with a grievance is motivated to redress the injustice that has been done and to deter similar antinormative actions by the offender and by other people in the future. Punishment is more likely if the costs are not too high, if deterrence is expected to be successful, and if the offender fails to show remorse or provide an acceptable account. The more blame attributed to offenders and the more harmful their actions, the more severe the punishment. The notion of retribution or negative reciprocity is probably also a human universal (Brown, 1991).

The development of grievances in a culture depends on beliefs about the rules of behavior and attributions of blame to people who are perceived as violating those rules. We first describe the source of grievances in different cultures. Then we describe some of the ways in which those grievances are expressed. Finally we consider the role of third parties in handling grievances.

***The Source of Grievances.*** For every norm there is the potential for its violation. In an attempt to classify norm violations, Mikula, Petri, and Tanzer (1989) asked respondents from Austria, Bulgaria, Finland, and Germany to recall experiences of injustice. Factor analysis revealed three basic types of injustice (or norm violations): distributive, procedural, and interactional. Distributive justice refers to a fair allocation of benefits and responsibilities, and recognition of performance. Procedural justice refers to the means used by individuals to resolve conflicts of interest. Interaction justice involves conformity to norms about demeanor, respect, and politeness toward other people.

Interaction justice was by far the most important category of unjust events reported by respondents in the data collected by Mikula, et al. (1989). The most frequent unjust experiences in these European societies referred to lack of loyalty, lack of regard for the feelings of others, selfishness, accusations or censure, hostility, and failure to keep agreements. Similar types of injustices were reported in a study by Messick, Bloom, Boldizar, and Samuelson (1985) in the United States and by Yeung (in press) among Hong Kong Chinese. Subjects listed vicious gossip, rudeness, lack of punctuality, exploitative behavior, and selfishness as unfair things that other people did. Suburban residents in the U.S. complain about dogs barking, noisy parties, and neighbors walking on their grass (Baumgartner, 1988).

The content of grievances between husbands and wives are likely to be somewhat different. Studies of American couples reveal differences between males and females in the types of offenses they attribute to each other. Buss (1989) found that men were likely to be angry when women were moody or when they rejected sexual overtures. Women were likely to complain about males being condescending, neglectful, and inconsiderate. Women were more likely than men to be angry about demands for sexual intimacy and touching of their bodies without permission.

Levinson (1989) examined sources of grievances in spousal violence in small scale and peasant societies. Data were collected from ethnographic reports in the Human Relations Area File for 90 societies. Allegations of adultery were a common source of grievances leading to wife beating in these societies (see also, Daly & Wilson, 1988). A husband was also likely to beat his wife when she failed to perform her duties, or when she failed to treat him with the degree of respect that he expected. In many societies, wife beating is seen as legitimate method for men to maintain their authority in the household, and it can occur in response to any offense, however minor.

The aggrieved party is likely to have a different perspective than the target of the grievance. For example, Mikula and Heimgartner (1992) asked husbands and wives to report instances of unfair behavior by their spouse. Each was also asked to respond to a series of questions about the events the other partner thought were unfair. Perpetrators rated the events as less serious and unjust, thought their causal contribution to the event was smaller, and considered their actions as more justified than did victims (see also Mummendey, Linneweber, & Loschper, 1984). The tendency for grievances to be concealed may also lead to a difference in perspective. An aggrieved party may have accumulated a set of grievances that he or she never expressed to the target. The unaware target may then perceive the anger expressed for the latest event as an unjustified overreaction (Baumeister, 1990). As a result of these differences in perspectives the dispute may escalate leading to physical violence.

Coercive actions themselves are sometimes a source of grievances, leading to retaliation and escalation. Among the Eskimo, collective killing is often directed at murderers or those suspected of sorcery (Hoebel, 1954).[9] Violence against persons accused of sorcery occurs in other tribal societies and is the most common motive of homicides among the Gebusi (Knauft, 1987). When a person dies from sickness, a sorcerer may be accused of causing the death. Observers believe someone must be responsible for a sickness death and they attempt to discover the identity of the sorcerer through spiritual inquest. If this supernatural investigation reveals that the accused is guilty, the person is killed. The example illustrates the tendency for people to assign human agency and blame for incomprehensible events, and to wreak retributive justice on those who are believed to be guilty. The discovered identity of sorcerers in Gebusi society is not random, however. Aggressive, outspoken or assertive males are particularly likely to be accused and killed. The homicide may also reflect grievances over imbalanced marital exchanges. The charge of sorcery typically serves two functions: it explains death and it punishes someone who violates other group norms. In this egalitarian society, violence is a strong leveling mechanism that prevents status rivalry between males (Knauft, 1987).

***The Inhibition of Grievance Expression.*** Many grievances are never openly expressed to the offender. People are often inhibited from expressing their grievances to an offender because of the costs. One of the costs of the expression of grievances is embarrassment. Rules of deference and politeness are strong regulators of smooth, nonconflicting relationships, and may inhibit the expression of grievances and thereby reduce the frequency of coercive interactions (Goffman, 1959). Lack of confidence that any action will restore justice or deter future offenses may also lead to inaction.

Survey studies in the United States suggest that people infrequently express their anger relative to the number of grievances they experience (e.g., Averill 1982). Respondents in one study reported that they frequently did not express their grievances because they did not want to induce conflict or damage the relationship with the offender (Deshields, Jenkins, & Tate, 1989). Unpublished data by the first author show that people are more likely to express grievances toward immediate family members than toward co-workers or relatives outside the immediate family.

When people do not express their grievances, others may continue to engage in their offensive behavior. This cost can be avoided if there is little contact with the offender. As a result grievances are less likely to be expressed when grievants are able to avoid contact with offenders. According to Baumgartner (1988), the ease with which suburban residents in the U.S. can avoid their neighbors leads them to frequently do nothing to redress injustices. Avoidance is generally difficult in tribal societies, because of their small size. Serious conflicts sometimes result in a fission in the group between the antagonists and their supporters, at least temporarily. Fission is probably less common in horticultural communities than in foraging communities, because group members in the former type of community are tied to a fixed food supply. When avoidance between grievant and offender is not possible, one would expect to observe higher incidence of violence. For example, among the !Kung, incorrigible persons could not be cast out, and therefore were assassinated (Draper, 1978).

The tendency to express grievances openly varies dramatically across cultures. Studies of the Dafla hill tribes of northeast India (Furer-Haimendorf, 1967) and of precolonial New Guinea society (DuBois, 1961) show that people immediately attack those who offend them. A person who does not seek redress for injustices acquires a reputation as weak and indecisive, and invites subsequent transgressions by others. In contrast, the expression of anger is perceived as antisocial by the Gebusi and by Central Eskimo groups (Knauft, 1987). Among the Eskimo, there is an ideological emphasis on patience, cooperation, equality, and peacefulness.

In Japanese society people are very concerned about maintaining good relationships with others and avoiding disrespect (Ohbuchi, 1991). Japanese generally wish to avoid open conflict with others and will often do nothing when they have grievances. On the other hand, Americans are more confrontational than Japanese when they have grievances. Some Americans feel the need to express their grievances more often, and purchase books and attend assertiveness training seminars that exhort them to do so.

The concealment of grievances does not necessarily lead to lower levels of violence. For example, the Gebusi do not publicly express their grievances, but they have an extremely high homicide rate (Knauft, 1987). Failure to openly express complaints makes it unlikely that there can be restitution, apologies, or other methods to redress injustices short of extreme forms of violence.

***The Expression of Grievances***. Grievances, even when expressed, do not necessarily lead to punishment by the aggrieved party. Grievants may first demand an account, an apology, or restitution. If the offender's response is satisfactory, grievants may forgive them. Grievants may also seek the assistance of third parties to mediate the dispute.

A variety of punishments can be used to express grievances and redress injustices. The Javanese handle disputes by not speaking to each other—the "satru" pattern (Geertz, 1961). Eskimos use song duels to settle some disputes (Hoebel, 1954). Each antagonist ridicules the other in a highly conventionalized singing style but with as much skill as possible. The person who receives the greatest applause is the winner of the song contest and gains in prestige. Sometimes the song duels are accompanied by regulated physical combat, such as head-butting and wrestling. Grievances, disputes, and identity contests may be settled by combat rather than by evidence and the determination of guilt. In a song duel the justice process is transformed into an identity contest. This process is not unlike the more informal and less ritualized transformation of coercive incidents that begin with a grievance and develop into escalating conflicts over identities that occur in American society (Luckenbill, 1977; Felson, 1984).

Trial by combat is also used by the Chukchee of Siberia (Sverdrup, 1938). An angry Chukchee accuses the alleged offender in a loud, insulting tirade. If the accused rejects the accusation, he responds in kind. The antagonists then grab each other and attempt to throw each other to the ground. The one who is thrown to the ground is beaten until he gives in. The winner's point of view is accepted and he lights his pipe and offers it to his antagonist as a peace-making gesture.

***Third party intervention***.  As indicated above, one alternative available to a grievant is to seek the aid of third parties to punish the offender and help restore justice. Sometimes these third parties serve as allies, sometimes they try to mediate the dispute or mete out punishment.

With the development of legal systems, the state assumes the role of third party in disputes involving violations of law, and determines guilt and punishment. Where legal systems are absent, undeveloped or ineffective, or when third party mediators are unavailable, grievants are more likely to engage in coercive actions themselves as a form of "self-help" (Black, 1983). Nevertheless, even in modern societies, the state never has a monopoly on the use of force. According to Black many acts of criminal violence reflect decisions of offenders to settle grievances themselves when they perceive that police are unavailable or ineffective. Thus, Black describes some homicides as "capital punishment administered on a private basis (1983, p. 35)."

Dollard (1957) suggested that the unavailability of law could explain the high level of violence among blacks in the Southern United States. He identified a double standard where crimes between blacks were ignored by authorities, while black crime against whites, which was rare, was punished severely. Outside the protection of the law, blacks were compelled to make and enforce their own law with other blacks.

The weaker party in a dispute is particularly likely to seek third party intervention, since direct confrontation is likely to be costly. The intervention of third parties changes the balance of power in favor of weaker antagonists, encouraging coercion on their part and discouraging coercion by stronger parties. The effects of these power inequalities can be illustrated in cases of domestic violence where husbands are usually stronger than wives. Cross-cultural evidence suggests that wives often seek the support of third parties when they have been assaulted by their husbands (Baumgartner, 1993). In some cultures, a male is designated at the marriage as the wife's protector. The closer the protector lives to the couple, the greater the probable cost to the husband for beating his wife. As a result, the further wives live from their families, who usually support them, the more likely they are to suffer abuse from their husbands. For example, Yanamomo women abhor being married to men in distant villages. They know that their father and brothers cannot protect them under these circumstances if they live too far away. Among the Ojibwa Indians of North America, newly married couples move to distant areas with virtually no neighbors or way of communicating to family members. Women in these arrangements are subjected to severe physical punishment by their husbands (Landes, 1971).

Power inequality is also a factor in third party intervention in sibling conflict, since older children are usually stronger than their younger siblings. In the United States, parents usually intervene on behalf of the younger sibling (Felson, 1983; Felson and Russo, 1988). Knowing that they enjoy parental protection, the younger sibling is more willing to fight the older sibling, and coercive interactions are frequent. By intervening, parents inadvertently encourage the behavior they are trying to deter.

In many cultures, the punitive actions by an aggrieved party leads to feuding involving the two antagonists and their kin. (Otterbein and Otterbein, 1965). As in disputes between individuals, the dispute can escalate, with each side retaliating. Grievances and identity concerns on both sides may produce a conflict that continues for a long period of time. In contrast, Boehm (1984) argues that many feuds do not continue indefinitely. When accompanied by compensation for the aggrieved party, feuds can lead to a resolution of conflict. Feuding can then be viewed as an alternative to law in settling grievances and maintaining social order.

Feuding may also deter people from engaging in behaviors that offend members of other groups. For example, Levine (1959) attributed an increase in rape among the Gusii of southwestern Kenya in part to the substitution of British law for feuding. Where formerly a rape or abduction might result in a feud bringing possible death to the offender and his clansmen, now these offenses bring an assault charge carrying a fine. The dramatically lower penalties apparently led to an increase in inter-clan rape.

The incidence of violence to settle conflicts in tribal societies is associated with the presence of fraternal interest groups. Fraternal interest groups are localized groups of related males having common interests. The presence of a group of males with common interests to defend leads to feuding as group members support each other's violent behavior (Otterbein & Otterbein, 1965). On the other hand, the dispersal of consanguineous males leads to conflicting loyalties and mediation by third parties.

The difference between illegitimate violence and violence supported by the group is often not clear, particularly in tribal societies without a legal apparatus. The grievant's kin may view punishment as legitimate and participate in its administration. The target's kin are likely to have a different point of view. Informal punishment, unlike punishments imposed by the state, often result in retaliation, and sometimes feuding between the two antagonists or their kin (Otterbein & Otterbein, 1965). However, informal punishment does not necessarily lead to retaliation from kin. Among the Gebusi, when a homicide is committed against a sorcerer or other wrong-doer, the dispute is viewed as settled

(Knauft, 1987). While the offender's kin may not approve of the killing, they do not attempt to retaliate.

## Identities and Coercion

As indicated above, an insult or other attack on identity is likely to lead to retaliation. Norms of politeness exist in all societies to prevent these events from occurring. Brown and Levinson (1987) classify these norms of politeness in terms of their implications for social identities. They distinguish between threats to negative face and threats to positive face. Negative face represents a desire to maintain autonomy and not be interfered with by other people. Acts that threaten a person's autonomy include orders and threats. Positive face refers to the identities claimed by the individual. Acts that threaten positive face include disapproval, criticism, disagreements, complaints and reprimands, accusation, insults, challenges, blatant non-cooperation in an activity, and interruptions or other signs of lack of attention. Norms relevant to positive face appear to be similar to Mikula et al.'s concept of interactional norms.

Individuals may violate norms of autonomy when they constrain the behavior of others. Many incidents of violence between police and civilians are instigated by civilians' resentment of being stopped and questioned by police (Toch, 1969). Research indicates that barroom violence in Irish and American bars begin when the bartender refuses to serve a customer, either because the customer is too intoxicated or underage (Felson, Baccaglini, & Gmelch, 1986). Violence sometimes results when the customer is offended by this constraint on their behavior.

Brown and Levinson show how easily common speech acts may inadvertently result in attacks on identity. Considerable effort and skill are required to avoid such attacks. For example, the Gebusi avoid taking any public stance which could be perceived as an imposition on others (Knauft, 1987). When people feel their autonomy has been constrained or their positive claims about themselves challenged they may believe they have been intentionally attacked. Violation of politeness norms not only create grievances (like other norm violations), they also attack identities, and thus elicit protective self-presentation.

Stress and other forms of aversive stimuli can have an indirect effect on coercive episodes because they inadvertently bring about disrespectful behavior. A survey study in an American city found that people who had experienced stressful life events were likely to be the victims of attacks by others, and that they engaged in higher levels of coercion in response (Felson, 1991). Because of their negative mood states distressed persons are less likely to be polite and friendly, to feign positive emotions, or to show ritualized support for others. If distressed persons are likely to perform less competently, violate expectations, or annoy others, they are likely to become the targets of grievances. These grievances are likely to lead to their involvement in coercive interactions, often, initially, as targets. In addition, when people are upset they are less likely to give as much thought to their decisions; they may act impulsively without considering costs or alternative choices. They may also be more irritable, less empathic, and more egocentric in interactions with other people.

***Third parties and social identities***. The role of third parties as allies in the redress of grievances was described earlier. Third parties also have an impact on social identities in coercive interactions. That influence is related to their role as an audience, or as mediators or instigators of coercive interactions.[10] Actors may also be motivated to defend the identities of third parties with whom they are associated.

Self-presentation to an audience is critical in "the dozens," an insult game observed among Afro-Americans (Dollard, 1939). Playing the dozens consists of an exchange of verbal insults between two adolescent males, usually in a public setting, in which each attempts to "win" by delivering insults in the form of one-liners or rhyming sentences. The audience evaluates the insults and urges the antagonists on. One of the parties may become physically violent if he is unable to come up with an adequate riposte. In some groups the antagonist who first turns to violence is viewed as weaker because he did not have an effective verbal retort and could not keep his "cool." In other instances the antagonists might be urged to fight. Physical altercations are more likely when the antagonists are from different groups.

Third party mediation may prevent coercive interactions from escalating by allowing antagonists to back down without losing face. This role of third parties is illustrated by Fox's (1989) description of fights on an island in Ireland. The fights usually involved two men with a history of antagonistic relations between themselves or between members of their families. A fight would not start unless there were enough third parties present who were close kin of each antagonist and who were kin related to both antagonists. When the two antagonists squared off the close kin would restrain them while the common kin would act as negotiators. The antagonist's attitude was always "Hold me back or I'll kill him." The fight would end without anyone hurt when the mother of one of the antagonists, or some other female relative, would plead with him to stop fighting. A "proper fight" involved two men who stood up to each other and showed they were willing to fight. If there were few people around, they sometimes came to blows, but rarely was anyone injured. On the other hand, it was unusual for two men to start a fight with no audience around, and when this occurred there was universal condemnation.

Third parties also play a role in assertive self-presentation. For example, bullies tend to seek out situations where their behavior can be witnessed by their peers (Besag, 1989). Violent men described by Toch (1969) initiated fights with strangers without provocation for the purpose of "rep building." These fights occurred in front of audiences so that the desired reputation could be publicized. Rep builders also habitually precipitated incidents in which they could legitimate demonstrations of their fighting ability and physical courage. Similar behavior was observed among Yanomamo men. It is important in this society for men to gain a reputation as fierce and intimidating. Thus, there are many fights involving head butting and clubs within the village, and periodic attacks against other villages. Wife beating may also be motivated to some extent by a desire to project an identity as a fierce man. Yanomamo men prefer to beat their wives in public.

Sometimes people retaliate for insults to third parties. In collectivist cultures, individuals are particularly likely to be concerned about affronts to their group. Semin and Rubini (1990) examined insults in Northern Italy which is characterized by individualism and in Southern Italy, which is a more collectivistic culture. Insults in the North were chiefly directed at some characteristic or identity of the individual, while those in the South frequently referred to members of the target person's family.

Bond and Venus (1991) examined the reactions of Chinese students in the collectivist culture of Hong Kong. Male students were more likely to directly retaliate with some form of negative verbal statement or indirectly retaliate by giving the antagonist a negative rating when the insult referred to their group identity and occurred in front of third parties than when the insult referred to them as individuals. In the latter case the individual is expected to show restraint and humility; retaliation would reveal too much self-concern.

An anthropological study of three tribes of West Cameroon indicates that any sexual insult by men directed at a woman (usually referring to genitalia) is considered as an affront to all women (Ardener, 1973). The insulted woman tells other women in the tribe about the incident and they collectively seek out the offender and publicly humiliate him. These character contests may involve grievances since there is a norm prohibiting such public insults to women. If the insulted woman can produce witnesses who heard the insult, the offender is required to pay damages in animals or cash. This restitution is divided among all the females of the tribe, including the female children.

## CONCLUSIONS

Examples from cross-cultural research of violent behavior suggest that the conditions for the use of coercion may be the same in all cultures—to gain compliance, to redress injustice, and to assert and defend identities. People use coercion to achieve compliance from others in all societies, especially when conflicts occur over scarce resources. The social organization and the availability of resources will affect the form, frequency, and intensity of conflicts, but we suggest that conflict is related to the use of coercion in all societies.

The existence of norms inevitably leads to their violation. When norms are violated, people become aggrieved and may punish the norm violator as a means of redressing the injustice and deterring future violations. Punishment as an aspect of informal social control is present in all societies (Brown, 1991). In modern societies, the legal system assumes some, but not all of this activity. The form that punishment takes varies across societies, but the conditions for eliciting the justice process may be the same everywhere.

Every society develops politeness norms to protect vulnerable social identities (Brown, 1991). Inevitably, mistakes are made, and people perceive they have been attacked. Attacks on identity also develop out of the grievance process, when the reproach of an offended party gives offense. In many societies, social identities are particularly salient for young men who have special concerns for appearing strong, fierce, and courageous.

The cross-cultural patterns of coercive behavior described in this chapter are not easily explained by a frustration-aggression mechanism. According to the most recent version of that approach aggressive behaviors are involuntary responses instigated by any form of aversive experiences. Physical pain, sadness, depression, embarrassment, and guilt (i.e., self-blame) do not instigate coercive behavior in these societies. Only particular types of aversive experience—identity attacks and other behaviors perceived as blameworthy—instigate coercive actions. When dispute-related violence occurs it is usually the result of an escalation process in which the social interaction between antagonists and sometimes the role of third parties are important.

For a long time there has been skepticism about frustration-aggression theory, based on both conceptual and empirical grounds. A social interactionist perspective provides an alternative framework for understanding all forms of coercive behavior, using ideas that are well-accepted in the social psychological literature.[11] The theory suggests that basic features of social life create incentives for coercive actions. If conflict, social control, and concerns for justice and self are features of every society, then the use of coercion is also likely to be a universal.

## NOTES

1. For a more detailed discussion of the frustration-aggression hypothesis, and its relationship to a social interactionist approach, see Tedeschi and Felson (1994).

2. We prefer a vocabulary of coercive actions to the traditional vocabulary of aggression or violence for a variety of reasons (see Tedeschi and Felson, 1994 for a more extended discussion). One advantage is that the language links other literatures to the aggression literature. In particular, it ties in the literature on conflict, grievances and social control, and other forms of social influence.

3. Our approach is also consistent with the rational choice approach to crime (e.g., Cornish and Clarke, 1986). It is also compatible with theories that focus on variation in the costs of crime (e.g., control theories, routine activity theory) and group differences in incentives for criminal behavior (e.g., subcultural theories; blocked opportunity theories).

4. Coercion may involve redistributive justice rather than retributive justice (see Tedeschi and Norman, 1985; Donnerstein and Hatfield, 1982). When individuals decide that the distribution of rewards and costs is unfair they may attempt to restore equity by harming the person perceived as privileged, even when that person is not held responsible for the injustice.

5. We shall use the present tense—the "ethnographic presence" to describe conditions in tribal cultures that may no longer exist.

6. There is substantial evidence that many acts of sexual coercion are sexually motivated (for reviews see Palmer, 1988; Felson, 1993).

7. However, deviant women are probably at greater risk for a variety of reasons (Kanin, 1985).

8. A person may also be blamed for negative actions that are unintentional if the outcomes are perceived as having been foreseeable.

9. Violence is also directed at chronic liars.

10. The importance of third parties as observers, mediators. and instigators of coercive interactions has been demonstrated in experimental research (see Tedeschi and Felson, 1994 for a review).

11. Human universals are often attributed to biological factors resulting from evolutionary processes. We are skeptical that some gene for aggression can account for the situational effects that we have described. Instead, biological factors probably play an indirect, facilitative role in the use of coercion (see Tedeschi and Felson, 1994).

## REFERENCES

Abelson, R. P. (1976). Script processing in attitude formation and decision making. In J. S. Carroll & I. W. Payne (Eds.), *Cognition and social behavior* (pp. 33-46). Hillsdale, NJ: Erlbaum.

Ardener, S. G. (1973). Sexual insult and female militancy. *Man, 8,* 422-440.

Arkin, R. M. (1981). Self presentation styles. In J. Tedeschi (Ed.) *Impression management theory and social psychological research.* New York: Academic Press.

Averill, J. R. (1982). *Anger and aggression: An essay on emotion.* New York: Springer-Verlag.

Bandura, A. (1973). *Aggression: A social learning analysis.* Englewood Cliffs, NJ: Prentice-Hall.

Baumgartner, M. P. (1988). *The moral order of a suburb.* New York: Oxford University Press.

Baumgartner, M. P. (1993). Violent networks: The origins and management of domestic conflict. In R. B. Felson & J. T. Tedeschi (Eds.), *Aggression and violence: Social interactionist perspectives.* Washington, DC: American Psychological Association.

Baumeister, R., A. Stillwell, & Wotman, S. R. (1990). Victim and perpetrator accounts of interpersonal conflict: Autobiographical narratives about anger. *Journal of Personality and Social Psvchology, 59,* 994-1005.

Berkowitz, L. (1993). *Aggression: Its causes, consequences, and control.* New York: McGraw Hill.

Besag, V. (1989). *Bullies and victims in school.* Philadelphia: Open University Press.

Bisanz, G. L. & Rule, B. G. (1989). Gender and the persuasion schema: A search for cognitive invariants. *Personality and Social Psychology Bulletin, 15,* 4-18.

Black, D. (1983). Crime as social control. *American Sociological Review, 48,* 34-45.

Boehm, C. (1984). *Blood Revenge: The Anthropology of feuding in Montenegro and other tribal societies.* Lawrence: University Press of Kansas.

Bond, M. H., & Venus, C. K. (1991). Resistance to group or personal insults in an ingroup or outgroup context. *International Journal of Psycholoqy, 26,* 83-94.

Briggs, J. L. (1970). *Never in anger: Portrait of an Eskimo family.* Boston: Harvard University Press.

Broude, G. J., & S. J. Greene. (1976). Cross-cultural codes on twenty sexual attitudes and Practices. *Ethnology, 15,* 409-429.

Brown, D. E. (1991). *Human universals.* New York: McGraw-Hill. Brown, P., & Levinson, S. C. (1987). *Politeness: Some universals in language usage.* New York: Cambridge University Press.

Buss, D. (1989). Conflict between the sexes: Strategic interference and the evocation of anger and upset. *Journal of Personality and Social Psychology, 56,* 735-747.

Chagnon, N. A. (1977). *Yanomamö: The fierce people.* New York: Holt, Reinhardt and Winston.

Cornish D., & Clarke, R. (1986). (Eds.), *The reasoning criminal: Rational choice perspectives on offending.* New York: SpringerVerlag.

Daly, M., & Wilson, M. (1988). *Homicide.* New York: Aldine De Gruyter.

Deshields, T. L., Jenkins, J. 0., & Tait, R. C. (1989). The experience of anger in chronic illness: A preliminary investigation. *International Journal of Psychiatry in Medicine, 19,* 299-309.

Dodge, K. A., & Crick, N. R. (1990). Social-information processing bases of aggressive behavior in children. *Personality and Social Psychology Bulletin, 16,* 8-22.

Dollard, J. (1957). *Caste and class in a southern town. 3rd ed.* Garden City, NY: Doubleday.

Donnerstein, E., & Hatfield, E. (1982). Aggression and inequity. In J. Greenberg, & R. Cohen (Eds.), *Equity and justice in social behavior.* (pp. 309-336) New York: Academic Press.

Draper, P. (1978). The learning environment for aggression and anti-social behavior among the !Kung (Kalahari Desert, Botswana, Africa). In Ashley Montagu (Ed.) *Learning on aggression* (pp. 31-53). New York: Oxford University Press.

DuBois, C. (1961). *The peoples of Alor*. New York: Harper & Row.

Felson, R. B. (1983). Aggression and violence between siblings. *Social Psychology Quarterly, 46*, 271-285.

Felson, R. B. (1984). Patterns of aggressive interaction. In A. Mummendey (Ed.), *Social psychology of aggression: From individual behavior to social interaction.* (pp. 107-126). Berlin: Springer-Verlag.

Felson, R. B. (1992). "Kick'em when they're down": Explanations of the relationship between stress and interpersonal aggression and violence. *Sociological Quarterly, 33*, 1-16.

Felson, R. B. (1993). Motives for sexual coercion. In R. B. Felson, & J. T. Tedeschi (Eds.), *Aggression and violence: Social interactionist perspectives.* (pp. 233-253). Washington, DC: American Psychological Association.

Felson, R. B., Baccaglini, W., & Gmelch, G. (1986). Bar-room brawls: Aggression and violence in Irish and American bars. In Anne Campbell and John J. Gibbs (Eds.) *Violent Transactions* (pp. 153-166). Oxford: Basil Blackwell.

Felson, R. B., & Russo, N. (1988). Parental punishment and sibling aggression. *Social Psychology Quarterly, 51*, 11-18.

Felson, R. B., & H. J. Steadman. (1983). Situations and processes leading to criminal violence. *Criminology, 21*, 59-74.

Felson, R. B., & Tedeschi, J. T., (1993). *Aggression and violence: Social interactionist perspectives*. Washington, DC: American Psychological Association.

Ferguson, T. J., & Rule, B. G. (1981). An attributional perspective on anger and aggression. In R. Geen, & R. E. Donnerstein (Eds.), *Perspectives on aggression: Theoretical and empirical reviews* (pp. 41-74). New York: Academic Press.

Fox, R. (1989). *The search for society: Quest for a biosocial science and morality.* New Brunswick, NJ: Rutgers University Press.

Furer-Haimendorf, C. (1967). *Moral and merit: A study of values and social control in South Asian Societies.* London: Wiedenfeld and Nicholson.

Geertz, H. (1961) The Javanese family. New York: Free Press.

Gregor, T. (1990). Male dominance and sexual coercion. In J. W. Stigler, R. A. Shweder, & G. Herdt (Eds.) *Cultural psychology: Essays on comparative human development* (pp. 477-495) Cambridge: Cambridge University Press.

Goffman, E. (1959). *The presentation of self in everyday life.* New York: Doubleday Anchor.

Heider, F. (1958). *The psychology of interpersonal relations.* New York: Wiley.

Hoebel, E. A. (1954). *The law of primitive man: A study in comparative legal dynamics.* Cambridge: Harvard University Press.

Huesmann, L. R. (1988). An information processing model for the development of aggression. *Aggressive Behavior, 14*, 13-24.

Kanin, E. (1983). Rape as a function of relative sexual frustration. *Psychology Reports, 52*, 133-134.

Kanin, E. (1985). Date rapists: Differential sexual socialization and relative deprivation. *Archives of Sexual Behavior, 6*, 67-76.

Knauft, B. M. (1987). Reconsidering violence in simple human societies: Homicide among the Gebusi of New Guinea. *Current Anthropology, 28*, 457-497.

Landes, R. (1971). *The Ojibwa woman.* New York: Norton.

Levine, R. A. (1959). Gusii sex offenses: A study in social control. American Anthropologist, 61, 189-226.

Levinson, D. (1989). *Family violence in cross-cultural perspective.* Newbury Park: Sage.

Luckenbill, D. F. (1977). Criminal homicide as a situated transaction. *Social Problems, 25,* 176-186.

Melburg, V., & J. T. Tedeschi. (1989). Displaced aggression: Frustration or impression management. *European Journal of Social Psychology, 19,* 139-145.

Messick, D. M., Bloom, S., Boldizar, J. P., & Samuelson, C. D. (1985). Why we are fairer than others. *Journal of Experimental Social Psychology, 21,* 480-500.

Mikula, G., & Heimgartner, A. (1991). Experiences of injustice in intimate relationships. Unpublished manuscript. University of Graz, Austria.

Mikula, G., Petri, B., & Tanzer, N. (1990). What people regard as unjust: Types and structures of everyday experiences of injustice. *European Journal of Social Psychology, 20* 133-149.

Mummendey, A., Linneweber, V., & Loschper, G. (1984). Actor or victim of aggression. Divergent perspectives—Divergent evaluations. *European Journal of Social Psychology, 14,* 291-311.

Murphy, R. F. (1959). Social structure and sex antagonism. *Southwestern Journal of Anthropology, 15,* 89-123.

Ohbuchi, K. (1991). Interpersonal conflicts among Japanese and Americans. unpublished paper, Tohoku University, Sendai, Japan.

Otterbein, K. F., & C. S. Otterbein, 1965. An eye for an eye, a tooth for a tooth: A cross-cultural study of feuding. *American Anthropologist, 67,* 1470-1482.

Palmer, C. T. (1988). Twelve reasons why rape is not sexually motivated: A skeptical examination. *The Journal of Sex Research, 25,* 512-530.

Sanday, P. R. (1981). The sociocultural context of rape: a cross-cultural study. *Journal of Social Issues, 37,* 5-27.

Schank, R., & Abelson, R. (1977). *Scripts, plans, goals and understanding.* Hillsdale, NJ: Erlbaum.

Semin, G. R., & Rubini, M. (1990). Unfolding the concept of person by verbal abuse. *European Journal of Social Psychology, 20,* 463-474.

Sverdrup, H. V. (1938). *With the people of the* Tundra (Human Relations Area Files, Trans.) Oslo: Gyldendal Norsk Forlag.

Tedeschi, J. T., & Felson, R. B. (1994). *Violence, aggression and coercive actions.* Washington, DC: American Psychological Association.

Tedeschi, J. T., & Norman, N. (1985). Self, self-presentation, and social power. In B. Schlenker (Ed.), *Self and identity. Presentation of self in social life.* New York: McGraw Hill.

Tedeschi J. T., Schlenker, B. R., & Bonoma, T. V. (1973). *Conflict, Power and games.* Chicago: Aldine.

Toch, H. (1969). *Violent men: An inquiry into the psychology of violence.* Chicago: Aldine.

Turnbull, C. (1965) *Wayward servants: The two worlds of the African Pygmies.* Garden City, NY: Natural History. Wills, T. A. (1981).

Wills, T. A. (1981) Downward comparison principles in social psychology. *Psychological Bulletin, 90,* 245-271.

Yeung, K., Wai-Hung, C., & Yuk-Fai, A. (In Press). Sympathy and support for industrial actions: A justice analysis. *Journal of Applied Psychology.*

# 10

# Inquiry Through a Comparative Lens: Unraveling the Social and Cultural Aspects of Interpersonal Violent Behaviors

Neil Alan Weiner
R. Barry Ruback

Scientific explanation progresses by moving from the simple to the complex. This complexity arises in many ways. Most basically, it arises from the common finding of multiple, direct causal influences. This kind of finding, however, accounts for only part of the complexity. Complexity also arises through recognizing that some causal influences are moderated by other causal influences; that is, the behaviors associated with some causes will occur under some (moderating) conditions but not under others (Baron and Kenny [1986] detail the conceptual and formal aspects of these relationships). For example, a study might reveal that a particular causal influence, such as a conflict between persons over money, drugs, sexual activity, family finances, or personal reputation (see Felson and Tedeschi, Kruttschnitt, and Wilson and Daly, in this volume), is more likely to lead to a particular type of violent behavior or to make the particular violent behavior used more lethal. The use and level of violence during these and other conflicts is moderated by certain social conditions and situations, such as group affiliation (e.g., gangs or other social groups), location (e.g., a barroom), presence of a firearm, and type of relationship between the parties (e.g., kin versus nonkin). In addition, the use and level of violence is moderated by the particular characteristics of the people involved, such as whether the incident involves only males or both males and females, whether the persons are very close or very far apart in their ages, and whether the persons all exhibit very high educational achievement or a mixture of very high and very low educational achievement. Thus, moderator influences are conditional causes: they explain when a particular causal influence, such as interpersonal conflict, will have an effect on a particular type of behavior, such as a completed aggravated physical attack.

In addition to moderated causal relationships, complexity arises from mediated causal relationships; these are relationships that specify the causal mechanism or intervention (the mediator) through which a causal influence affects behavior. When only this mechanism is operating, the social or cultural causal influence affects the behavior through this, and no other, mechanism. For example, a study might report that a particular type of violent behavior, a completed aggravated physical attack, is produced by a social or cultural influence only when another intervening causal mechanism or capacity is operating (e.g., a certain kind of distorted or pathological thinking, low cognitive and intellectual functioning, heightened physiological arousal, attitudinal preference for interpersonal domination) but not in its absence. The mediating causal process has a transformational effect on the social or cultural influence. Mediated causal influences are, therefore, dynamic influences on violent behaviors: they explain how and why a particular causal influence (the mediated influence), such as the social preference for physically punitive child rearing and the social perception that one's most important membership group (or groups) is under attack, will be transformed and then realized as one or another type of violent behavior, such as a completed aggravated physical attack.

## THE NEED FOR A COMPARATIVE STRATEGY

Clearly, society and culture influence violent behaviors through a rich, dense array of causal relationships—direct, moderated, and mediated—as well as through reciprocal processes that can also be direct, moderated, and mediated. A comparative social and cultural approach to understanding violent behaviors permits one to identify the forces that shape their trajectories and component transitions over the life course with greater specificity and confidence.

Different disciplines search for complexity in different ways. Social and cultural sciences, for example, have tended to focus on moderated relationships, especially on societal and cultural conditions (e.g., social stratification, gender roles and statuses, child-rearing practices) that can influence when certain types of violent behaviors are more likely to occur. Psychology, on the other hand, has tended to focus on mediator relationships, especially on how the individual processes information—cognitive, affective, and normative—that influences both the chances that the individual will engage in violent behaviors and the seriousness of these behaviors. This contrast is clearly overdrawn, but it does underscore that there are dimensions of causal complexity beyond those that are typically considered within traditional disciplinary boundaries. These differences do not, however, invariably lead to disciplinary myopia; rather, they often have the opposite effect of expanding and altering scientific vision and paradigm. For these salutary effects to occur, scientists with diverse disciplinary skills will need to build bridges, both analytical and methodological, that reinforce and capitalize on one another's strengths and advancements.

There are several reasons why social and cultural research should proceed in tandem, especially in broadly envisioned comparative work. Through comparative social and cultural studies, scientists achieve a number of goals (Corsaro, 1992; Kohn, 1989; Triandis, 1980). First, they catalog the different types of violent behaviors and their relative frequencies across societies and cultures as a way of gauging the generality of these behaviors. Such work yields insights into many wide-ranging issues: among others, the biological and, relatedly, evolutionary bases of violent behaviors. Second, scientists can investigate the moderating and mediating causal effects of societal and cultural influences, as well as of other types of influences. Third, only comparative studies can test hypotheses of the broadest social and cultural theoretical generality, doing so through what are essentially natural quasi-experiments (e.g., studies of the effects of spatial dispersion or relocation of social and cultural groups with very high or very low rates of violent behaviors, studies of the impact of industrialization on agrarian societies). These studies take advantage of the fact that influences that are causally confounded in their relationships to violent behaviors within one society or culture are often unconfounded when many societies or cultures are examined together.

For these core scientific goals to be realized, other more limited but nonetheless critical objectives must be identified and realized. Many of these objectives became apparent while reading the chapters in this volume. Not surprisingly, these objectives fall into two groups: *methodological* and *conceptual*.

## METHODOLOGICAL OBJECTIVES

Perhaps first and foremost with respect to methodology, large-scale surveys (see Gartner, this volume) and ethnographies (see Ember and Ember, this volume) need to be more fully integrated. Studies need to tie together these two approaches from the outset in order to exploit their respective advantages, producing knowledge that eclipses what can be yielded by either one separately. The broad social and cultural snapshots provided by large-scale surveys are most suited to surveillance. They can help monitor quantitatively broad social and cultural trends and patterns in violent behaviors and can identify persistent correlates of these behaviors. Special samples can also be selected to focus attention on specific social and cultural groups, for example, those at greatest and least risk of engaging in or being victimized by a particular type of violent behavior. While no one doubts that surveys can provide information regarding both causal moderation and mediation, in fact, practical problems have generally limited the kinds of questions asked. Large-scale surveys, at least as they have been implemented, seem to be best tailored, then, to identifying those social and cultural influences moderating the many causal pathways to violent behaviors.

The value of large surveys notwithstanding, they cannot provide the detailed, nuanced knowledge issuing from the direct and in-depth observations reported in ethnographies. Ethnographies can be thought of as social and cultural case studies, whether they are of communities, tribes, or other social and cultural entities. As such, ethnographies possess the same strengths as clinical case histories of individuals. One central strength is to pinpoint narrower social and cultural dynamics influencing violent behaviors. Ethnographies seem to be best tailored, then, to identifying those social and cultural influences mediating the many causal pathways to violent behaviors.

The central challenge of a comparative social and cultural analysis that is both eclectic and inclusive in its methods and conceptualizations is to meld the telescopic insights of large-survey research with the microscopic ones of ethnography. Such an integration might reveal how individual processes produce aggregate patterns, as, for example, in the chapter by Archer and McDaniel (this volume).

One way to accomplish this merger of methods is to launch targeted ethnographies in societies and cultures exhibiting causally relevant characteristics flagged by large surveys (e.g., very high or very low levels of violent behaviors, a very high level of one type of violent behavior and a very low level of another type of violent behavior, very high levels of violent behaviors at one point in time and very low levels at another point). Another way to meld the two approaches is to incorporate into large-scale surveys questions that are shown to be relevant by ethnographies (e.g., ritual vs. nonritual violence, drug-related vs. non-drug-related violence, tribal vs. nontribal violence).

The success of methodological integration depends upon capitalizing on the strengths of the complementary methods while minimizing their respective weaknesses. Large-survey research must avoid the usual potential pitfalls: poorly or incompletely defined population universes, biased or insufficient samples, too few cases for identifying infrequently occurring but significant violent behaviors and related causal processes, difficulties in documenting errors in official and nonofficial data due to misrecording and under- and overreporting, and the absence of information about types of violent behaviors ignored or neglected by official agencies (see Gartner, this volume). Ethnography must also avoid its potential flaws and contaminants: overgeneralization, biased or incomplete field observations, and unsubstantiated statements of historical or contemporary facts (see Ember and Ember, this volume).

The integration of large-scale surveys and ethnographies needs to be complemented by a greater focus on specific types of violent behaviors. Researchers presently know enough about interpersonal violent behaviors to realize that their undifferentiated grouping is not likely to result in much if any new knowledge. Although there is evidence that violent offenders frequently engage in different types of violent (and nonviolent) crimes, the causes may nonetheless vary by the type of violent crime. It therefore makes little sense to ignore these differences. In order to advance knowledge, scientists will need to fence off separate groupings: among others, familial, sexual, and hate-motivated violence (see Kruttschnitt, Ember and Ember, and Wilson and Daly, this volume).

The success of the strategies just discussed will hinge crucially on the capacity of researchers (a) to collect multiple kinds of data for use in multilevel causal analyses and (b) to apply multiple kinds of analyses at each of the levels at which data are collected. First, information needs to be collected at multiple analytical levels so that the various kinds of causal relationships described earlier (direct, moderated, mediated, and reciprocal) can be traced: (a) societies and cultures (macro-level), (b) institutions and groups within these societies and cultures (mid-level), and (c) individuals within these institutions and groups (micro-level). Second, at each of these analytical levels, information needs to be collected from different disciplinary approaches and from different perspectives within these approaches. Absent such a nested systematic strategy, the collected information will be too infested by confounding to permit a clear delineation of mediating and moderating causes.

Finally, whenever possible, at each level of social and cultural analysis, information must be collected in multiple ways. For example, at the macro-level, the collection of official, self-report, and victimization data should be coordinated in order to leverage more reliable and therefore robust analyses of comparative patterns and trends in individuals' violent behaviors and of their causes and correlates. Methodological and conceptual multiplism is, then, the best path to knowledge of the diverse and complex social and cultural roots of violent behaviors.

## CONCEPTUAL OBJECTIVES

One of the central aspects of a comparative social and cultural analysis of violent behaviors has already been mentioned. We refer to the pressing need for analyses to be conducted at multiple conceptual levels. The tight web of methods and conceptualization made it impossible to avoid discussing this aspect in our earlier comments about the core methodological strategies required to produce breakthroughs in knowledge. Here, without belaboring this important point, we will expand upon it a bit.

At each level of social and cultural analysis, regardless of disciplinary approach or perspective within an approach, a developmental orientation will be a crucial component of understanding violent behaviors (see Laub and Lauritsen, this volume). The longitudinal, or sequential, feature of the developmental orientation (other features include notions of maturation and function) permits the most rigorous causal analysis; in order to establish social and cultural causality, information is needed about trajectories, that is, the temporal and spatial pathways of violent behaviors and of social and cultural phenomena hypothesized to influence them. Scientists will therefore need to plot the trajectories of many specific kinds of behaviors, violent as well as nonviolent, and of social and cultural processes. Scientists will also need to describe the constituent transitions of these many trajectories. For example, scientists will need to track the trajectory of sexual assaults and link this trajectory to concomitant social (e.g., educational) and cultural (e.g., child-rearing) trajectories. Key transitional milestones within social and cultural trajectories will also need to be tracked. The main idea, of course, is to sort out the causal progressions and relationships among these trajectories and transitions. That is the only way to pinpoint the comparative directions and strengths of social and cultural influences.

Whenever possible, developmental studies of violent behaviors should focus on violent individuals rather than only on violent incidents. Doing so facilitates the identification of causal aspects of individual stability and change as well as of situational stability and change. This is because developmental studies usually aim to understand the trajectories and transitions of violent behaviors over the life course which, of course, involves an individual focus. Unfortunately, the bulk of comparative research, notably large-survey studies, uses official records, often of arrests. These records summarize what happened during criminal incidents. However, these incident-level records do not usually clearly identify which participants in the incidents engaged in specific behaviors, particularly the violent behaviors. Unless arrest narratives are also available, which is rarely the case, it is virtually impossible to know how many individuals were involved in the incidents and, importantly, which individuals were responsible for which specific acts of violence. Developmental research requires self-reports or third-party accounts of violent behaviors to surmount this difficulty of linking behaviors to individuals. Obtaining undistorted accounts of interpersonal violence is a tall order even when a single society or culture is under study, let alone when many societies or cultures are under study. Future developmental work, especially of a comparative focus, will need to remedy this weakness of aggregate analyses based on official records.

The need for individual- rather than incident-level data is also important for another reason: it signals the need for a social psychological analysis of violent behaviors. For both methodological and theoretical reasons, future research on interpersonal violent behaviors will have to focus on interpersonal interactions and on individuals' perceptions and attitudes. Such a social-psychological perspective can act as a bridge between the macro and micro levels of analysis, because social psychologists are concerned with both societal-level questions of moderator influences and individual-level questions of mediating influences. Despite the pivotal analytical location of social psychology, very little research, especially comparative, has been conducted based on this perspective.

As is apparent from many of the articles in this volume (see especially Gartner), most of the research on interpersonal violent behaviors has been conducted using large-survey data collected at a highly aggregated level (e.g., nation). From such data bases, especially those that have information about both offender(s) and victim(s), one can draw some inferences about individuals' perceptions of each others' intentions and motives. These inferences are based on officially recorded aspects of the participants and circumstances, such as whether the participants are strangers and whether the violent behavior was committed in conjunction with another felony. However, inferences based on aggregate data have numerous limitations, the ecological fallacy being only the most obvious one. Even the ethnographic data sets that have examined individual behavior (see Ember and Ember, this volume) have tended to ignore individuals' judgments about intentions and motives.

A social psychological perspective, for example, as formulated by Felson and Tedeschi (this volume), would provide more insight into the development and maintenance of individual-level perceptions of social interactions, especially of those perceptions that most directly and powerfully influence the use of violent behaviors. One of the central tenets of social psychology is that beliefs, attitudes, and behaviors are affected by the physical, imagined, and implied presence of other people (Allport, 1985). Social psychology can help to pinpoint how these beliefs, attitudes, and behaviors are shaped and modified within different types of social and cultural contexts and within different situations within these contexts. Unfortunately, this line of inquiry has infrequently been pursued in ways that are relevant to understanding violent behaviors, particularly their most serious forms. This perspective deserves to be discussed here because it is likely to be a source of innovative theory and research in the coming years. We decided to do this ourselves because so little research has been done in this area that a paper could not be drafted for inclusion in the volume.

## AN EXPERIMENTAL APPROACH TO THE STUDY OF INTERPERSONAL VIOLENT BEHAVIORS

Like other disciplines, social psychology endorses a variety of methodologies. However, the discipline's unique contribution to the study of human behavior, and the technique most associated with it, is the laboratory experiment. Social psychologists prefer the experiment because it provides the most unambiguous evidence of causation. Not only is the temporal sequence of events known, but potential confounding variables can be controlled, thereby permitting better tests of, for example, the distinction between causal moderation and mediation

(Baron & Kenny, 1986). Further, within a particular experimental paradigm, replicating and extending findings are relatively straightforward. Social psychologists are also aware, however, of the weaknesses of the laboratory experiment: artificial settings, nonrepresentative subject populations (mainly white, middle-class college students), and subjects who may be responding to experimenters' demands rather than to aspects of the experimental situation. Furthermore, there are often limitations on what can ethically be investigated, both about socially and culturally relevant variables like ethnicity, race, gender, and age and about types and levels of interpersonal violent behaviors.

Within the experimental approach, there have been numerous investigations of aggression, usually defined as "any form of behavior that is intended to injure someone physically or psychologically" (Berkowitz, 1993, p. 3). This research literature is vast; however, the crucial question is the degree to which this literature augments the understanding of interpersonal violent behaviors outside the laboratory setting.

## Experiments on Aggression

Typically, experimental research on aggression has involved a naive subject delivering a hostile response, frequently an electric shock, to another person, allegedly as part of an investigation of the effects of punishment on learning. In these studies, the subject is generally free to choose the level of punishment that the other person will ostensibly receive. The intensity and duration of the shock constitute the dependent variables. There are several well-known variations of this procedure (e.g., using other types of noxious stimuli, such as noise or heat).

Questions about the validity of these experimental procedures have been raised because, on their face, electric shocks administered in a laboratory setting seem to share very little with violent behaviors outside the laboratory setting in which weapons or fists are used to inflict physical harm on others (Berkowitz, 1993, pp. 414–418). For example, it has been argued that laboratory measures of aggression are inversely related to violent behavior in natural settings (Gottfredson & Hirschi, 1993).

However, there is reason to believe that subjects' behavior in experimental situations mirrors aggression in nonexperimental situations. First, in terms of construct validity, there is evidence that subjects who have been insulted deliver more punishment than do subjects who have not been insulted. Second, some research indicates that individuals who are the most aggressive outside the laboratory setting (e.g., individuals with histories of violence) are also the most aggressive in the laboratory setting (e.g., Gully & Dengerink, 1983). Also, consistent with the pattern found outside the laboratory setting, in the laboratory setting males show more physical aggression than do females (Eagly & Steffen, 1986). Third, some researchers have argued that, even if the harm inflicted in the laboratory setting is not similar in type and degree to harm inflicted outside the laboratory setting, study subjects believe they are harming the supposed victim. This psychological similarity ("experimental realism") is one of the most important bases on which rest inferences drawn from experiments about violent behaviors (Berkowitz & Donnerstein, 1982).

## Extending Experimental Research to Interpersonal Violent Behaviors

To increase our ability to draw valid inferences from laboratory experiments on aggression, several factors will need to be investigated. For example, studies will have to incorporate variables such as high arousal, independent of the aggression itself. These studies will also need to manipulate the degree to which violent behaviors are instrumental, that is, rationally serve some end other than the infliction of punishment. Future laboratory research should also investigate aggression in which the victim and the offender are not clearly differentiated. In nonexperimental settings, interpersonal violent behaviors are often reciprocal and continuing; victims and offenders commonly have histories of prior violence against one another, so that labeling a particular person a victim in a particular incident is in some sense arbitrary. Relatedly, future work needs to examine more closely the distinction between offensive and defensive violence, because a person's willingness to engage in violent behavior will depend in part on whether it is viewed as justified. Defensive violent behavior may be more widely viewed by society as justified than offensive violent behavior, and because of this, individuals are less often required to justify its use. There is also a need for experimental analogues of situations in which aggression is necessary or even socially supported or demanded, such as protecting a child's life. Moreover, research should examine how interpersonal violent behaviors are differentially affected by rewards (e.g., bolstering legitimacy) as opposed to disinhibitions (Megargee, 1983).

Although it is possible that some of these aspects of violent behaviors can be investigated in the laboratory setting, others cannot be investigated there. For good reason, experimental studies do not tread beyond aggression and anger. Because offenders and victims must both be protected in these studies, it is virtually impossible to span the entire violence continuum, ranging from threats to attempts to actual physical harm. While it is true that laboratory experiments are able to study subjects who believe they are inflicting relatively minor harm on others, these experiments cannot inflict on, attempt, or even threaten serious harm to a subject. Thus, with respect to the continuum of violent behaviors, there is compelling reason to bar direct laboratory tests of serious violent behaviors.

Further, because of similar ethical considerations, phenomena such as sexual violent behavior and mental illness and violent behavior cannot be fully studied in the laboratory setting. Moreover, laboratory studies can only touch on questions such as how the levels of actually inflicted victim harm and suffering affect the offender's decision to inflict further harm. This limitation cannot be circumvented even by studies involving animal targets (e.g., Sheridan & King, 1972) because these studies cannot be ethically conducted.

Despite these research impediments, it is important to recognize that the overwhelming majority of assaults in nonexperimental settings involve relatively minor harms, precisely the kinds of harms that can be most closely approximated in the laboratory. Also, many children are likely to engage in impulsive, disorderly, aggressive, and nonserious violent behaviors before engaging in serious violent behaviors. From a developmental perspective, then, studying nonserious violent behaviors makes sense. Finally, to the extent that violent behaviors escalate as social interactions unfold, with minor physical harms leading to more serious physical harms, understanding the dynamics of the less serious types of physical harms may result in significant insights about how to defuse interactions before they irrevocably spiral upward in intensity, both over the life course and during specific encounters. The bottom line, then, is that experimental social psychology potentially has much to contribute to our understanding of violent behaviors, even if it is limited in the types that it can directly study.

## Extending Experimental Research to Social and Cultural Contexts

Generalizing laboratory experiments to interpersonal violent behaviors is problematic. It is even more problematic to generalize these experiments to interpersonal violent behaviors across societies and cultures. Unfortunately, most of the experimental work that has been conducted fails to address directly the effects of social and cultural factors. Furthermore, this work is neither explicitly nor systematically linked to macro-level factors. Although it might be argued, for example, that research on the effects of pornography on males' violence against women (Linz & Malamuth, 1993) is of this type, the major line of experimental work in this area concerns research on prejudice and discrimination.

There is evidence that aggression against a target motivated by prejudice depends on both individual factors (e.g., the subject's race) and situational factors (e.g., the target's ability to retaliate). For example, when teaching white and black subjects in an experimental setting, white subjects use different amounts of electric shocks only when the learner cannot retaliate or does not know who administered the shocks (Crosby, Bromley, & Saxe, 1980). As another example, Rogers and Prentice-Dunn (1981) found that when white subjects had not been angered, they gave less shock to black subjects than to white subjects. However, when white subjects had been angered, they gave more shock to black subjects than to white subjects. As a third example, Dovidio and Gaertner (1986) found that if their aggression cannot be justified, subjects will be less aggressive toward blacks than toward whites. However, if their aggression can be justified, subjects will be more aggressive toward blacks. In summaries of these and other studies, reviewers have concluded that discrimination is likely to occur only when there is some other apparent motive for the discriminatory behavior. Similar studies conducted in Israel have also found less aggression against minorities when retaliation is expected but more aggression when retaliation is not possible (Bizman, Schwarzwald, & Zidon, 1984).

Although these studies of hostility toward minorities and, more generally, the powerless in the United States and Israel suggest that researchers have been thinking about the roles of society and culture in influencing violent behaviors, the research itself does not investigate the process by which society and culture affect individuals' use of aggression, perception of aggression in others, and motivation to retaliate. A cross-cultural comparative social psychology of aggression would require the systematic investigation of the situational and contextual factors (e.g., incitements, restraints) that increase or decrease aggression. One would expect this kind of systematic investigation to yield sound and searching insights about both moderating and mediating causal relationships.

More generally, there is a knowledge gap that can be filled by a comparative experimental social-psychological approach to the study of aggression. In addition to the types of worthwhile questions to investigate in experimental settings within the United States, there is a need to conduct these same investigations in diverse social and cultural contexts. For example, the original subculture-of-violence hypothesis, formulated by Wolfgang and Ferracuti (1967), suggested that individuals who grow up in violent subcultures are more likely to interpret social interactions as provocations, more likely to become angry, and more likely to respond aggressively to these presumed provocations in order to preserve or enhance their social status and identity. However, no one has yet investigated experimentally whether this presumed sequence actually occurs and whether it differs for individuals from violent as compared to non-violent subcultures.

There is also a need to conduct these types of studies across different societies and cultures. Although ease of replication is generally an advantage of the experimental approach, there will almost certainly be formidable problems in translating across societies and cultures the cues and situational conditions that incite or restrain aggression. The problem, then, is one of creating and measuring psychologically comparable contexts, stimuli, and definitions of violent behaviors.

We have argued that an experimental social psychological approach is needed for the study of interpersonal violent behaviors. Ideally, however, such a research program would involve multiple methods. Nisbett's research (Nisbett, Polly, & Lang, this volume) is certainly one example of this multiple-method approach. This program represents the kind of theoretical and methodological integration that could be productively used to illuminate other aspects of the linkages between society, culture, and violent behaviors. These linkages are especially likely to be made if the kinds of individual-level data now collected in the experimental setting were also collected from aggregate populations by national surveys. The research yield would be further enhanced if data about moderating and mediating influences were also collected from and about the members of these populations.

## IMPLICATIONS OF THE BOOK

When reading these chapters we were struck not only by the obvious need for more and better research but also by the conceptual, methodological, and practical obstacles to actually doing that research. In particular, there are six critical issues facing scholars in this area. These issues should be familiar because they have already surfaced in this discussion in one form or another.

1.  **The Fundamental Importance of Comparative Social and Cultural Research.** It is no longer the case that cross-societal, cross-cultural, and cross-national studies are simply window dressing that make for interesting anecdotes in textbooks. The field must rescue these studies from their marginality. The field must further recognize more widely than it now does that understanding violent behaviors requires broadly conceived societal and cultural research designed to investigate questions of behavioral generality, relative frequency, the moderating role of context and of situation within context, and the mediating role of intervening social and cultural processes.
2.  **The Need for Multimethod, Multilevel Research.** Because of the complexities of behavior within a single society or culture, scientists need to use mul-

tiple methods to study them (Campbell & Stanley, 1966). Obviously, when research questions involve multiple societies and cultures, additional levels of multiplism—contexts, methods, and analyses—are required (Cook, 1985).

3. **The Need for Better Data Collection.** A truly comparative approach requires a coordinated data-collection strategy, specifically designed to reduce the weaknesses of current data sets. For example, it would be worthwhile to collect data combining the benefits of large surveys (e.g., quantitative data, large samples) with those of ethnographies (e.g., qualitative data, detailed information). Moreover, future data sets will need to include information about the interplay and overlap of offenders and victims over their life spans and the diverse motivations (e.g., offensive, defensive) underlying violent behaviors.

4. **The Need for Multitalented Research Teams.** Conducting cross-cultural and cross-societal research requires not only knowledge of one or more substantive areas, research design, and statistical techniques but also language skills and intimate familiarity with the behavioral patterns and traditions of the social and cultural groups being studied. No one scholar or group of scholars from a single country or a single academic discipline is likely to possess all of the needed expertise.

5. **The Need for an Administrative Structure.** Assembling and maintaining teams of experts will require an enduring organization. Encouraging, nurturing, and coordinating such long-term collaborations might involve regional organizations and some combination of public and private funding. Models already exist for inaugurating combined public and private funding ventures, but these are typically at the national level. Violent behaviors possess regional as well as international aspects, which makes cooperative efforts at these geopolitical levels a promising approach.

6. **The Need to Conduct Research on Intervention Effectiveness.** The scientific understanding of violent behaviors can benefit from both basic and applied research. The contributors to this volume have concentrated on basic research questions and strategies. However, experimental and quasi-experimental studies of policies, procedures, and practices implemented to curtail violent behaviors in different societies and cultures can also add much to what we know about the causal influences of these behaviors. When studied from a comparative perspective, interventions, both failures and successes, can help in identifying general and specific causal pathways, both moderating and mediating.

Until a research program incorporating these elements is launched, the study of interpersonal violent behaviors will be fettered by inadequate conceptualization, methodology, data, research cadre, and institutional support. The result will be an inability to test crucial questions of causality, ranging from elemental direct effects to more complex moderated and mediated ones. We hope that this book stimulates further thinking about the social and cultural aspects of violent behaviors and ways in which these questions can be better investigated.

## REFERENCES

Allport, G. W. (1985). The historical background of social psychology. In G. Lindzey & E. Aronson (Eds.), *Handbook of social psychology* (3rd ed., Vol. 1, pp. 1–46). New York: Random House.

Baron, R. M., & Kenny, D. A. (1986). The moderator-mediator variable distinction in social psychological research: Conceptual, strategic, and statistical considerations. *Journal of Personality and Social Psychology, 51*, 1173–1182.

Berkowitz, L. (1993). *Aggression: Its causes, consequences, and control.* Philadelphia: Temple University Press.

Berkowitz, L., & Donnerstein, E. (1982). External validity is more than skin deep: Some answers to criticism of laboratory experiments. *American Psychologist, 37*, 245–257.

Bizman, A., Schwarzwald, J., & Zidon, A. (1984). Effects of the power to retaliate on physical aggression directed toward Middle-Eastern Jews, Western Jews, and Israeli Arabs. *Journal of Cross-Cultural Psychology, 15*, 65–78.

Campbell, D. T., & Stanley, J. C. (1966). *Experimental and quasi-experimental designs for research.* Skokie, IL: Rand McNally.

Cook, T. D. (1985). Postpositivist critical multiplism. In R. L. Shotland & M. M. Mark (Eds.), *Social science and social policy* (pp. 21–62). Beverly Hills, CA: Sage.

Corsaro, W. A. (1992). Cross-cultural analysis. In E. F. Borgatta & M. L. Borgatta (Eds.), *Encyclopedia of sociology* (pp. 391–395). New York: Macmillan.

Crosby, F., Bromley, S., & Saxe, L. (1980). Recent unobtrusive studies of black and white discrimination and prejudice: A literature review. *Psychological Bulletin, 87*, 546–563.

Dovidio, J. F., & Gaertner, S. L. (1986). *Prejudice, discrimination, and racism.* Orlando, FL: Academic Press.

Eagly, A. H., & Steffen, V. J. (1986). Gender and aggressive behavior: A meta-analytic review of the social psychological literature. *Psychological Bulletin, 100*, 309–330.

Gottfredson, M. R., & Hirschi, T. (1993). A control theory interpretation of psychological research on aggression. In R. B. Felson & J. T. Tedeschi (Eds.), *The psychology of aggression* (pp. 47–67). Washington, DC: American Psychological Association.

Gully, K. J., & Dengerink, H. A. (1983). The dyadic interaction of persons with violent and nonviolent histories. *Aggressive Behavior, 9*, 13–20.

Kohn, M. L. (1989). *Cross-cultural research in sociology.* Newbury Park, CA: Sage.

Linz, D., & Malamuth, N. (1993). *Pornography.* Newbury Park, CA: Sage.

Megargee, E. I. (1983). Psychological determinants and correlates of criminal violence. In M. E. Wolfgang & N. A. Weiner (Eds.), *Criminal violence* (pp. 81–170). Beverly Hills, CA: Sage Publications.

Rogers, R. W., & Prentice-Dunn, S. (1981). Deindividuation and anger-mediated interracial aggression: Unmasking regressive racism. *Journal of Personality and Social Psychology, 41*, 63–73.

Sheridan, C. L., & King, R. G., Jr. (1972). Obedience to authority with an authentic victim [Summary]. *Proceedings of the 80th Annual Convention of the American Psychological Association, 7*, 165–166.

Triandis, H. C. (1980). Introduction. In H. C. Triandis & W. W. Lambert (Eds.), *Handbook of cross-cultural psychology* (Vol. 1, pp. 1–14). Boston: Allyn and Bacon.

Wolfgang, M. E., & Ferracuti, F. (1967). *The subculture of violence: Towards an integrated theory in criminology.* London: Tavistock Publications.

# Index